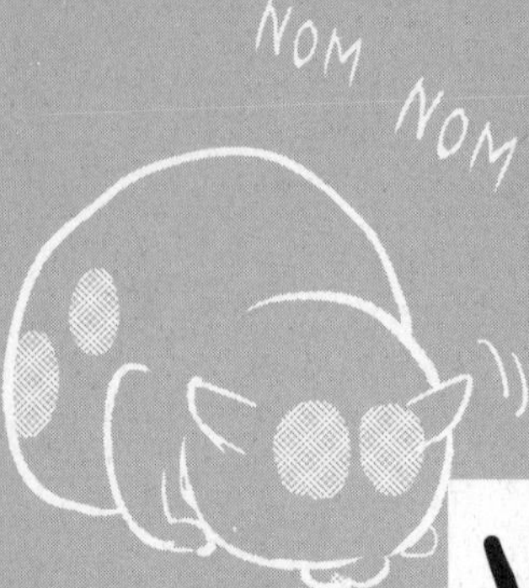
NOM NOM

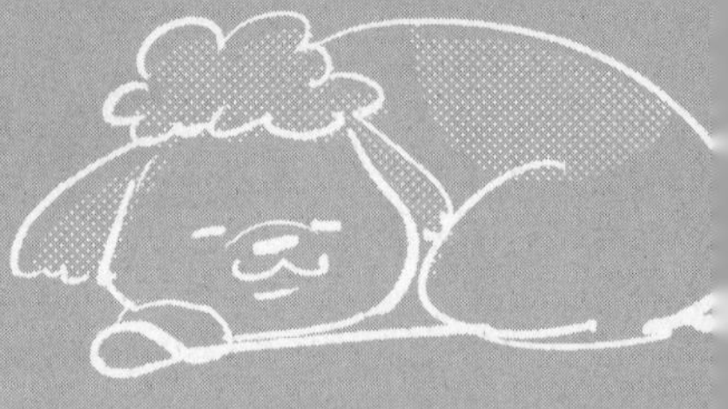

With a Dog AND a Cat, Every Day is Fun

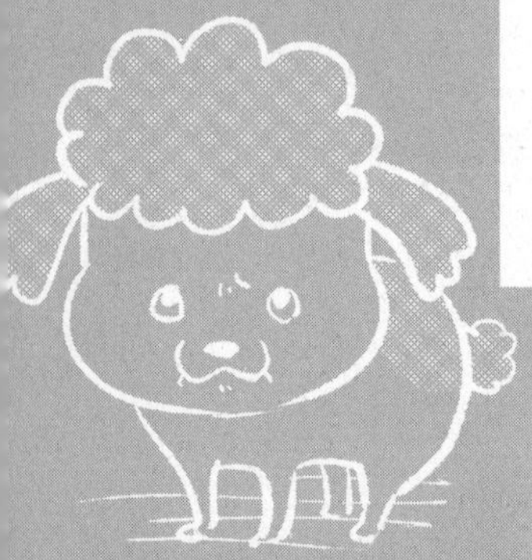

⑥

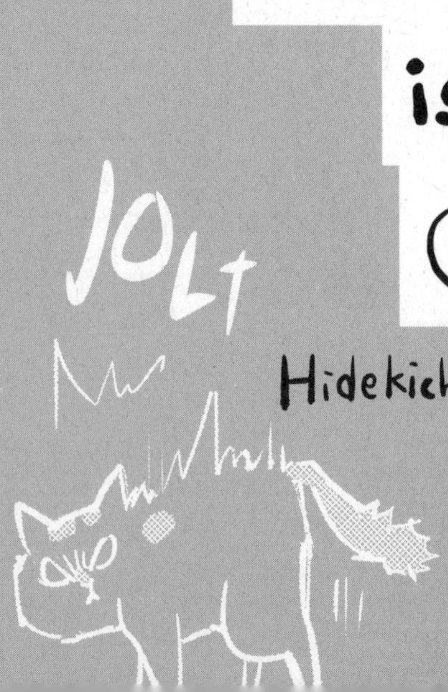
JOLT

Hidekichi Matsumoto

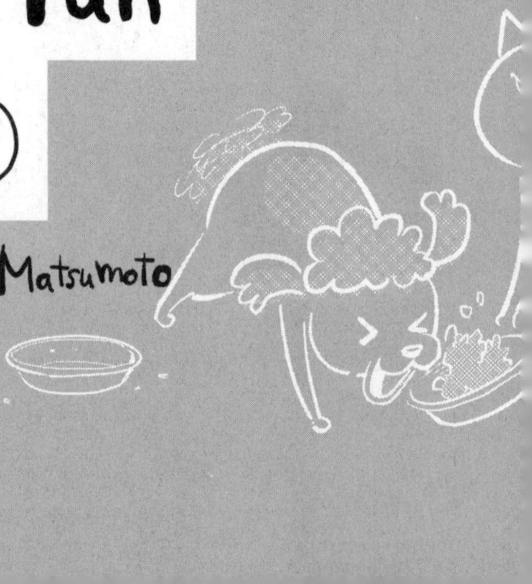

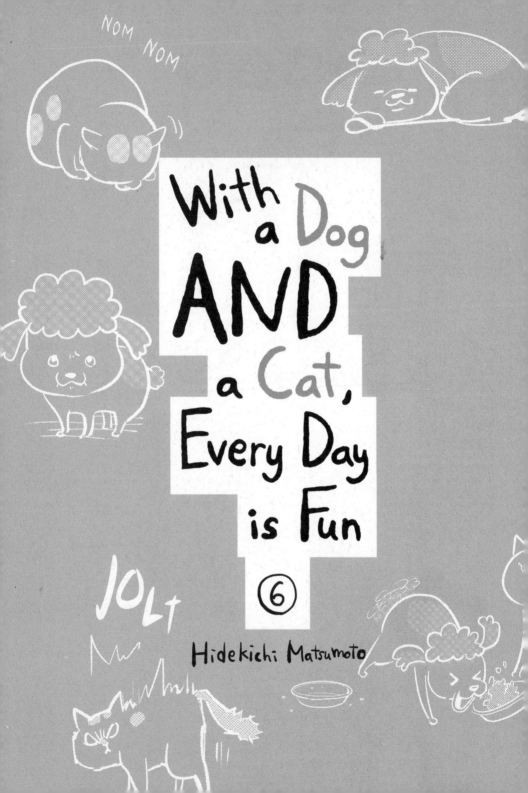

CAST

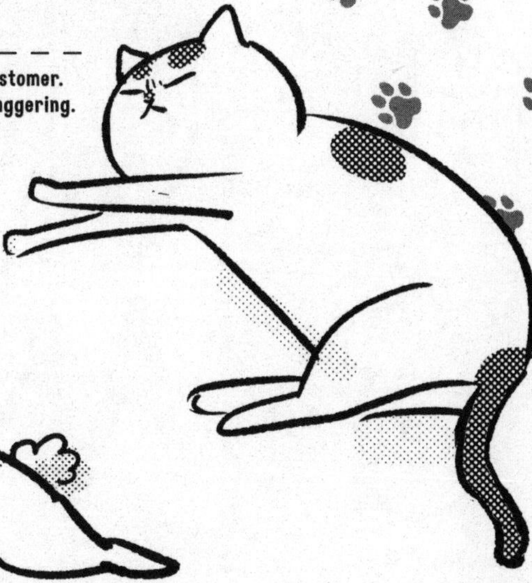

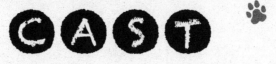

NEKO-SAMA

A fearsome face. A cool customer.
His passion for theft is staggering.

INU-KUN

Loves Neko. Even when he doesn't like something, if you sing and dance, he soon forgets about it.

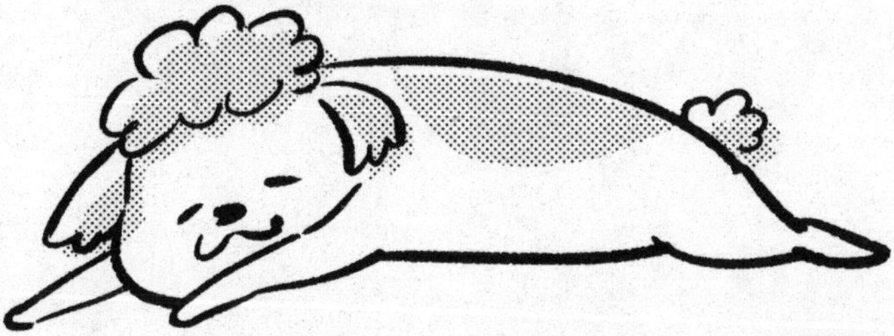

LEOPA

Nickname: Tokage-chan.
A constant object of Neko's gaze.
Has none of the cool composure you expect from reptiles.

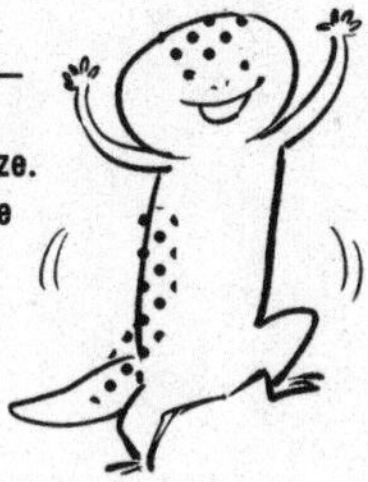

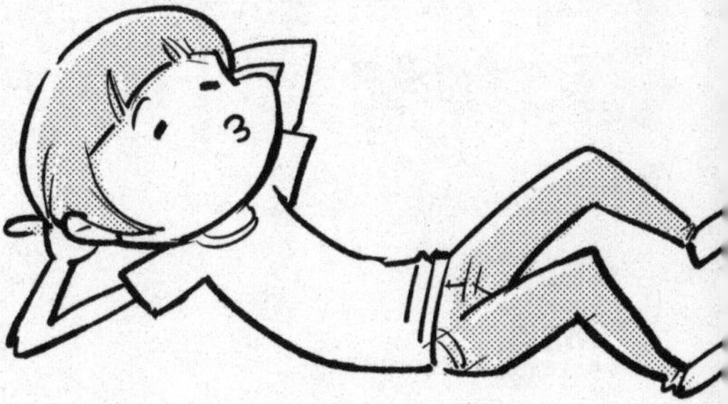

HIDEKICHI MATSUMOTO

Manga artist. Loves animals.

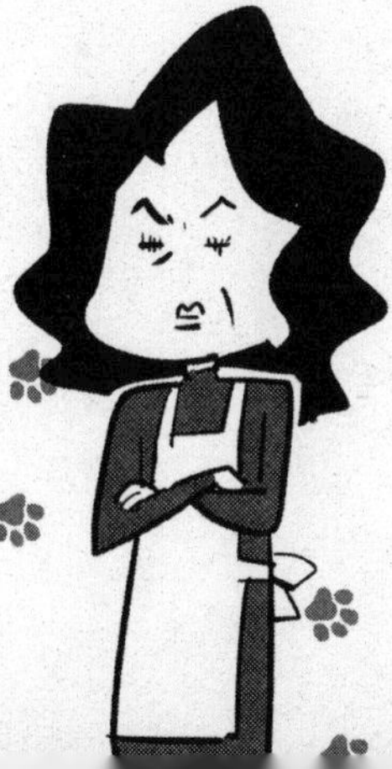

MOM

Hidekichi's mother. Holds the #1 ranking in the Matsumoto household.

DAD

Hidekichi's father.
A very kind man.

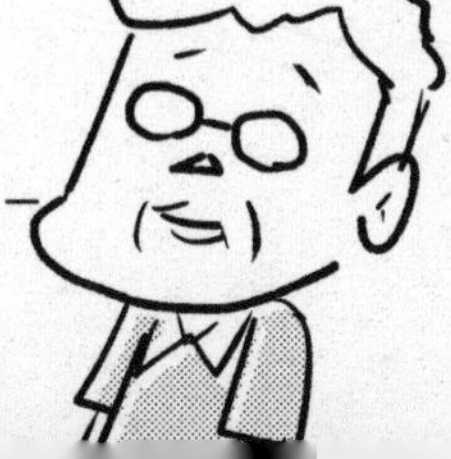

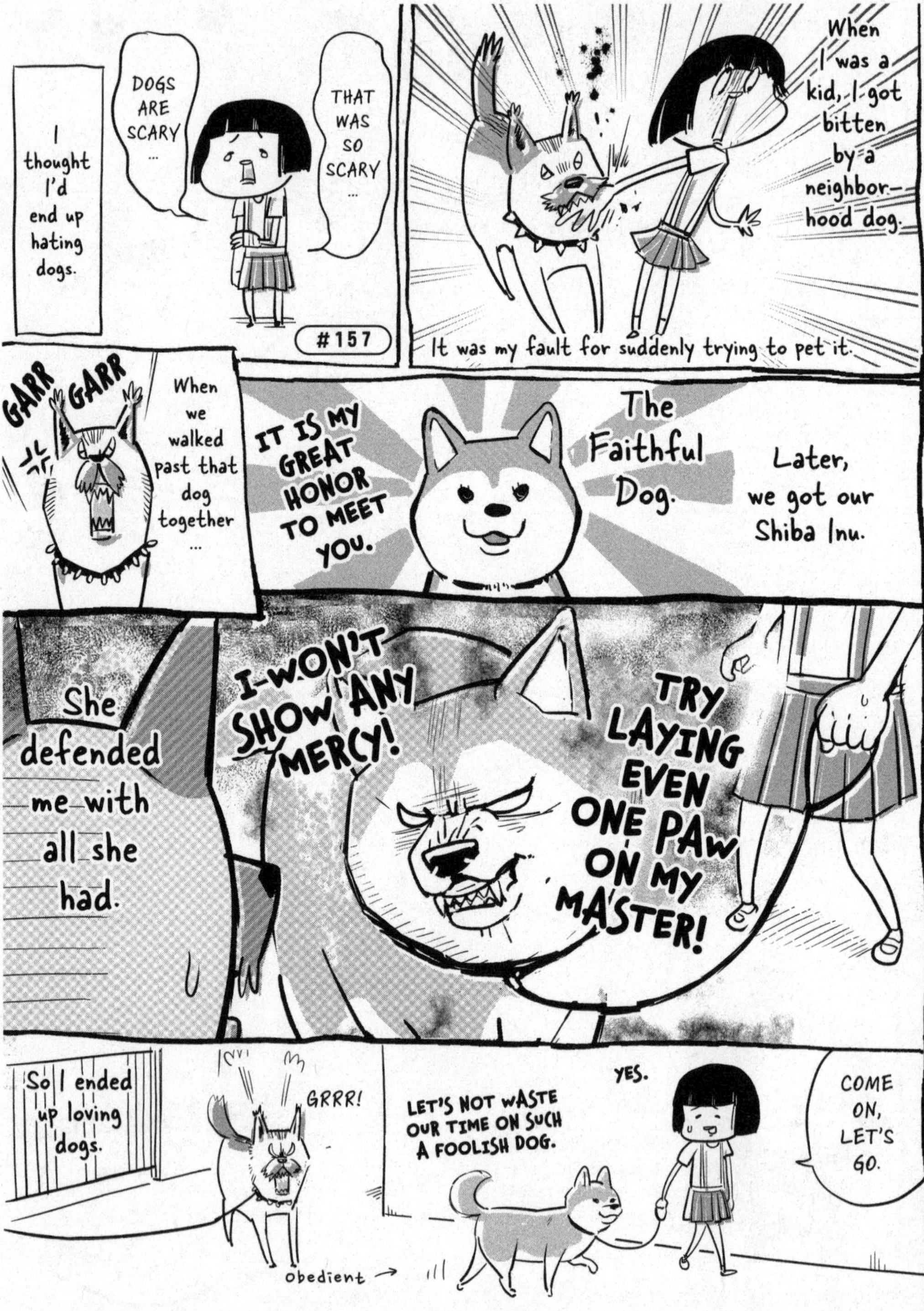
When I was a kid, I got bitten by a neighborhood dog.
It was my fault for suddenly trying to pet it.
I thought I'd end up hating dogs.
THAT WAS SO SCARY ...
DOGS ARE SCARY ...
#157
Later, we got our Shiba Inu.
The Faithful Dog.
IT IS MY GREAT HONOR TO MEET YOU.
When we walked past that dog together ...
GARR GARR
TRY LAYING EVEN ONE PAW ON MY MASTER!
I-WON'T SHOW ANY MERCY!
She defended me with all she had.
COME ON, LET'S GO.
YES.
LET'S NOT WASTE OUR TIME ON SUCH A FOOLISH DOG.
GRRR!
So I ended up loving dogs.
obedient →

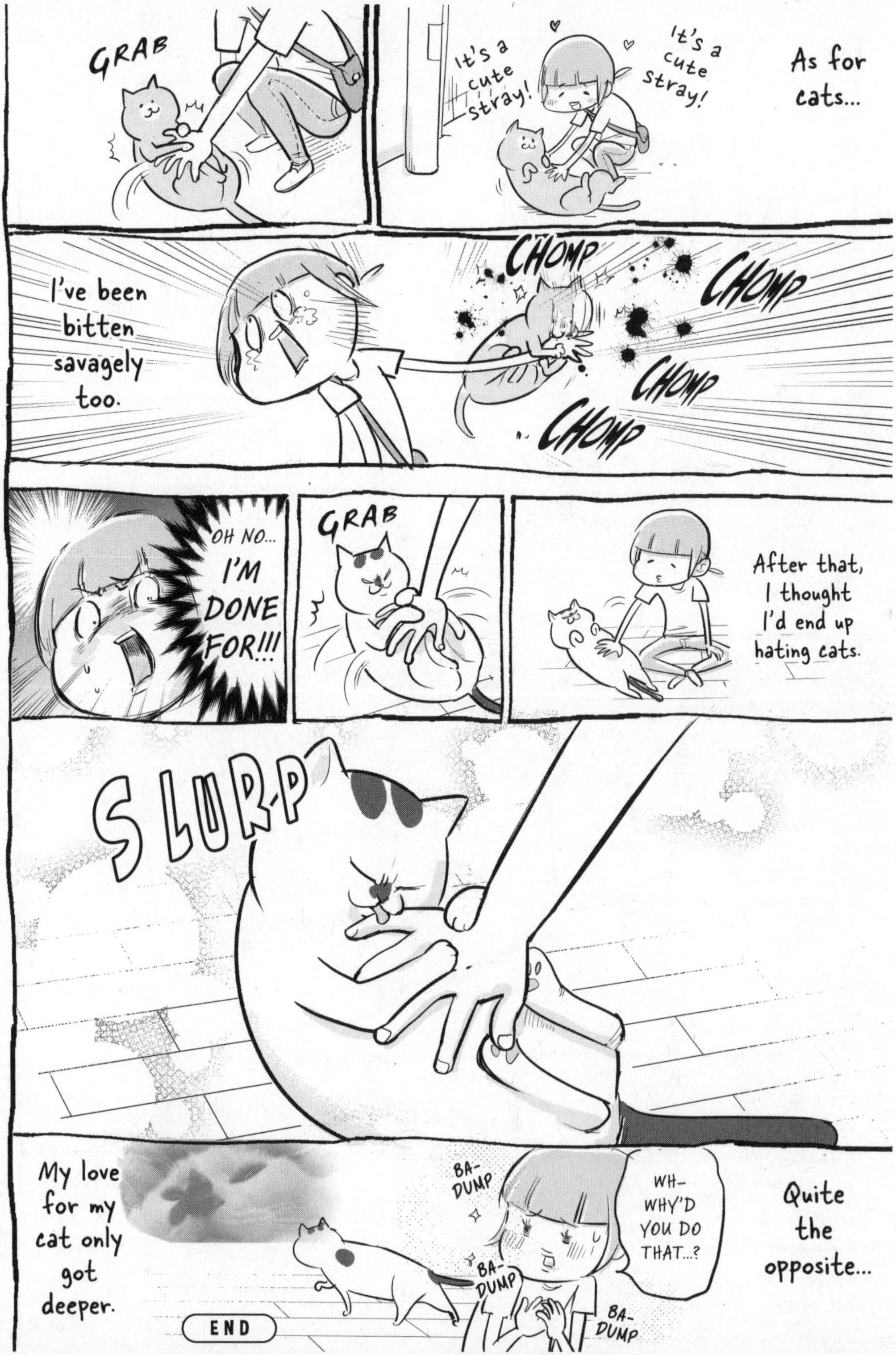
As for cats...
It's a cute stray!
It's a cute stray!
GRAB
CHOMP
CHOMP
CHOMP
CHOMP
I've been bitten savagely too.
After that, I thought I'd end up hating cats.
GRAB
OH NO... I'M DONE FOR!!!
SLURP
Quite the opposite...
WH- WHY'D YOU DO THAT...?
BA-DUMP
BA-DUMP
BA-DUMP
My love for my cat only got deeper.
END

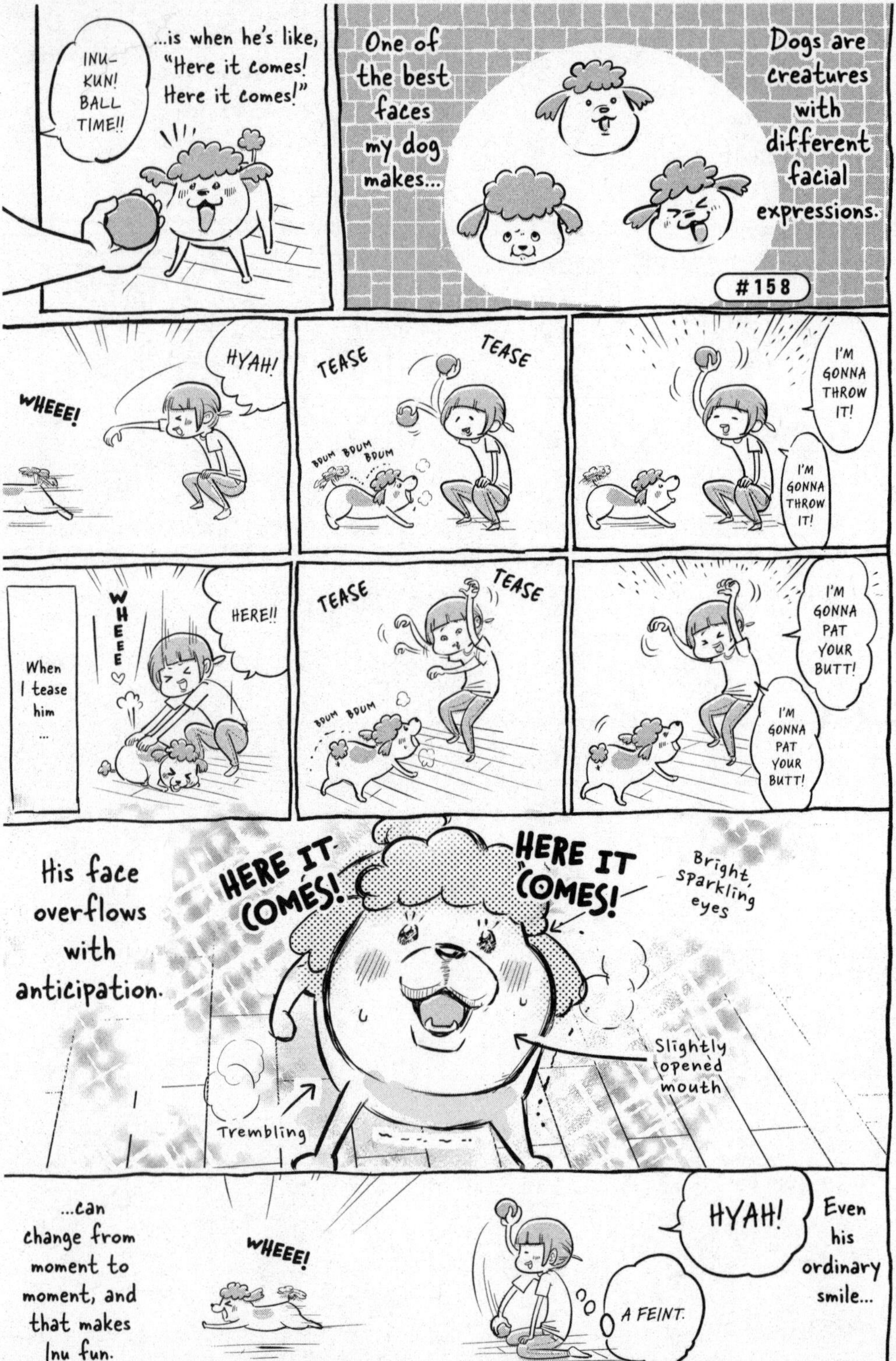
Dogs are creatures with different facial expressions.
One of the best faces my dog makes...
#158
...is when he's like, "Here it comes! Here it comes!"
INU-KUN! BALL TIME!!
I'M GONNA THROW IT!
I'M GONNA THROW IT!
TEASE
TEASE
BDUM BDUM BDUM
HYAH!
WHEEE!
I'M GONNA PAT YOUR BUTT!
I'M GONNA PAT YOUR BUTT!
TEASE
TEASE
BDUM BDUM
HERE!!
WHEEE ♡
When I tease him ...
Bright, sparkling eyes
HERE IT COMES!
HERE IT COMES!
His face overflows with anticipation.
Slightly opened mouth
Trembling
Even his ordinary smile...
HYAH!
A FEINT.
WHEEE!
...can change from moment to moment, and that makes Inu fun.

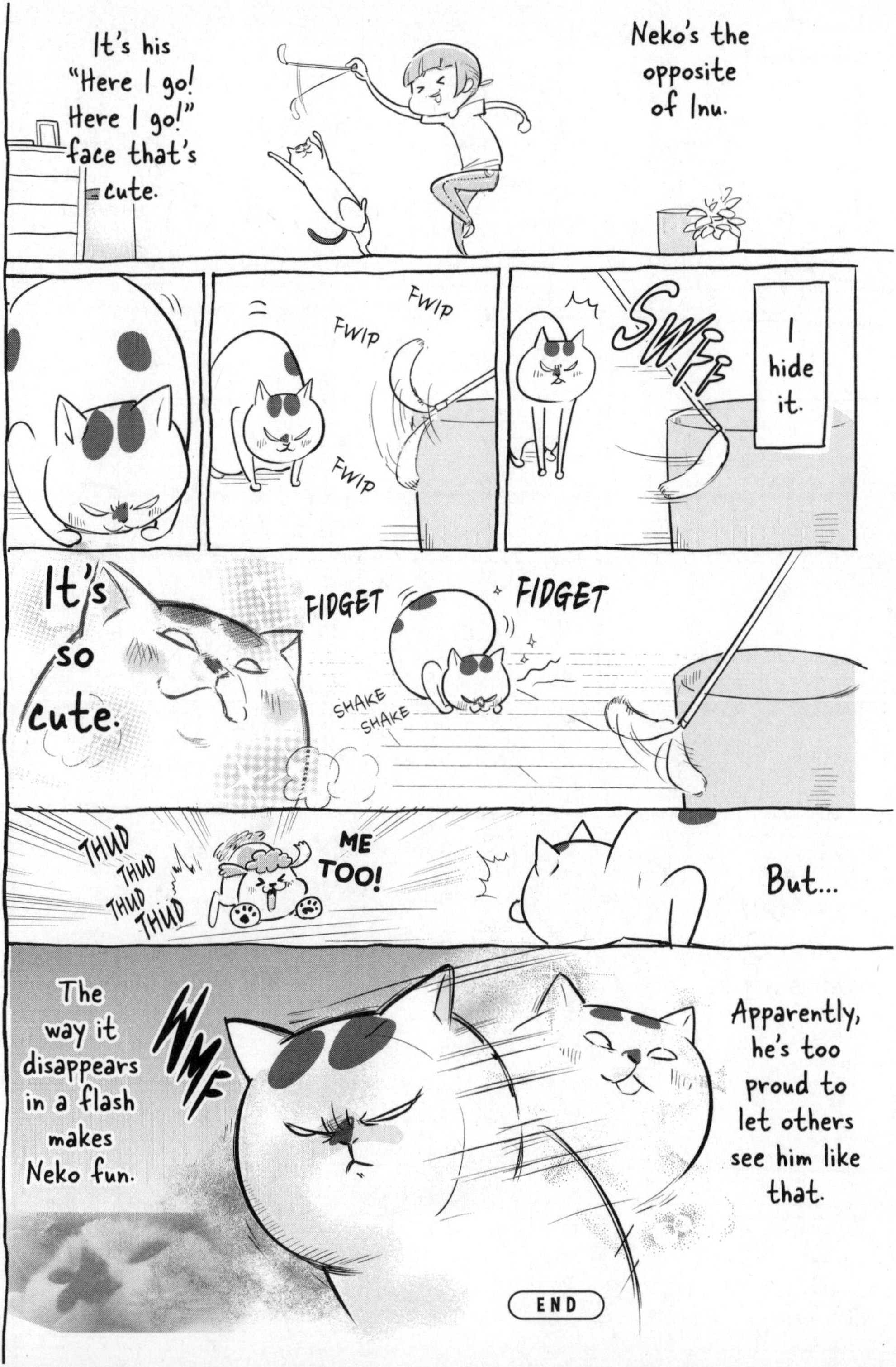
Neko's the opposite of Inu.
It's his "Here I go! Here I go!" face that's cute.
I hide it.
SWFF
FWIP
FWIP
FWIP
FIDGET
FIDGET
SHAKE SHAKE
It's so cute.
But...
ME TOO!
THUD THUD THUD THUD
Apparently, he's too proud to let others see him like that.
WMF
The way it disappears in a flash makes Neko fun.
END

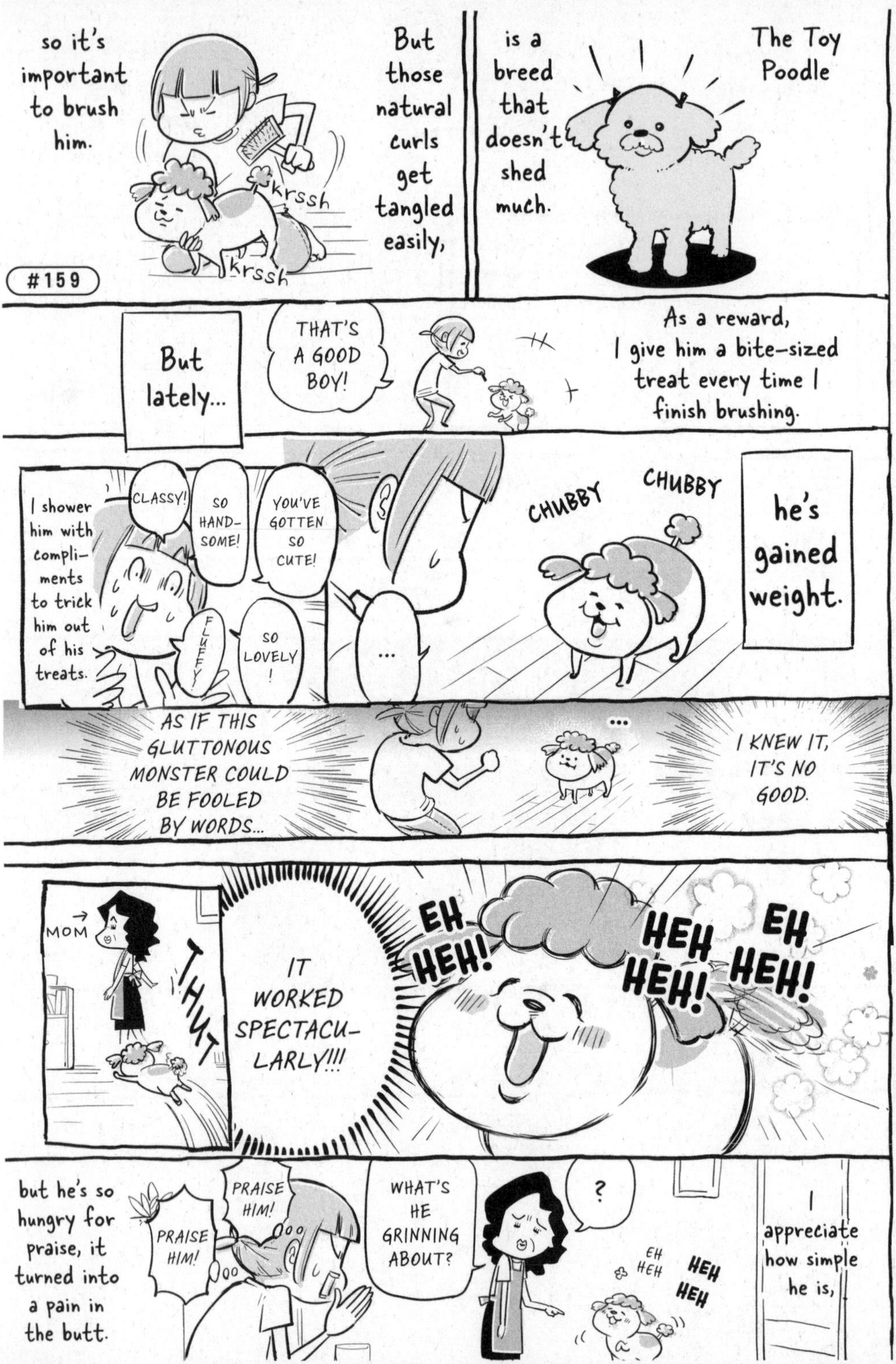
The Toy Poodle
is a breed that doesn't shed much.
But those natural curls get tangled easily,
so it's important to brush him.
krssh
krssh
#159
As a reward, I give him a bite-sized treat every time I finish brushing.
THAT'S A GOOD BOY!
But lately...
he's gained weight.
CHUBBY
CHUBBY
...
I shower him with compliments to trick him out of his treats.
YOU'VE GOTTEN SO CUTE!
SO HANDSOME!
CLASSY!
SO LOVELY!
FLUFFY!
I KNEW IT, IT'S NO GOOD.
...
AS IF THIS GLUTTONOUS MONSTER COULD BE FOOLED BY WORDS...
EH HEH!
HEH HEH!
EH HEH!
IT WORKED SPECTACULARLY!!!
MOM
THUNT
I appreciate how simple he is,
?
EH HEH
HEH HEH
WHAT'S HE GRINNING ABOUT?
PRAISE HIM!
PRAISE HIM!
but he's so hungry for praise, it turned into a pain in the butt.

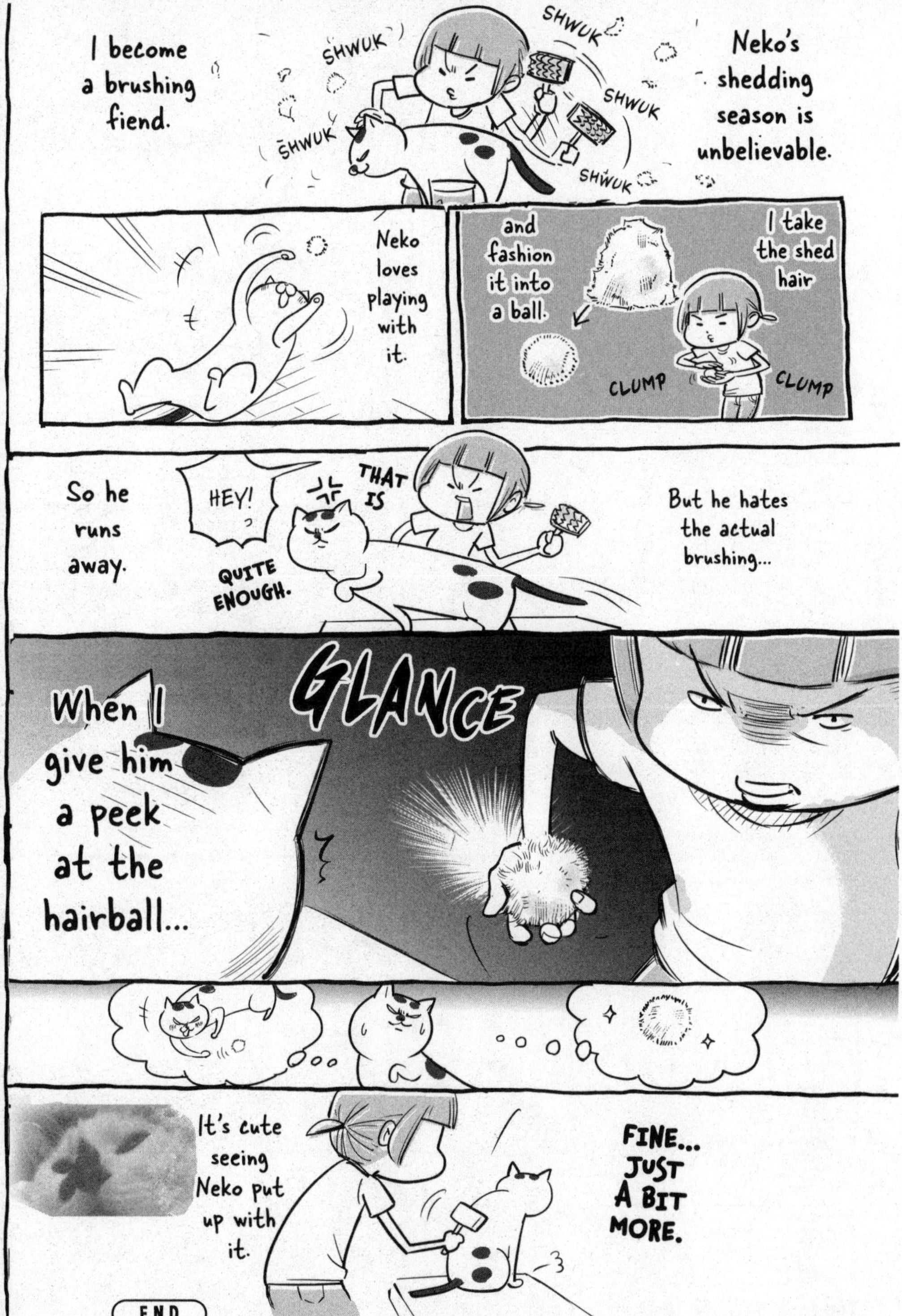
Neko's shedding season is unbelievable.
SHWUK
SHWUK
SHWUK
SHWUK
SHWUK
I become a brushing fiend.
I take the shed hair
and fashion it into a ball.
CLUMP
CLUMP
Neko loves playing with it.
But he hates the actual brushing...
THAT IS QUITE ENOUGH.
HEY!
So he runs away.
GLANCE
When I give him a peek at the hairball...
FINE... JUST A BIT MORE.
It's cute seeing Neko put up with it.
END

You look like you wanna say something.

Newly-Drawn 4-Panel Strip

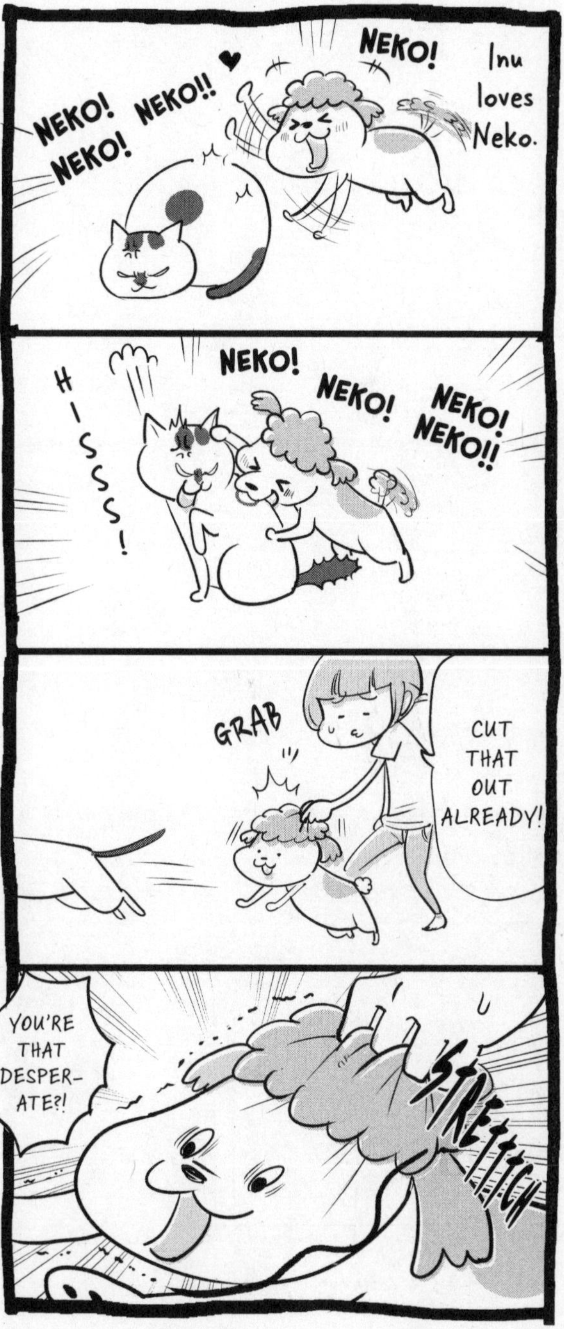
Inu loves Neko.
NEKO!
NEKO!!
NEKO!
NEKO!
NEKO!
NEKO!
NEKO!
NEKO!!
HISSS!
CUT THAT OUT ALREADY!
GRAB
YOU'RE THAT DESPERATE?!
STRETTCH

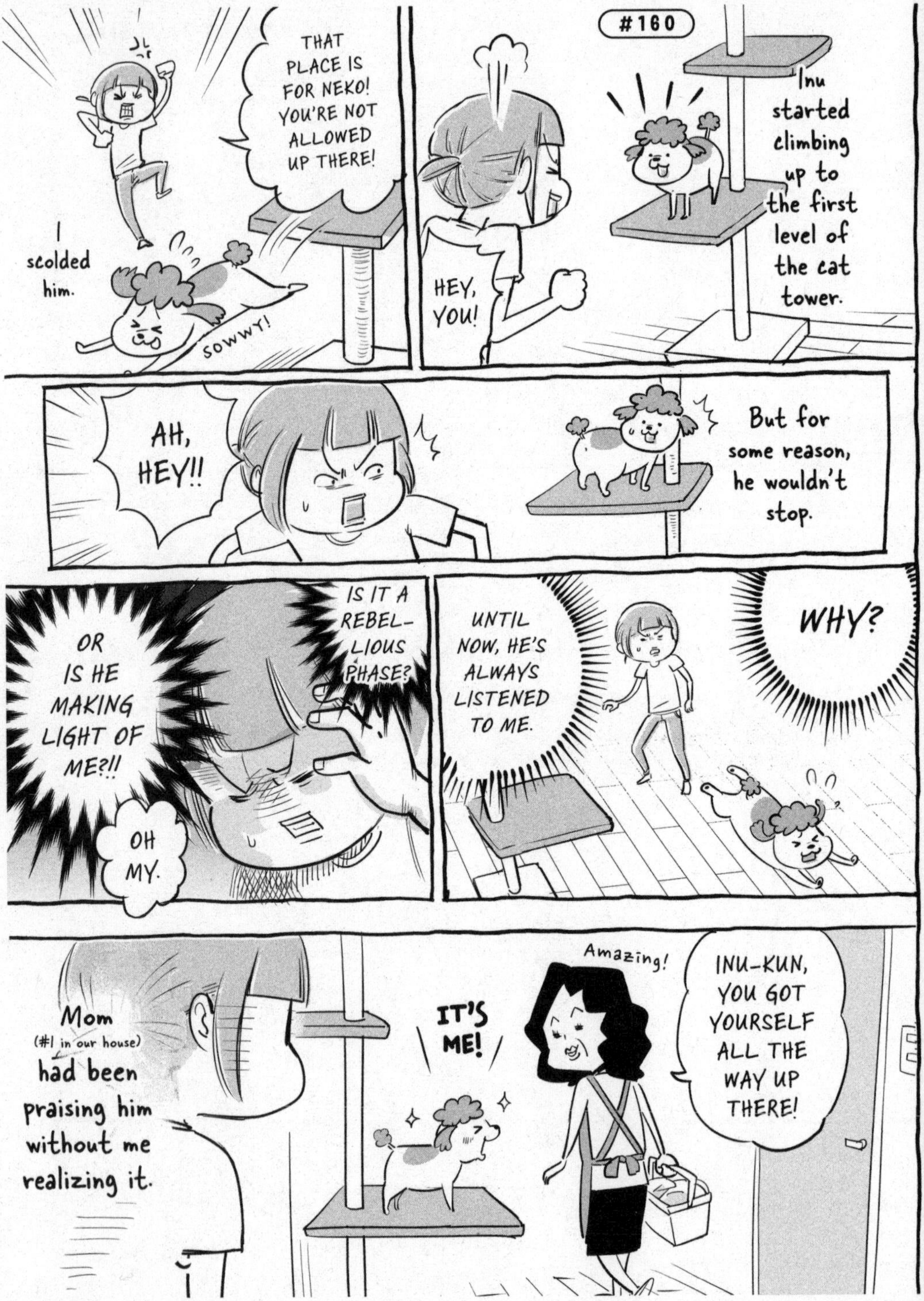
#160
Inu started climbing up to the first level of the cat tower.
HEY, YOU!
THAT PLACE IS FOR NEKO! YOU'RE NOT ALLOWED UP THERE!
SOWWY!
I scolded him.
But for some reason, he wouldn't stop.
AH, HEY!!
WHY?
UNTIL NOW, HE'S ALWAYS LISTENED TO ME.
IS IT A REBEL-LIOUS PHASE?
OR IS HE MAKING LIGHT OF ME?!!
OH MY.
INU-KUN, YOU GOT YOURSELF ALL THE WAY UP THERE!
Amazing!
IT'S ME!
Mom (#1 in our house) had been praising him without me realizing it.

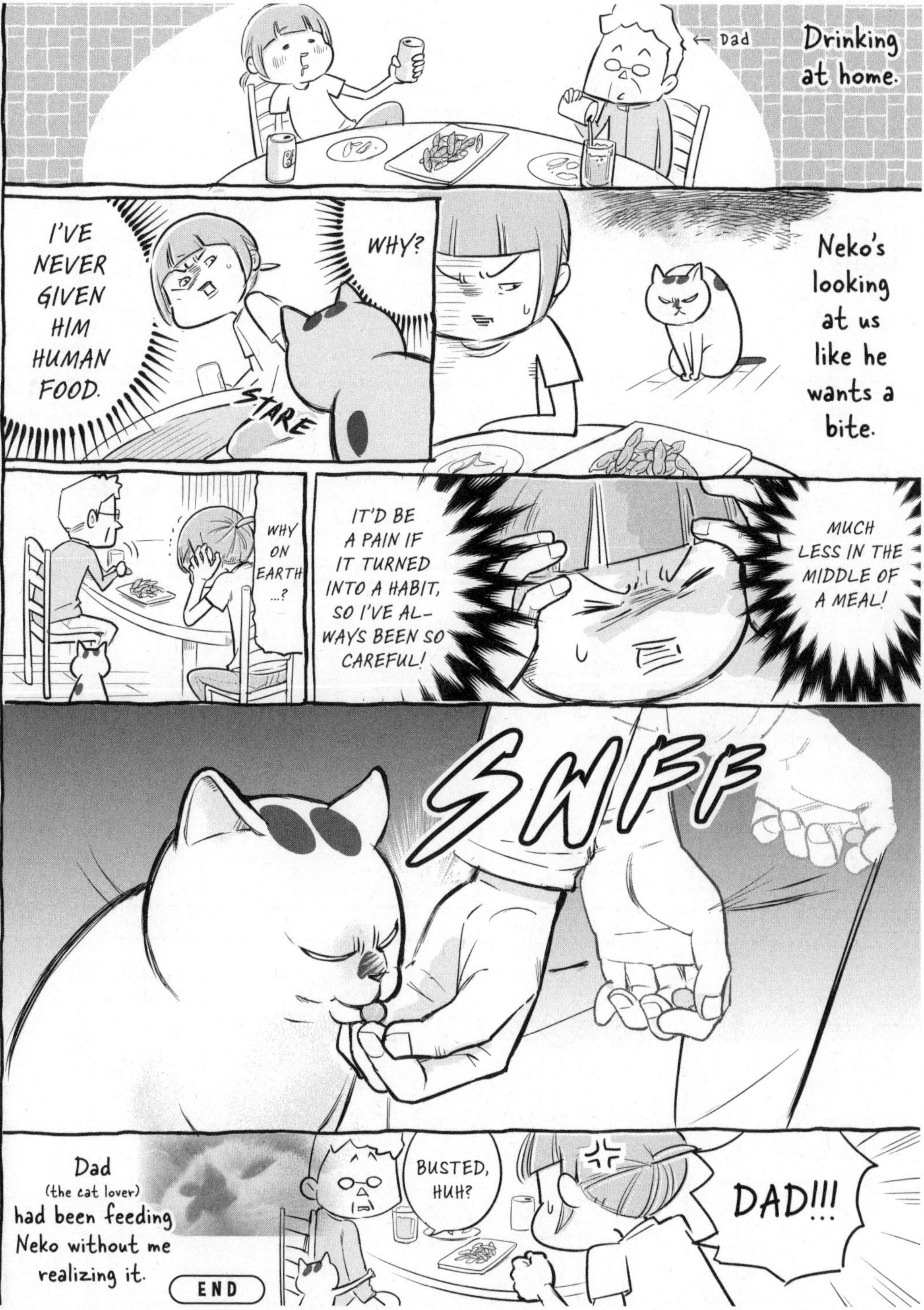
Drinking at home.
← Dad
Neko's looking at us like he wants a bite.
WHY?
I'VE NEVER GIVEN HIM HUMAN FOOD.
STARE
IT'D BE A PAIN IF IT TURNED INTO A HABIT, SO I'VE AL-WAYS BEEN SO CAREFUL!
MUCH LESS IN THE MIDDLE OF A MEAL!
WHY ON EARTH ...?
SNFF
DAD!!!
BUSTED, HUH?
Dad (the cat lover) had been feeding Neko without me realizing it.
END

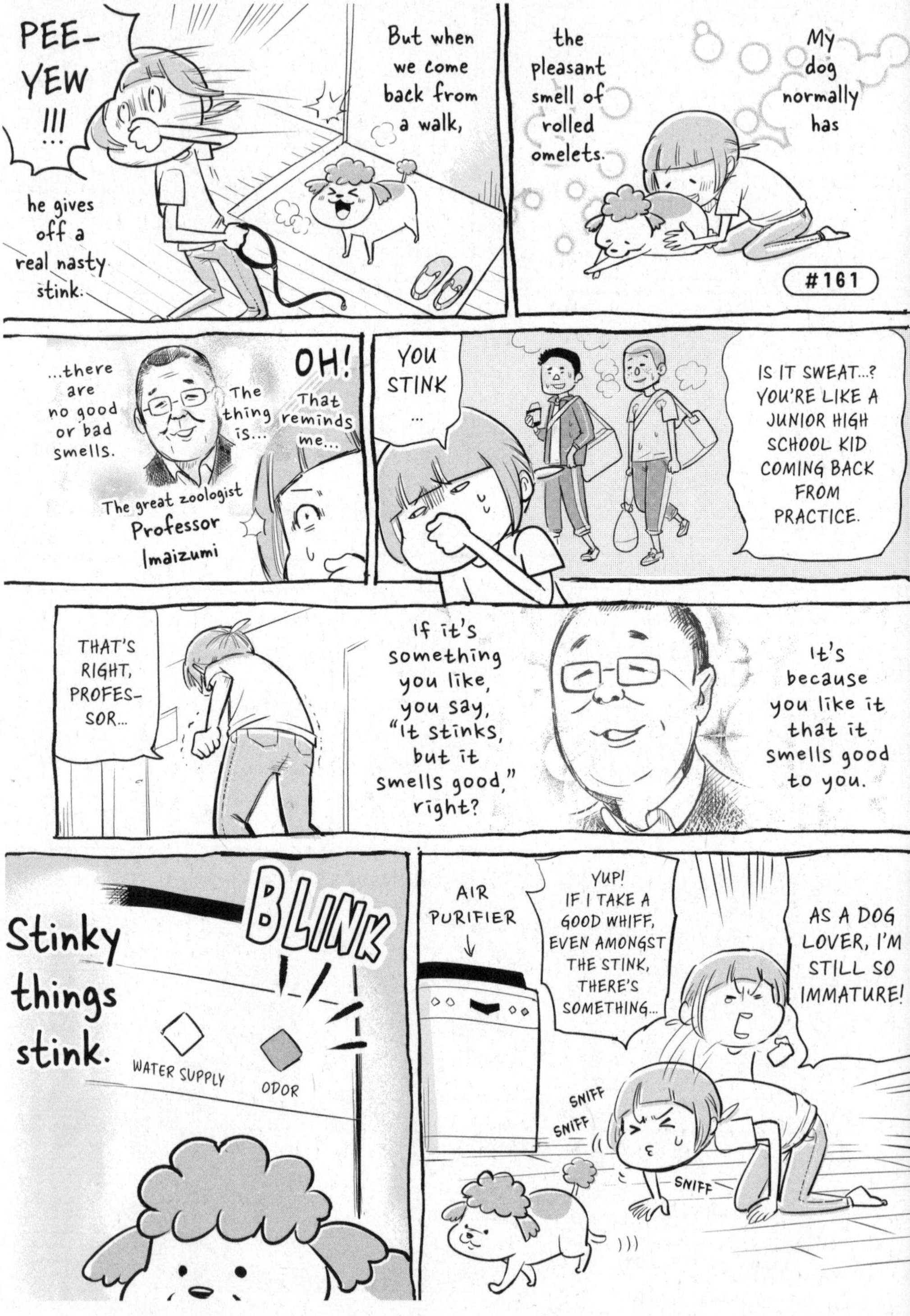

My dog normally has
the pleasant smell of rolled omelets.
#161
But when we come back from a walk,
PEE-YEW!!!...
he gives off a real nasty stink.
IS IT SWEAT...? YOU'RE LIKE A JUNIOR HIGH SCHOOL KID COMING BACK FROM PRACTICE.
YOU STINK...
OH! That reminds me...
The thing is...
...there are no good or bad smells.
The great zoologist Professor Imaizumi
It's because you like it that it smells good to you.
If it's something you like, you say, "It stinks, but it smells good," right?
THAT'S RIGHT, PROFESSOR...
AS A DOG LOVER, I'M STILL SO IMMATURE!
YUP! IF I TAKE A GOOD WHIFF, EVEN AMONGST THE STINK, THERE'S SOMETHING...
AIR PURIFIER
SNIFF
SNIFF
SNIFF
BLINK
WATER SUPPLY
ODOR
Stinky things stink.

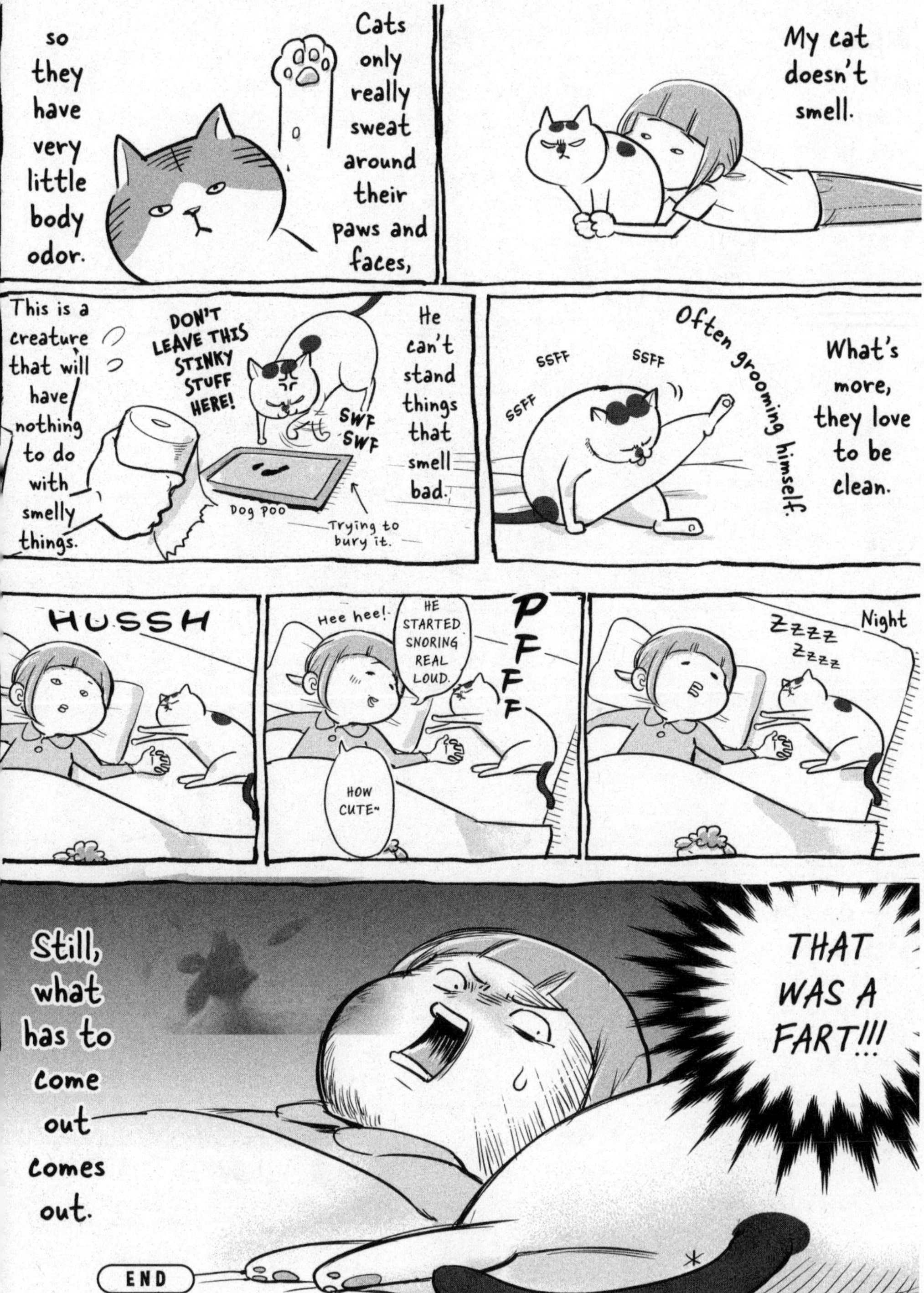
My cat doesn't smell.
Cats only really sweat around their paws and faces,
so they have very little body odor.
What's more, they love to be clean.
Often grooming himself.
SSFF
SSFF
SSFF
He can't stand things that smell bad.
DON'T LEAVE THIS STINKY STUFF HERE!
SWF SWF
Dog poo
Trying to bury it.
This is a creature that will have nothing to do with smelly things.
Night
Zzzz Zzzz
PFFF
HE STARTED SNORING REAL LOUD.
Hee hee!
HOW CUTE~
HUSSH
THAT WAS A FART!!!
Still, what has to come out comes out.
END

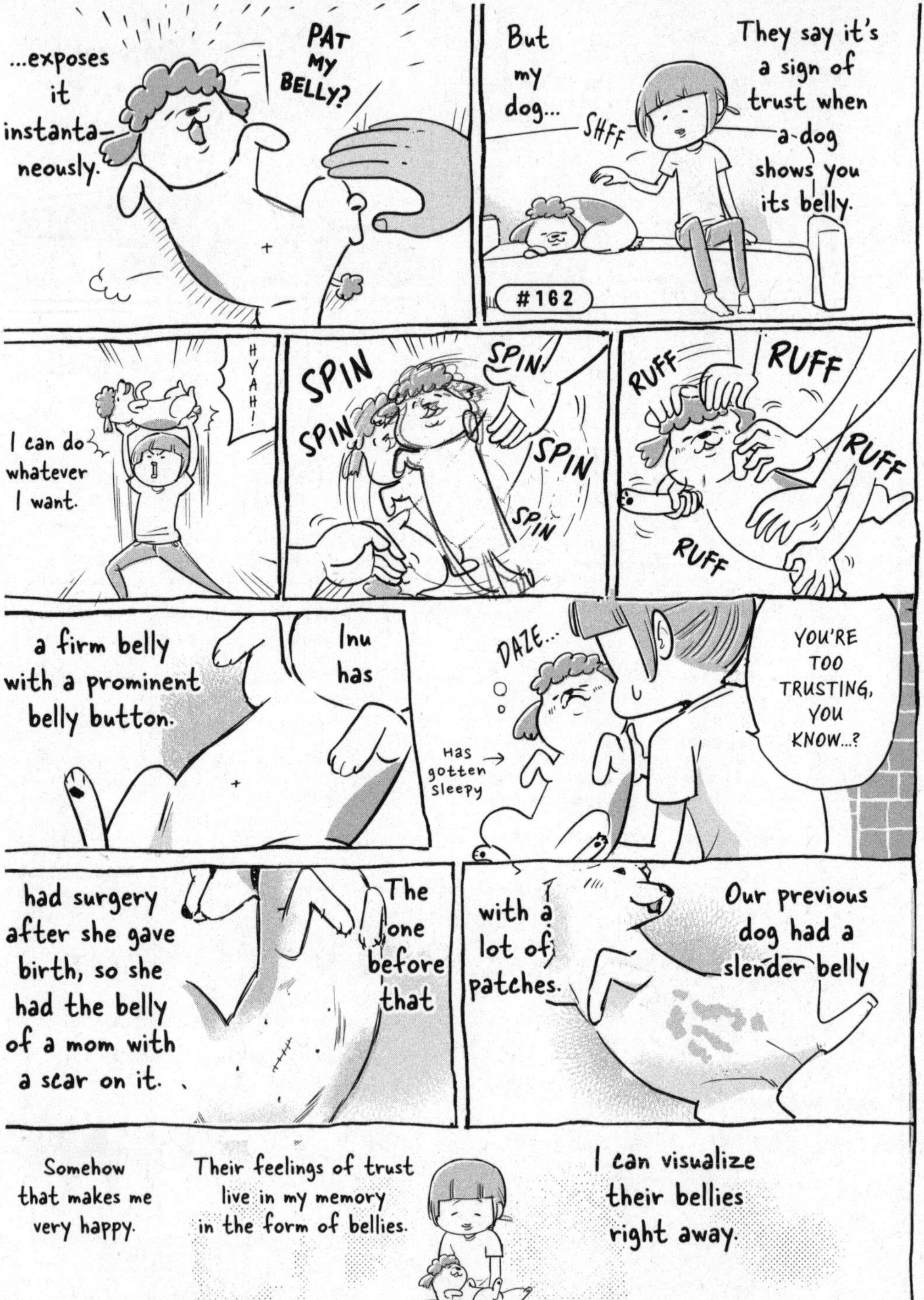
#162
They say it's a sign of trust when a dog shows you its belly.
But my dog...
SHFF
PAT MY BELLY?
...exposes it instantaneously.
RUFF
RUFF
RUFF
RUFF
SPIN
SPIN
SPIN
SPIN
SPIN
HYAH!
I can do whatever I want.
YOU'RE TOO TRUSTING, YOU KNOW...?
DAZE...
Has gotten sleepy
Inu has
a firm belly with a prominent belly button.
Our previous dog had a slender belly
with a lot of patches.
The one before that
had surgery after she gave birth, so she had the belly of a mom with a scar on it.
I can visualize their bellies right away.
Their feelings of trust live in my memory in the form of bellies.
Somehow that makes me very happy.

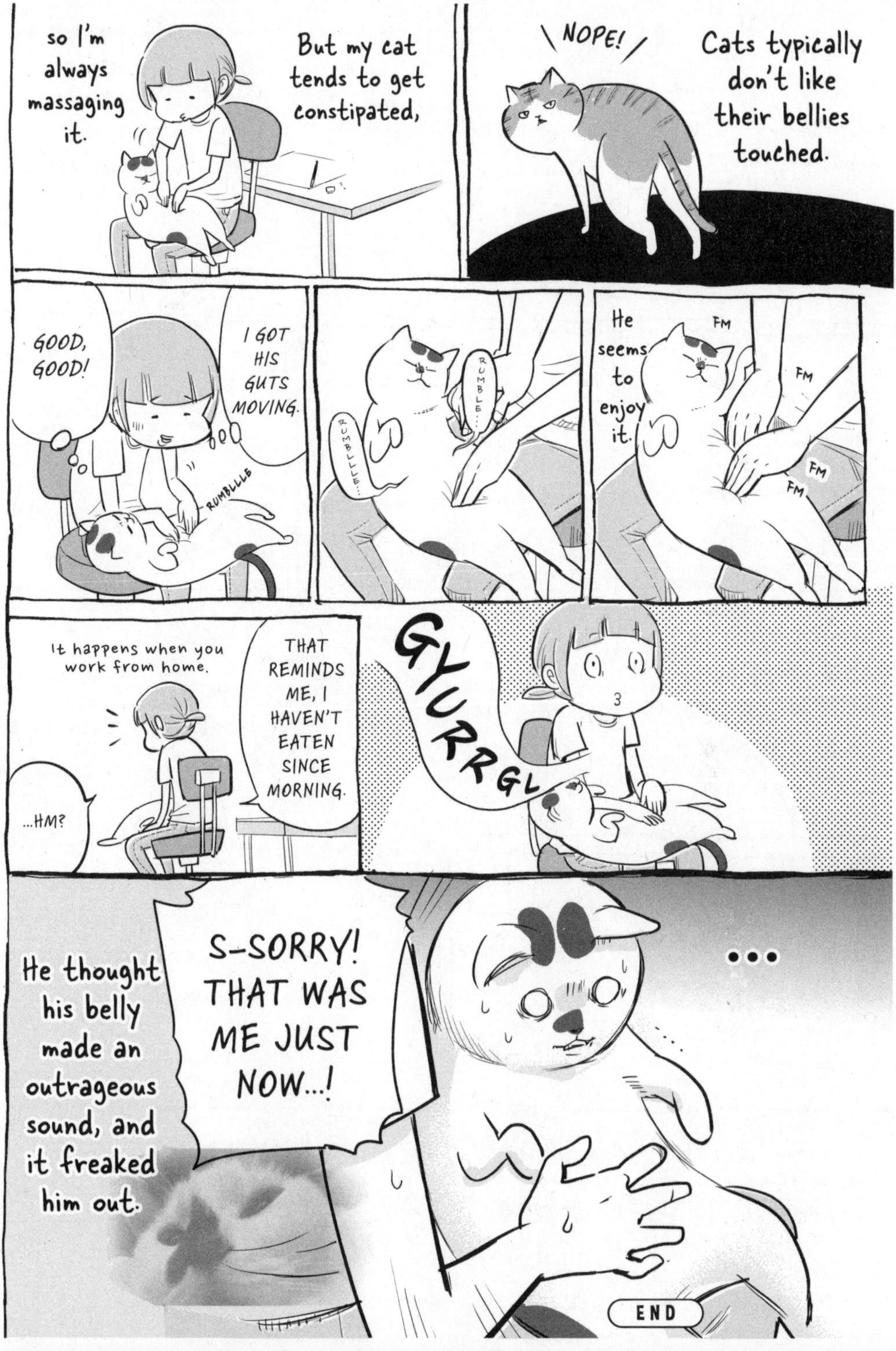
Cats typically don't like their bellies touched.
NOPE!
But my cat tends to get constipated,
so I'm always massaging it.
He seems to enjoy it.
FM
FM
FM
FM
RUMBLE...
RUMBLLLE...
I GOT HIS GUTS MOVING.
GOOD, GOOD!
RUMBLLLE
GYURRRGL
THAT REMINDS ME, I HAVEN'T EATEN SINCE MORNING.
It happens when you work from home.
...HM?
...
S-SORRY! THAT WAS ME JUST NOW...!
He thought his belly made an outrageous sound, and it freaked him out.
END

You're not angry... right?

Newly-Drawn 4-Panel Strip

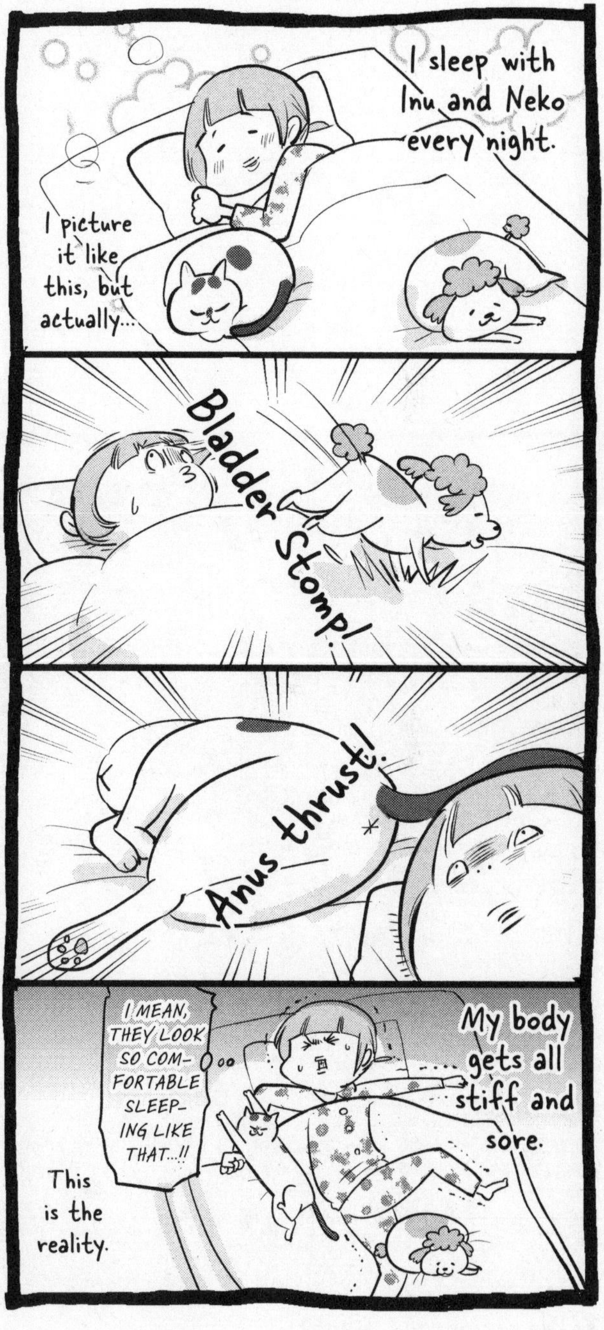

I sleep with Inu and Neko every night.
I picture it like this, but actually...
Bladder Stomp!
Anus thrust!
My body gets all stiff and sore.
I MEAN, THEY LOOK SO COM-FORTABLE SLEEP-ING LIKE THAT...!!
This is the reality.

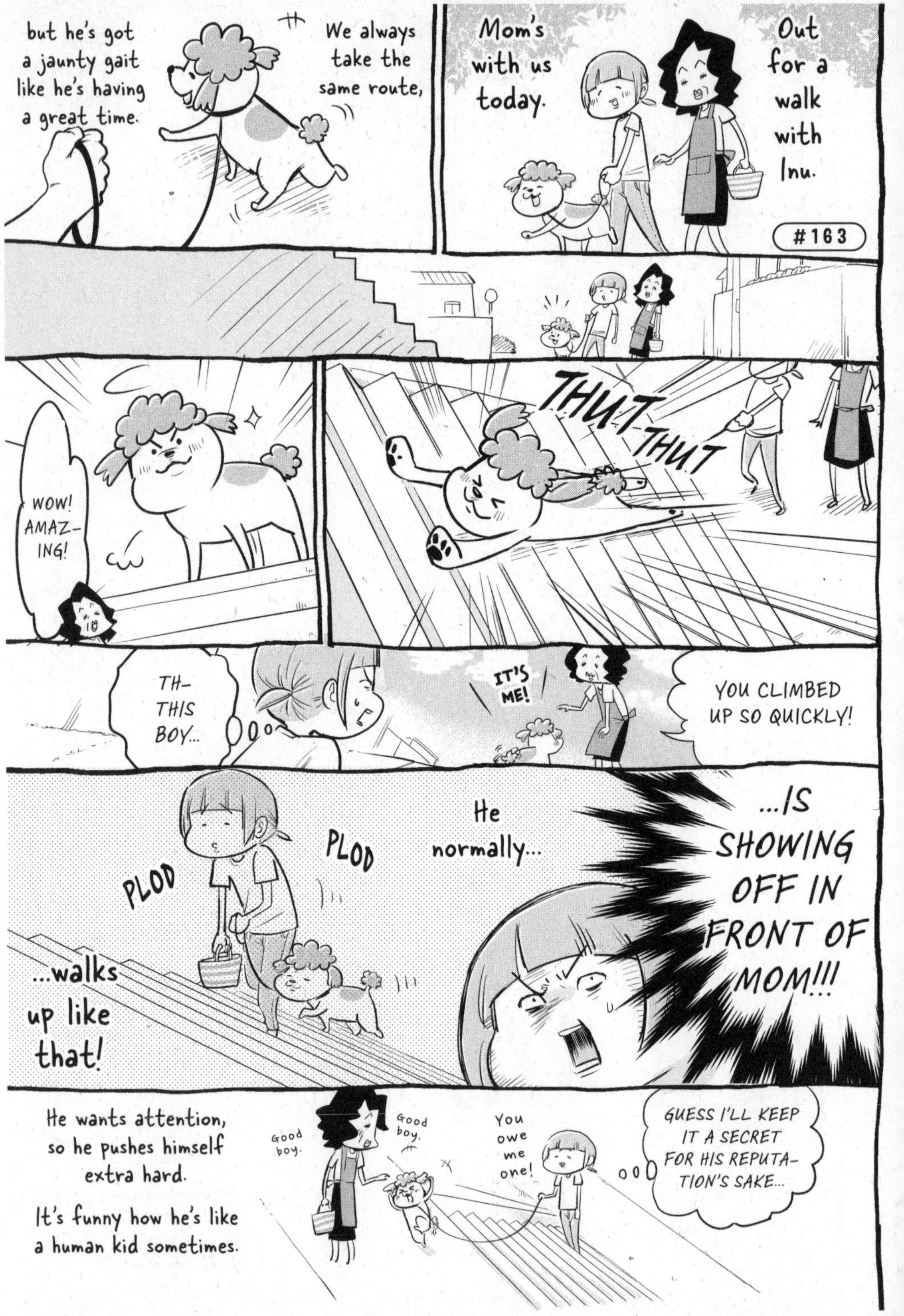

Out for a walk with Inu.
Mom's with us today.
#163
We always take the same route,
but he's got a jaunty gait like he's having a great time.
THUT
THUT
WOW! AMAZ-ING!
YOU CLIMBED UP SO QUICKLY!
IT'S ME!
TH-THIS BOY...
He normally...
PLOD
PLOD
...walks up like that!
...IS SHOWING OFF IN FRONT OF MOM!!!
GUESS I'LL KEEP IT A SECRET FOR HIS REPUTA-TION'S SAKE...
You owe me one!
Good boy.
Good boy.
He wants attention, so he pushes himself extra hard.
It's funny how he's like a human kid sometimes.

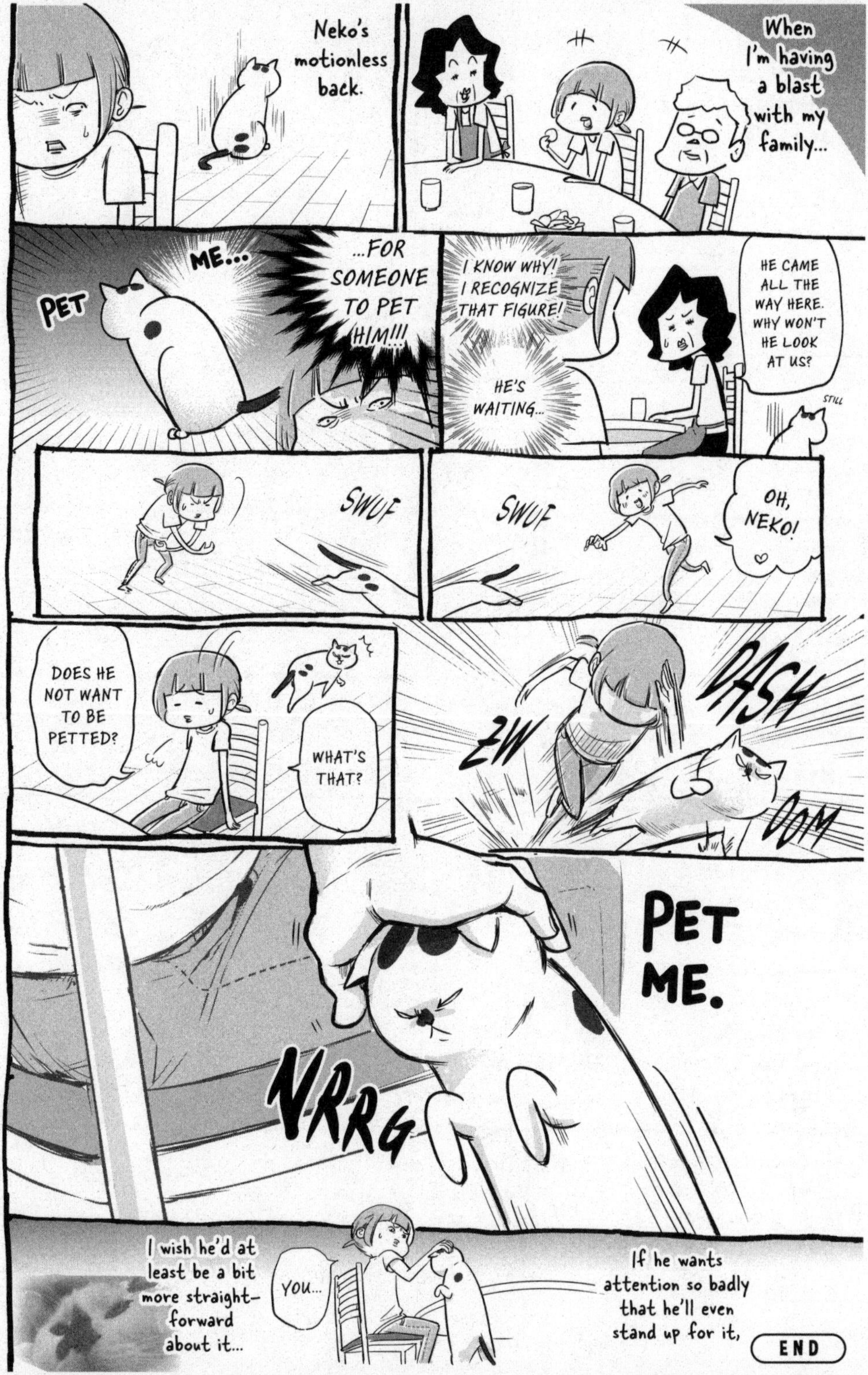
When I'm having a blast with my family...
Neko's motionless back.
HE CAME ALL THE WAY HERE. WHY WON'T HE LOOK AT US?
STILL
I KNOW WHY! I RECOGNIZE THAT FIGURE!
HE'S WAITING...
...FOR SOMEONE TO PET HIM!!!
PET ME...
OH, NEKO! ♡
SWUF
SWUF
DASH
ZWOOM
WHAT'S THAT?
DOES HE NOT WANT TO BE PETTED?
PET ME.
NRRG
If he wants attention so badly that he'll even stand up for it,
YOU...
I wish he'd at least be a bit more straight-forward about it...
END

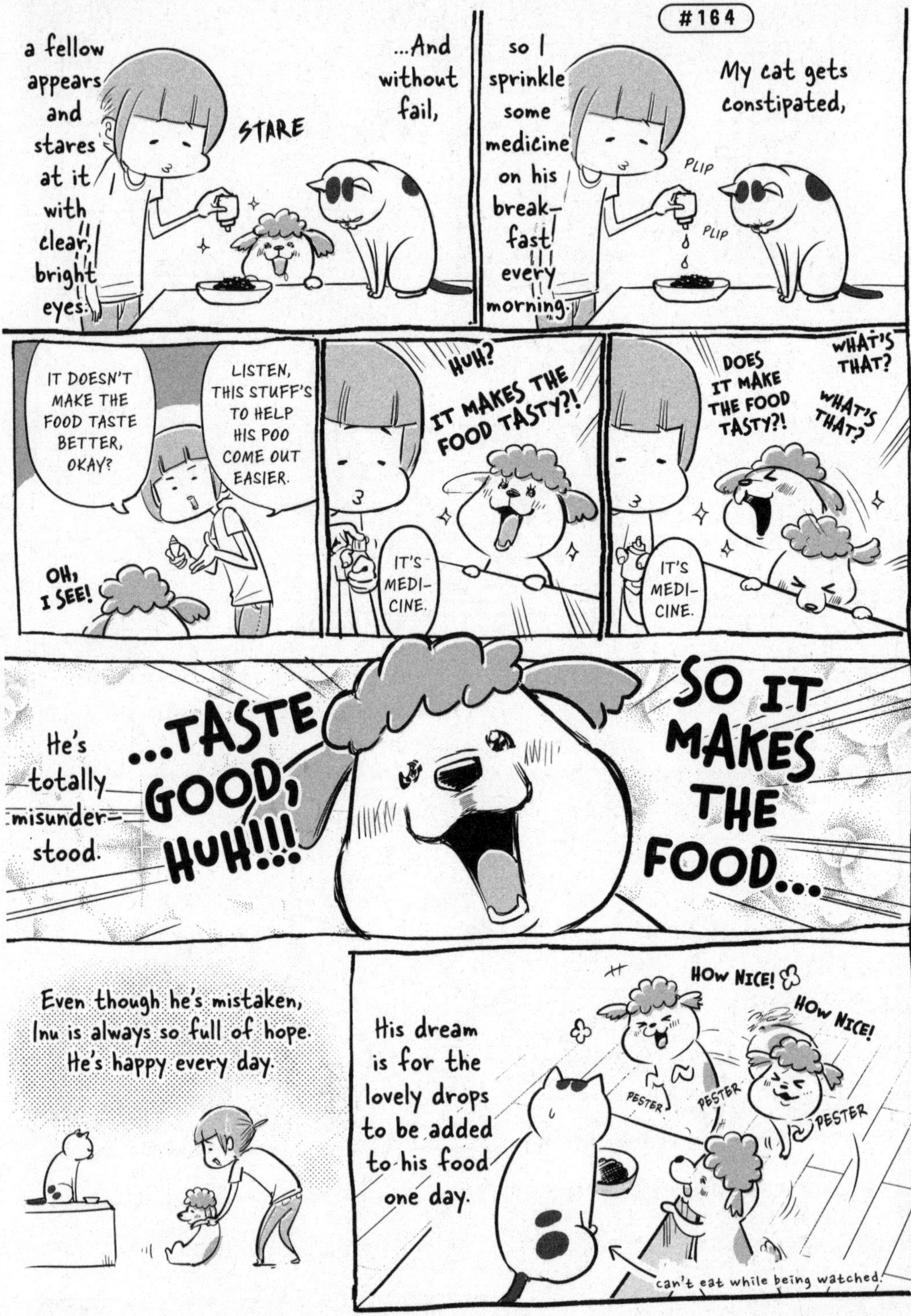
#164
My cat gets constipated,
so I sprinkle some medicine on his breakfast every morning.
PLIP
PLIP
...And without fail,
a fellow appears and stares at it with clear, bright eyes.
STARE
DOES IT MAKE THE FOOD TASTY?!
WHAT'S THAT?
WHAT'S THAT?
IT'S MEDI-CINE.
HUH?
IT MAKES THE FOOD TASTY?!
IT'S MEDI-CINE.
LISTEN, THIS STUFF'S TO HELP HIS POO COME OUT EASIER.
IT DOESN'T MAKE THE FOOD TASTE BETTER, OKAY?
OH, I SEE!
SO IT MAKES THE FOOD...
...TASTE GOOD, HUH!!!
He's totally misunder-stood.
His dream is for the lovely drops to be added to his food one day.
HOW NICE!
HOW NICE!
PESTER
PESTER
PESTER
can't eat while being watched.
Even though he's mistaken, Inu is always so full of hope. He's happy every day.

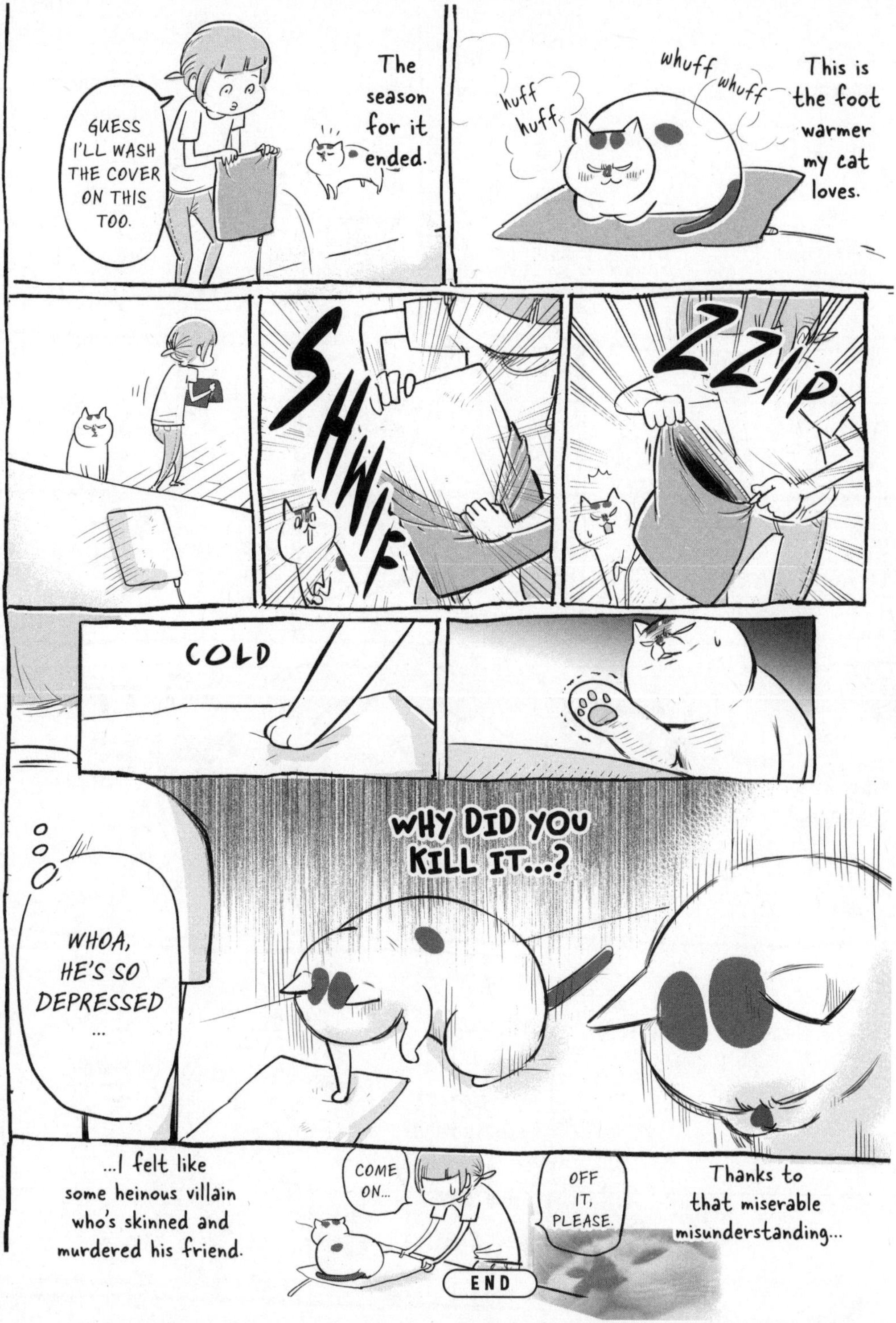
This is the foot warmer my cat loves.
whuff whuff
whuff
huff huff
The season for it ended.
GUESS I'LL WASH THE COVER ON THIS TOO.
ZZZIP
SHWIF
COLD
WHY DID YOU KILL IT...?
WHOA, HE'S SO DEPRESSED ...
Thanks to that miserable misunderstanding...
OFF IT, PLEASE.
COME ON...
...I felt like some heinous villain who's skinned and murdered his friend.
END

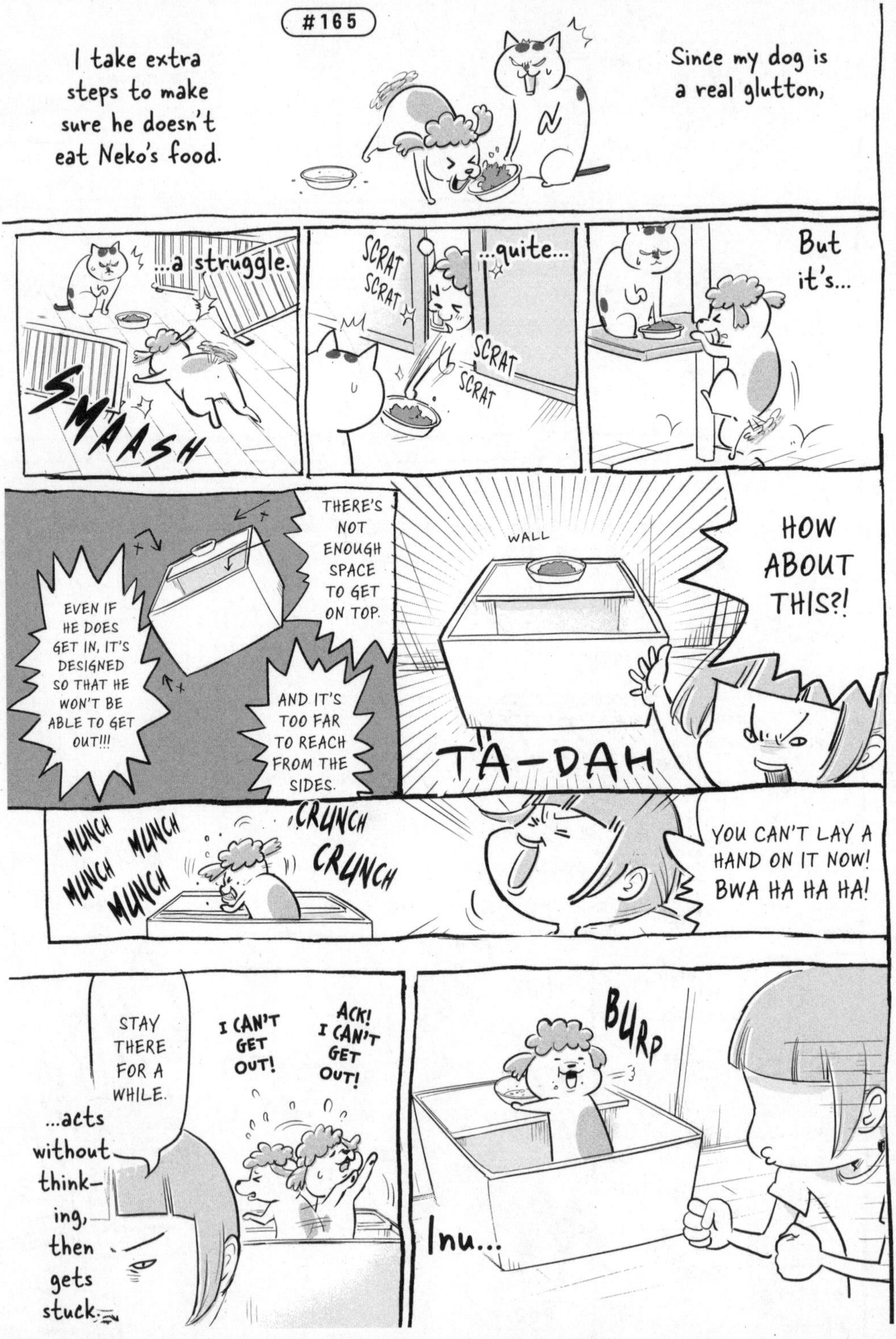
#165
Since my dog is a real glutton,
I take extra steps to make sure he doesn't eat Neko's food.
But it's...
...quite...
SCRAT SCRAT
SCRAT SCRAT
...a struggle.
SMAASH
HOW ABOUT THIS?!
WALL
TA-DAH
THERE'S NOT ENOUGH SPACE TO GET ON TOP.
EVEN IF HE DOES GET IN, IT'S DESIGNED SO THAT HE WON'T BE ABLE TO GET OUT!!!
AND IT'S TOO FAR TO REACH FROM THE SIDES.
YOU CAN'T LAY A HAND ON IT NOW! BWA HA HA HA!
CRUNCH CRUNCH
MUNCH MUNCH MUNCH MUNCH
BURP
Inu...
ACK! I CAN'T GET OUT!
I CAN'T GET OUT!
STAY THERE FOR A WHILE.
...acts without think-ing, then gets stuck.

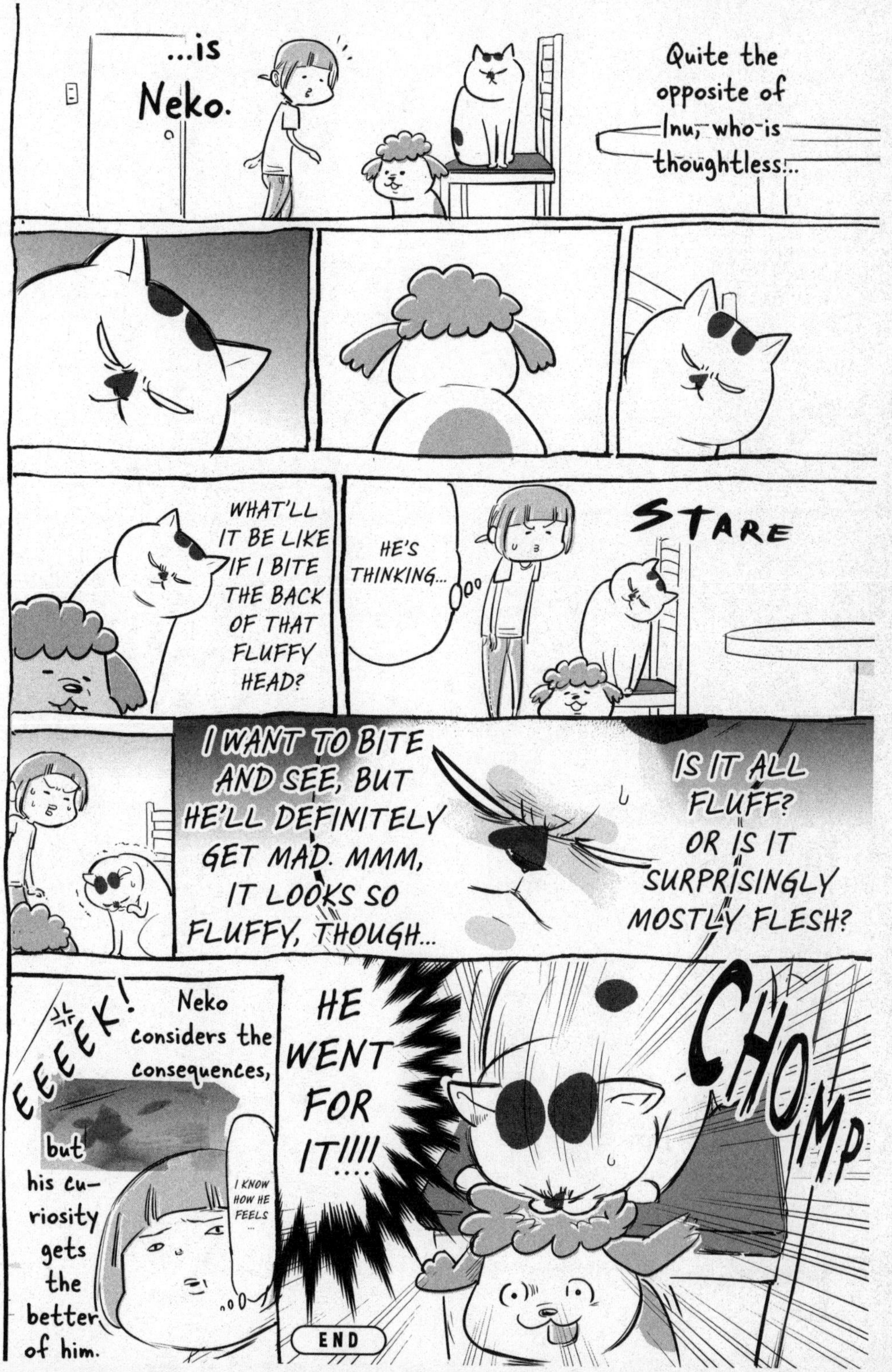
Quite the opposite of Inu, who is thoughtless...
...is Neko.
STARE
HE'S THINKING...
WHAT'LL IT BE LIKE IF I BITE THE BACK OF THAT FLUFFY HEAD?
IS IT ALL FLUFF? OR IS IT SURPRISINGLY MOSTLY FLESH?
I WANT TO BITE AND SEE, BUT HE'LL DEFINITELY GET MAD. MMM, IT LOOKS SO FLUFFY, THOUGH...
CHOMP
HE WENT FOR IT!!!!
EEEEK!
Neko considers the consequences,
but
his curiosity gets the better of him.
I KNOW HOW HE FEELS ...
END

Heh.

Newly-Drawn 4-Panel Strip

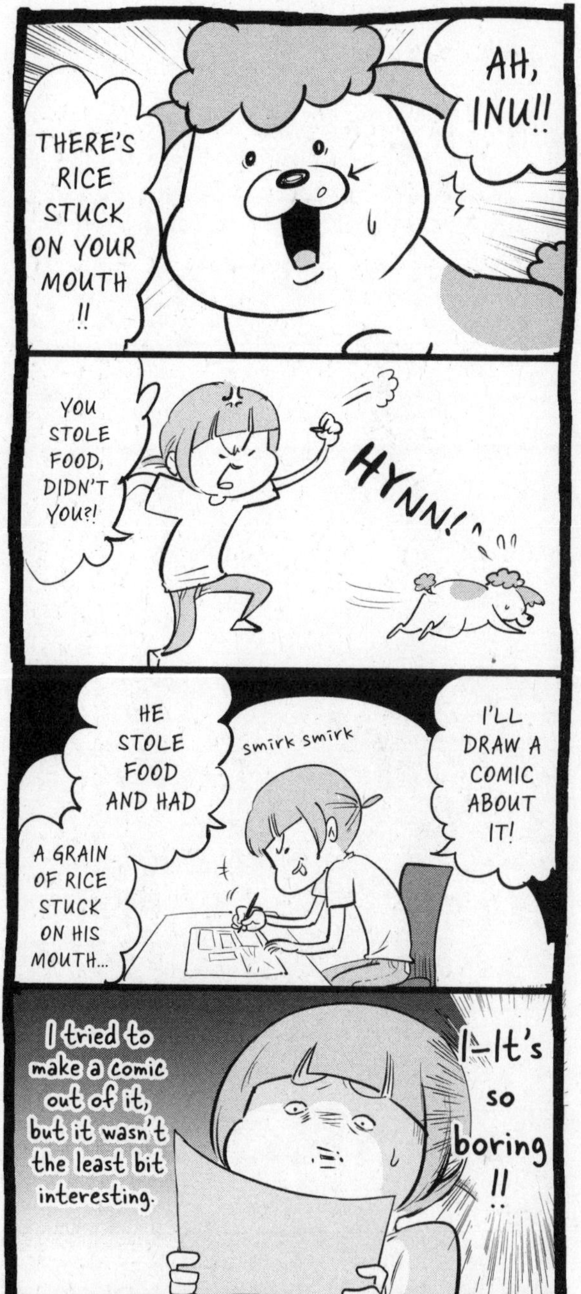

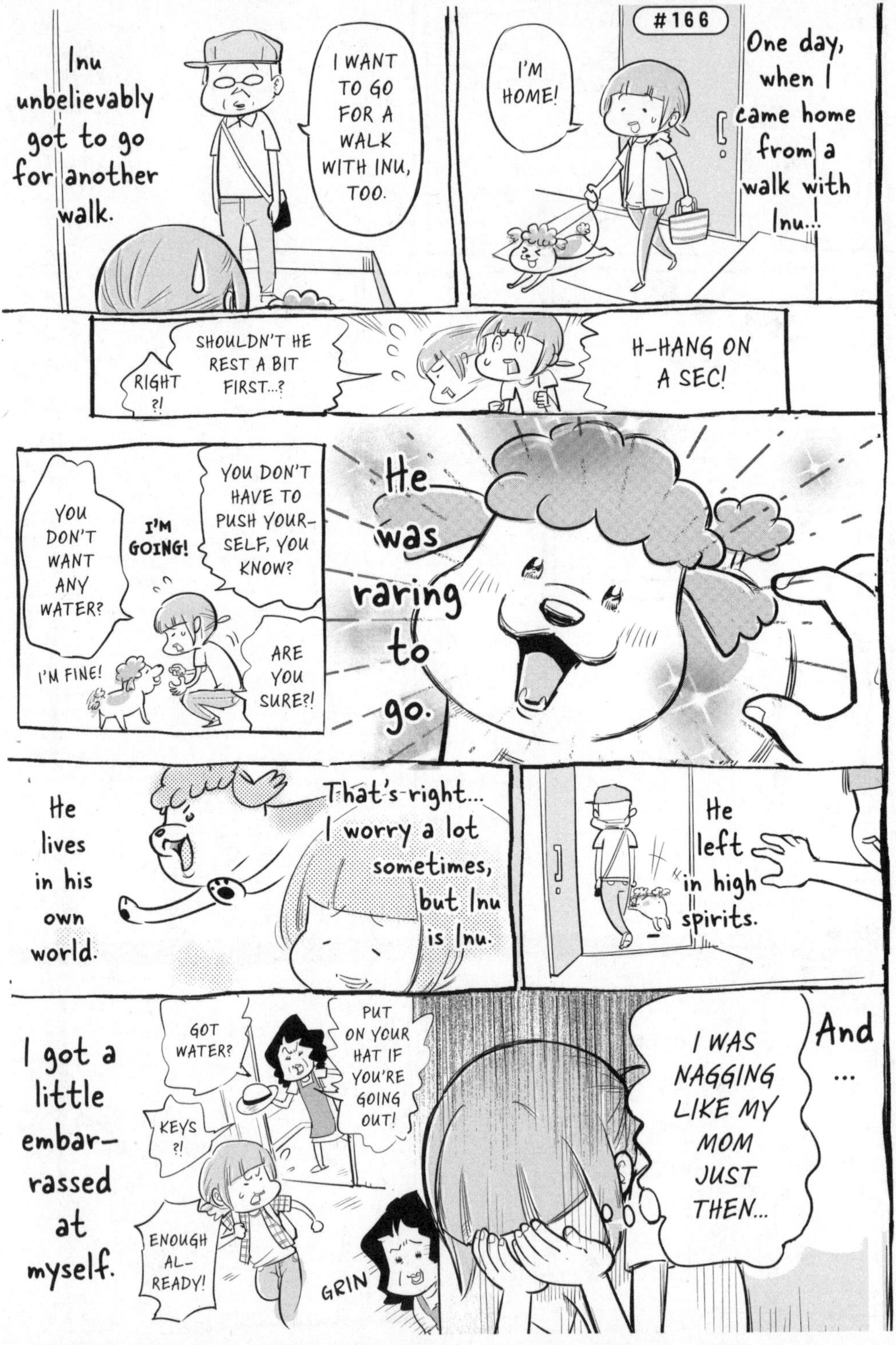

#166
One day, when I came home from a walk with Inu...
I'M HOME!
I WANT TO GO FOR A WALK WITH INU, TOO.
Inu unbelievably got to go for another walk.
H-HANG ON A SEC!
SHOULDN'T HE REST A BIT FIRST...?
RIGHT?!
He was raring to go.
YOU DON'T HAVE TO PUSH YOUR-SELF, YOU KNOW?
I'M GOING!
YOU DON'T WANT ANY WATER?
ARE YOU SURE?!
I'M FINE!
He left in high spirits.
That's right... I worry a lot sometimes, but Inu is Inu.
He lives in his own world.
And ...
I WAS NAGGING LIKE MY MOM JUST THEN...
PUT ON YOUR HAT IF YOU'RE GOING OUT!
GOT WATER?
KEYS?!
ENOUGH AL-READY!
GRIN
I got a little embar-rassed at myself.

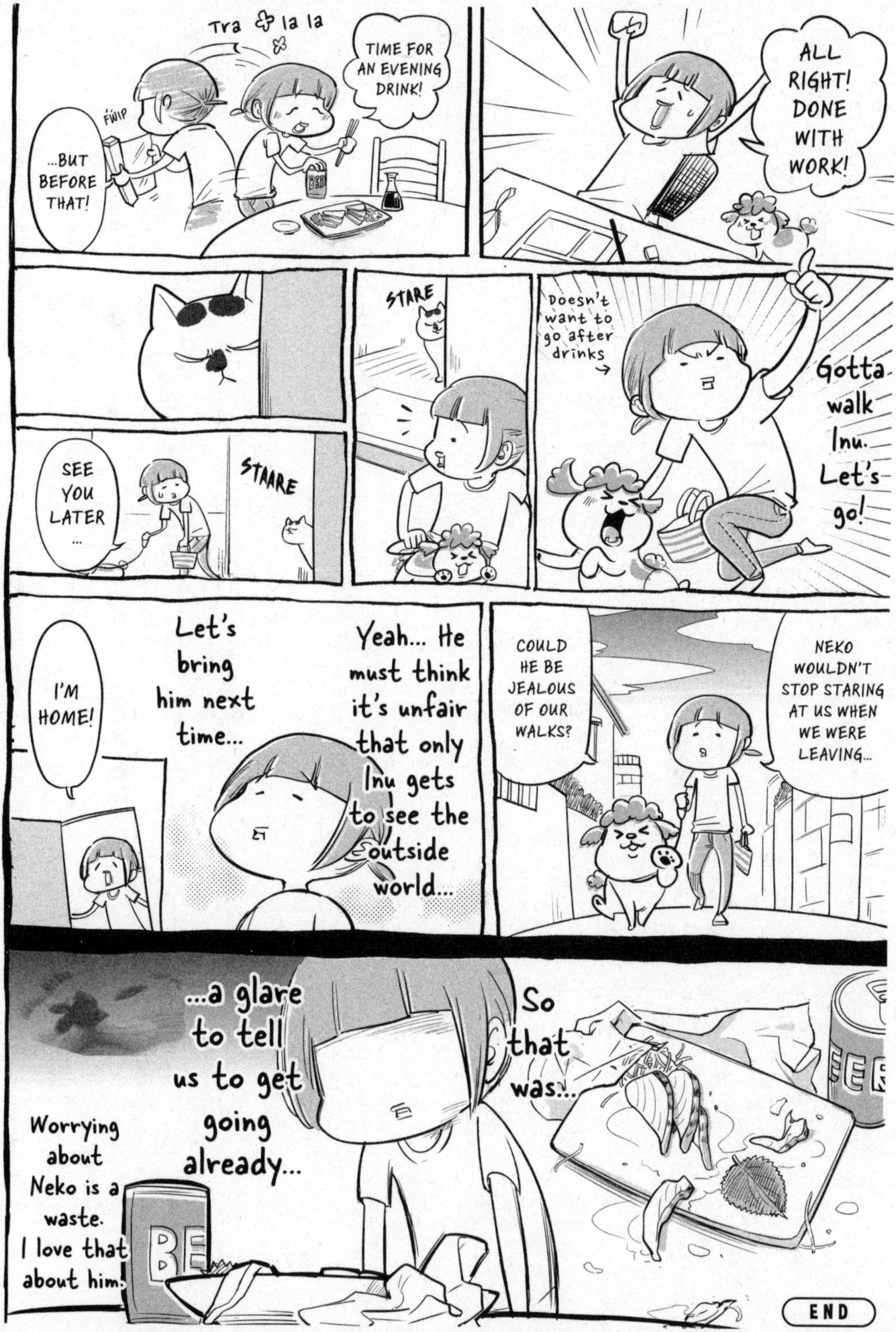
ALL RIGHT! DONE WITH WORK!
TIME FOR AN EVENING DRINK!
Tra la la
FWIP
...BUT BEFORE THAT!
Gotta walk Inu. Let's go!
Doesn't want to go after drinks
STARE
STAARE
SEE YOU LATER ...
NEKO WOULDN'T STOP STARING AT US WHEN WE WERE LEAVING...
COULD HE BE JEALOUS OF OUR WALKS?
Yeah... He must think it's unfair that only Inu gets to see the outside world...
Let's bring him next time...
I'M HOME!
So that was...
...a glare to tell us to get going already...
Worrying about Neko is a waste. I love that about him.
END

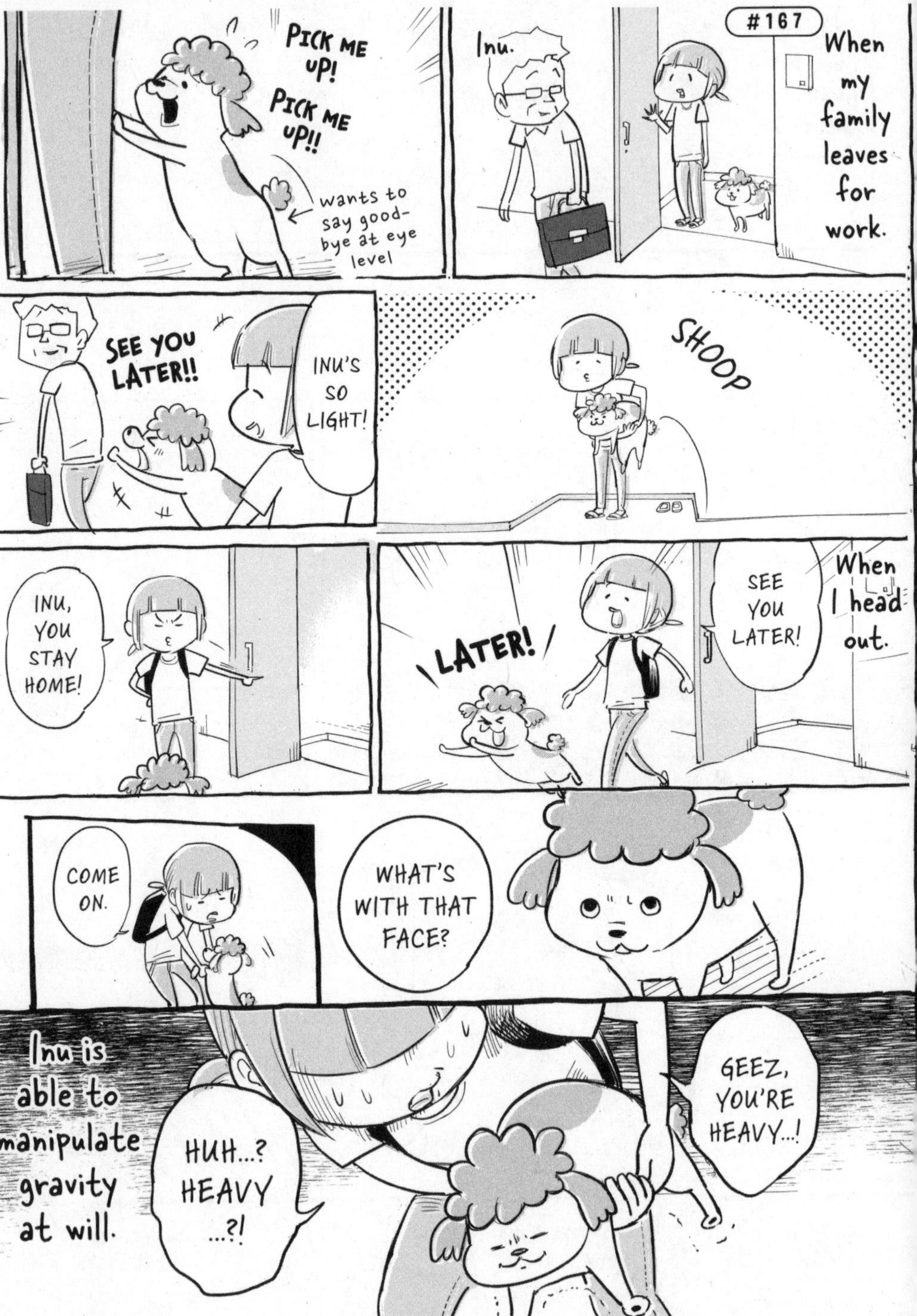
#167
When my family leaves for work.
Inu.
PICK ME UP! PICK ME UP!!
wants to say good-bye at eye level
SHOOP
INU'S SO LIGHT!
SEE YOU LATER!!
When I head out.
SEE YOU LATER!
LATER!
INU, YOU STAY HOME!
WHAT'S WITH THAT FACE?
COME ON.
GEEZ, YOU'RE HEAVY...!
HUH...? HEAVY ...?!
Inu is able to manipulate gravity at will.

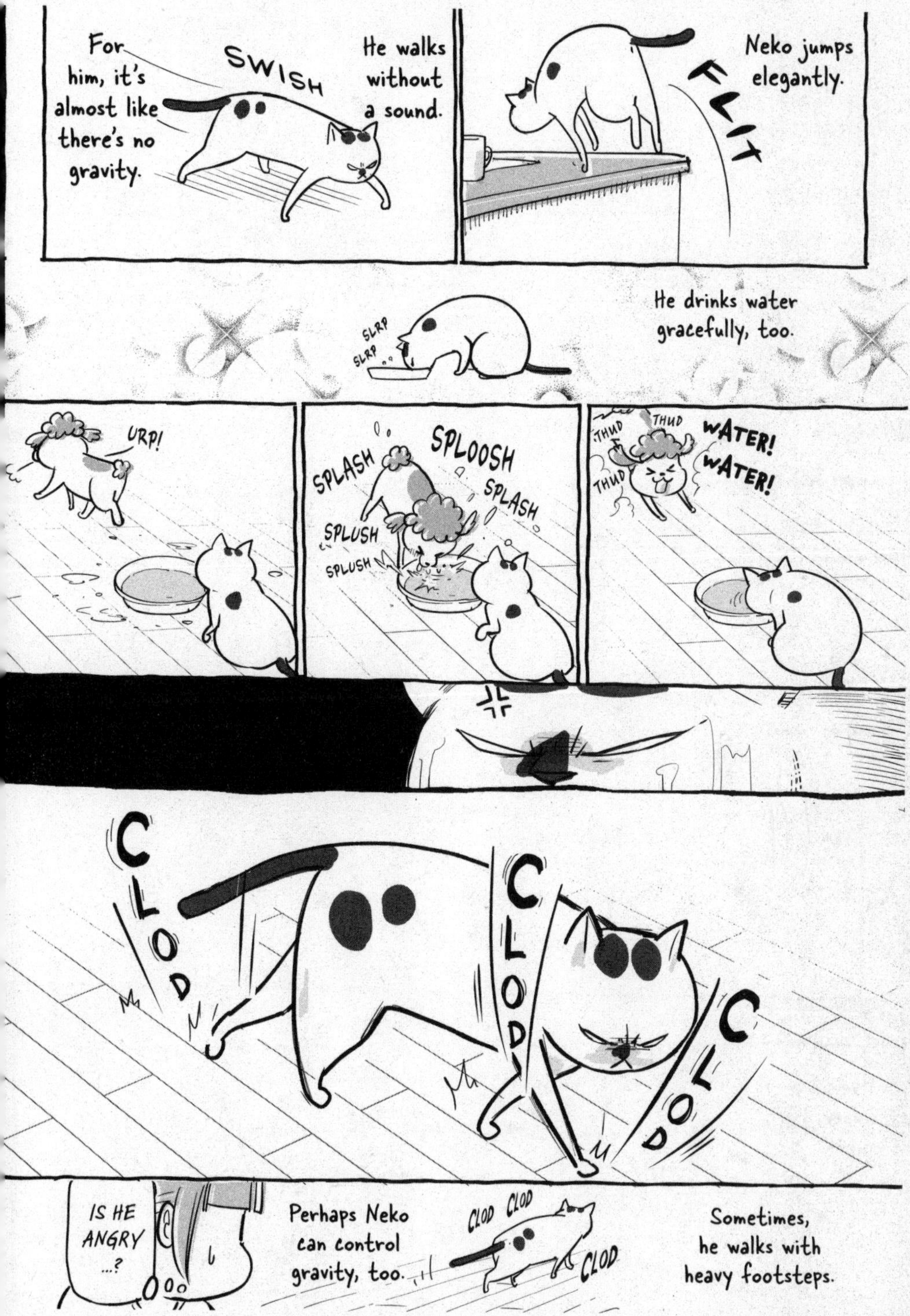

Neko jumps elegantly.
FLIT
He walks without a sound.
SWISH
For him, it's almost like there's no gravity.
He drinks water gracefully, too.
SLRP
SLRP
THUD
THUD
THUD
WATER! WATER!
SPLOOSH
SPLASH
SPLASH
SPLUSH
SPLUSH
URP!
CLOD
CLOD
CLOD
Sometimes, he walks with heavy footsteps.
CLOD CLOD
CLOD
Perhaps Neko can control gravity, too.
IS HE ANGRY ...?

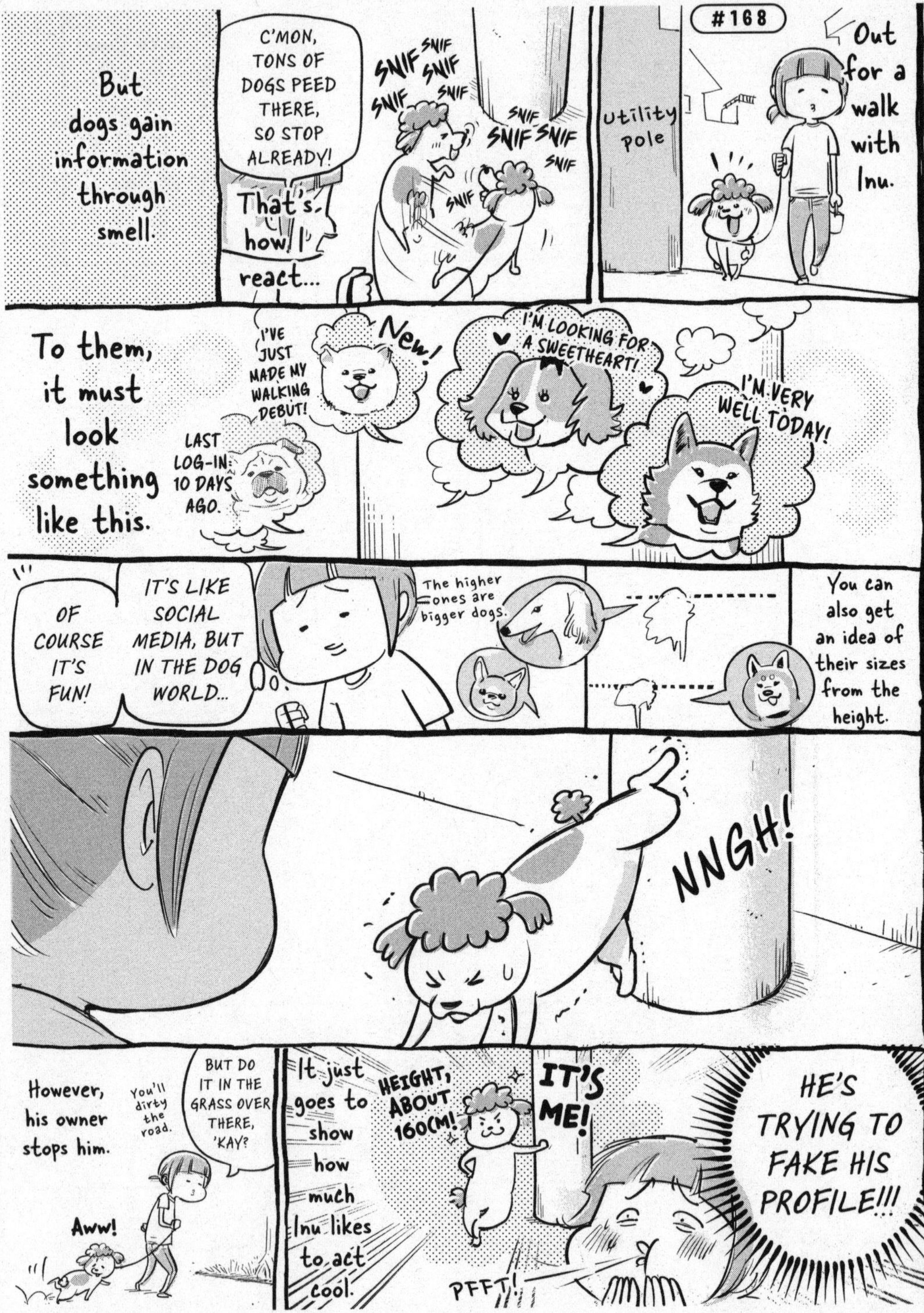
#168
Out for a walk with Inu.
Utility pole
SNIF SNIF SNIF SNIF SNIF
SNIF SNIF SNIF SNIF SNIF
C'MON, TONS OF DOGS PEED THERE, SO STOP ALREADY!
That's how I react...
But dogs gain information through smell.
I'M VERY WELL TODAY!
I'M LOOKING FOR A SWEETHEART!
New!
I'VE JUST MADE MY WALKING DEBUT!
LAST LOG-IN: 10 DAYS AGO.
To them, it must look something like this.
You can also get an idea of their sizes from the height.
The higher ones are bigger dogs.
IT'S LIKE SOCIAL MEDIA, BUT IN THE DOG WORLD...
OF COURSE IT'S FUN!
NNGH!
HE'S TRYING TO FAKE HIS PROFILE!!!
IT'S ME!
HEIGHT, ABOUT 160CM!
PFFT!
It just goes to show how much Inu likes to act cool.
BUT DO IT IN THE GRASS OVER THERE, 'KAY?
You'll dirty the road.
However, his owner stops him.
Aww!

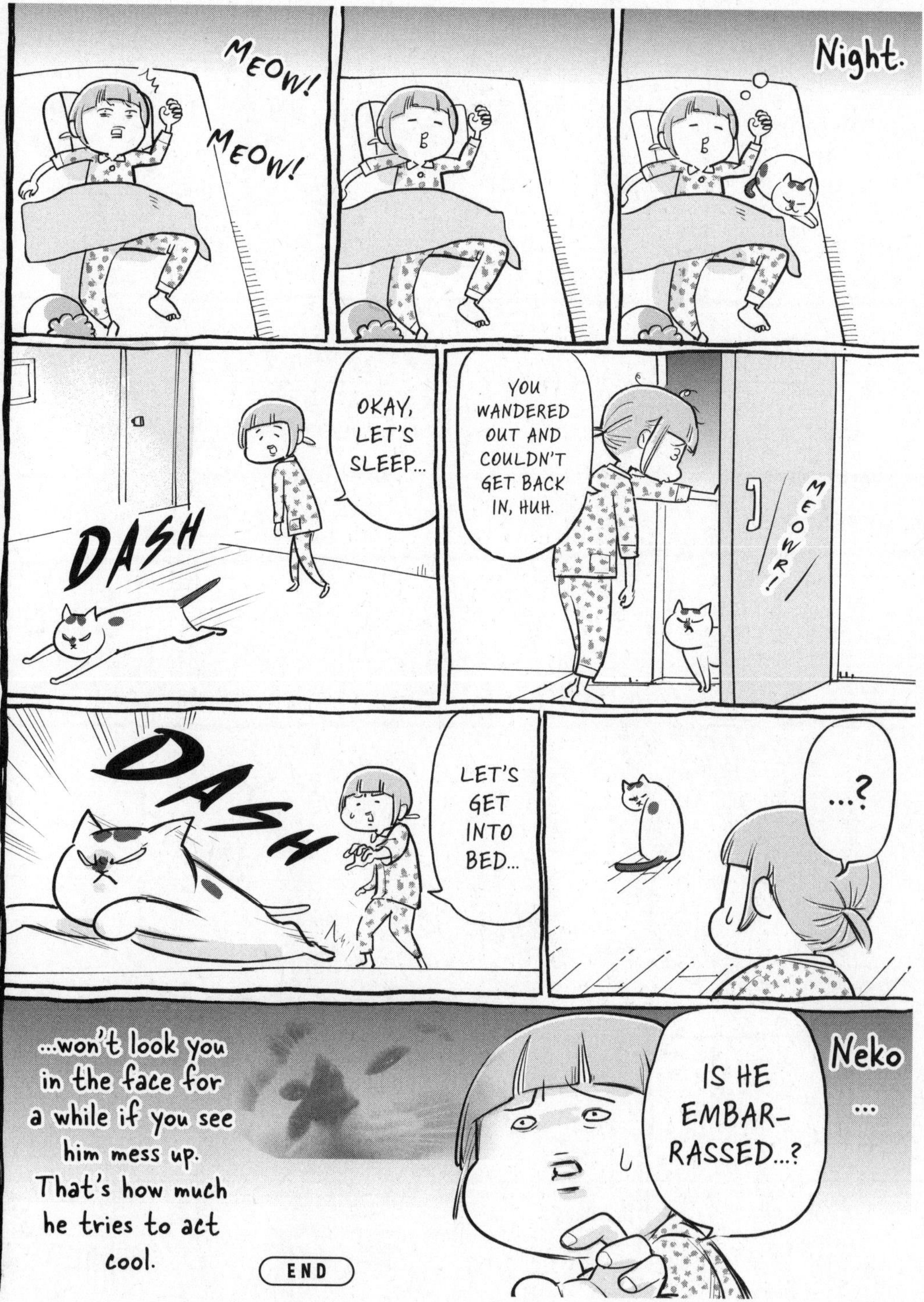
Night.
MEOW!
MEOW!
YOU WANDERED OUT AND COULDN'T GET BACK IN, HUH.
MEOWR!
OKAY, LET'S SLEEP...
DASH
...?
LET'S GET INTO BED...
DASH
Neko ...
IS HE EMBARRASSED...?
...won't look you in the face for a while if you see him mess up. That's how much he tries to act cool.
END

That funny face is unfair.

Newly-Drawn 4-Panel Strip

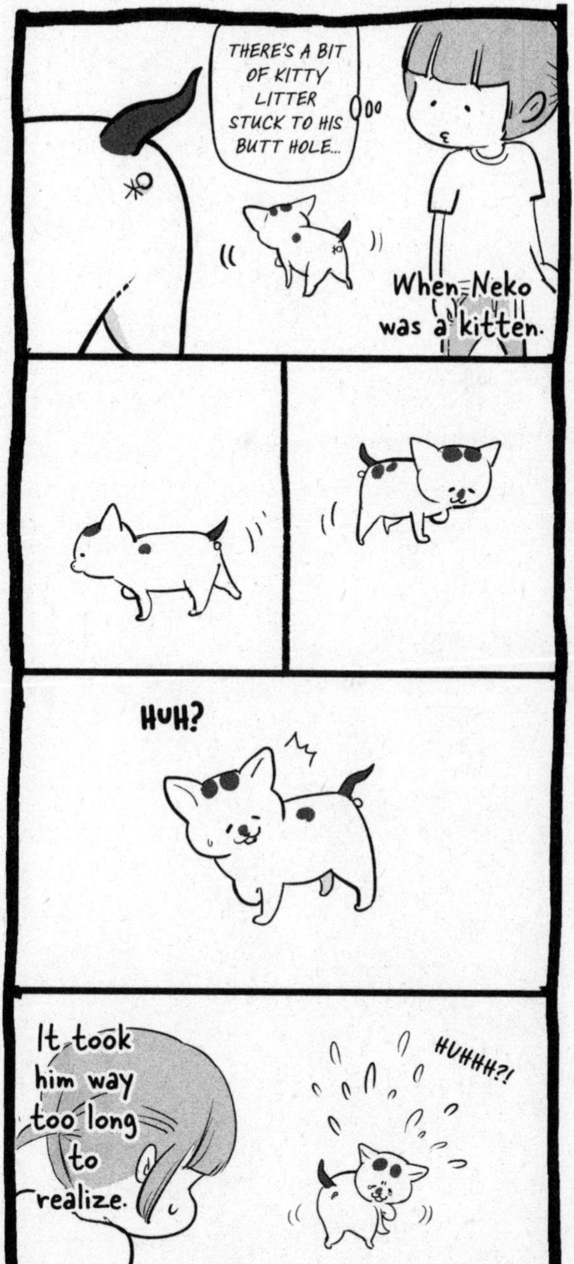

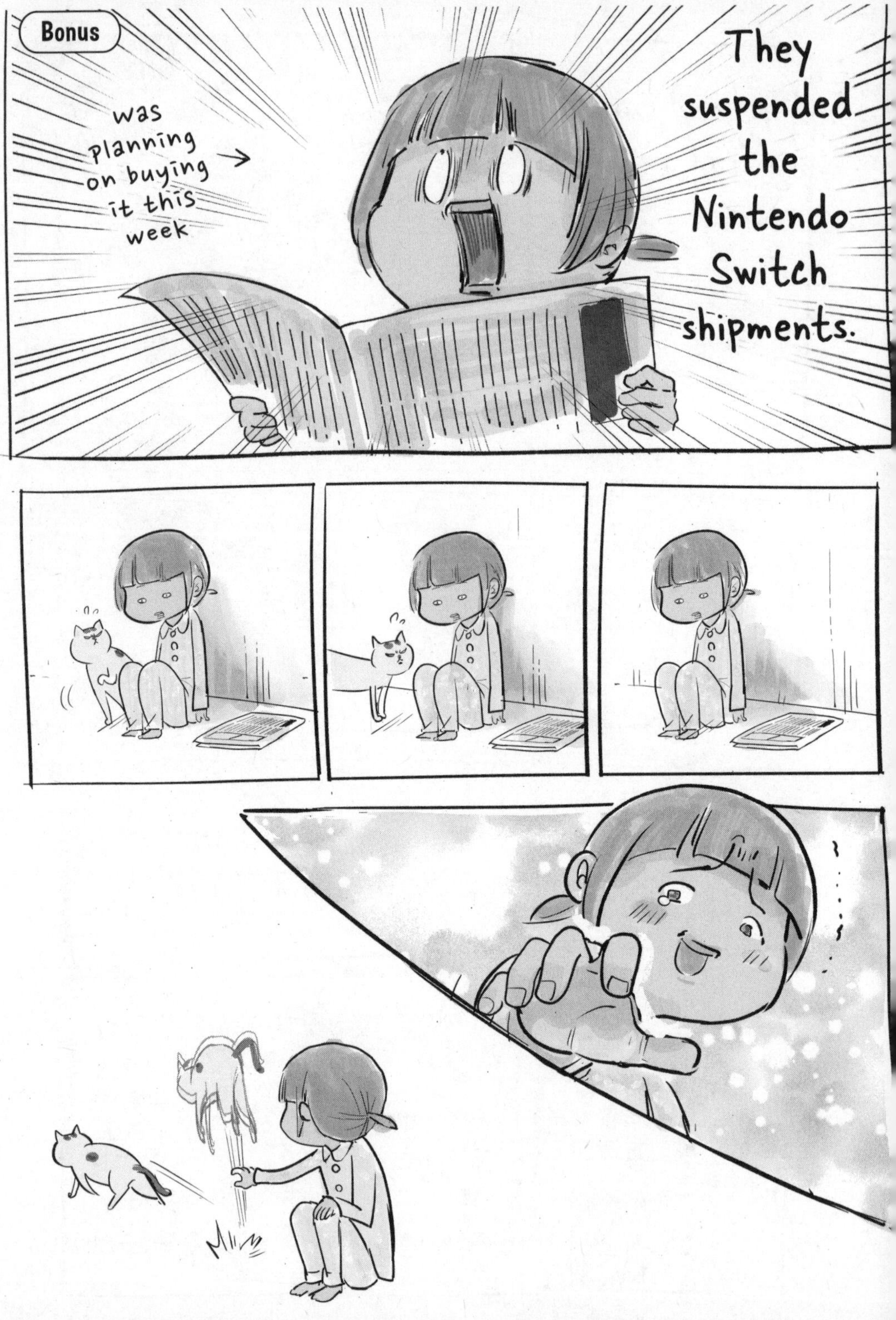
Bonus
They suspended the Nintendo Switch shipments.
was planning on buying it this week
. . . . .

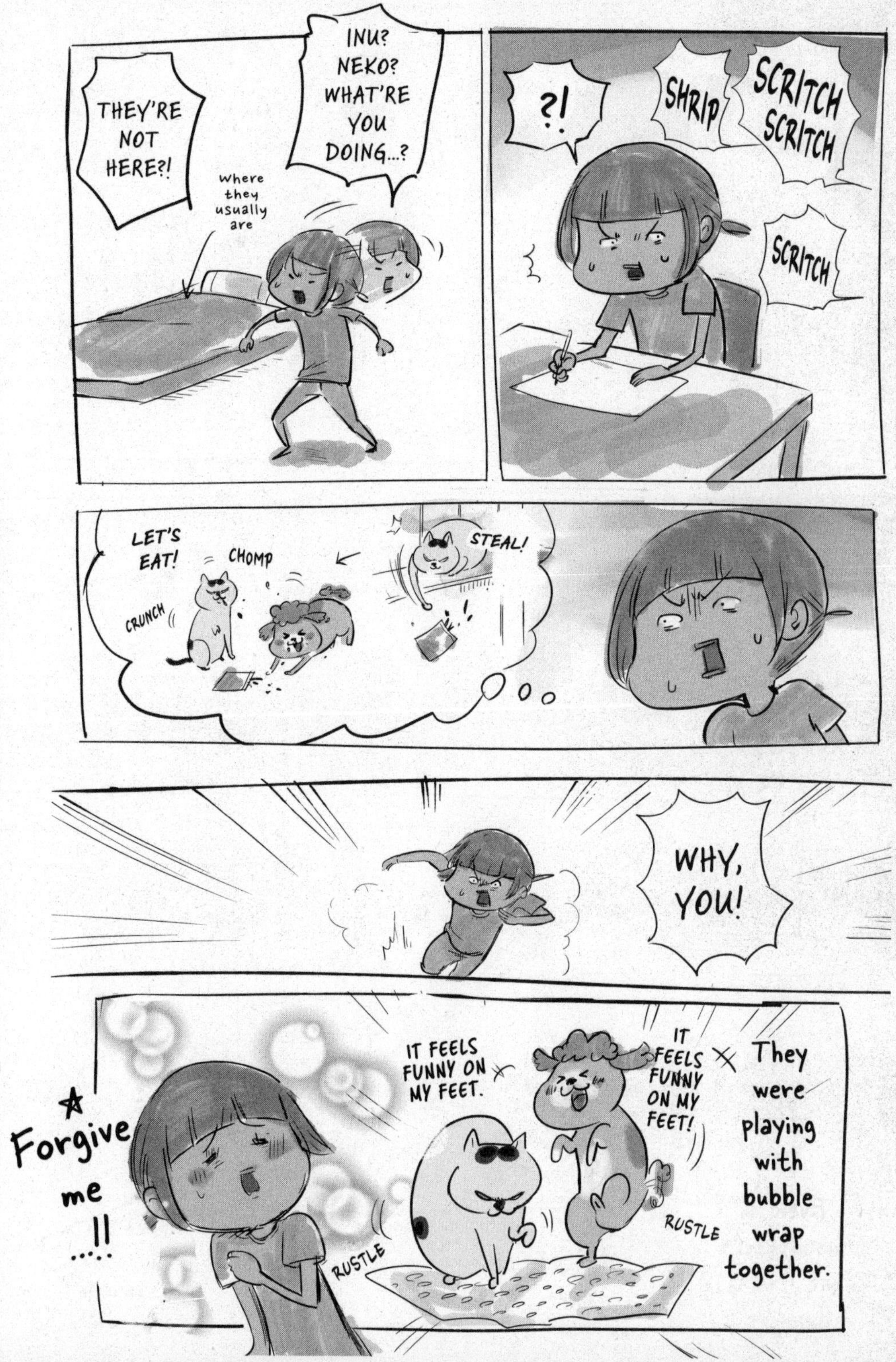
?!
SHRIP
SCRITCH SCRITCH
SCRITCH
INU? NEKO? WHAT'RE YOU DOING...?
THEY'RE NOT HERE?!
where they usually are
STEAL!
LET'S EAT!
CHOMP
CRUNCH
WHY, YOU!
They were playing with bubble wrap together.
IT FEELS FUNNY ON MY FEET!
IT FEELS FUNNY ON MY FEET.
RUSTLE
RUSTLE
Forgive me!! ....

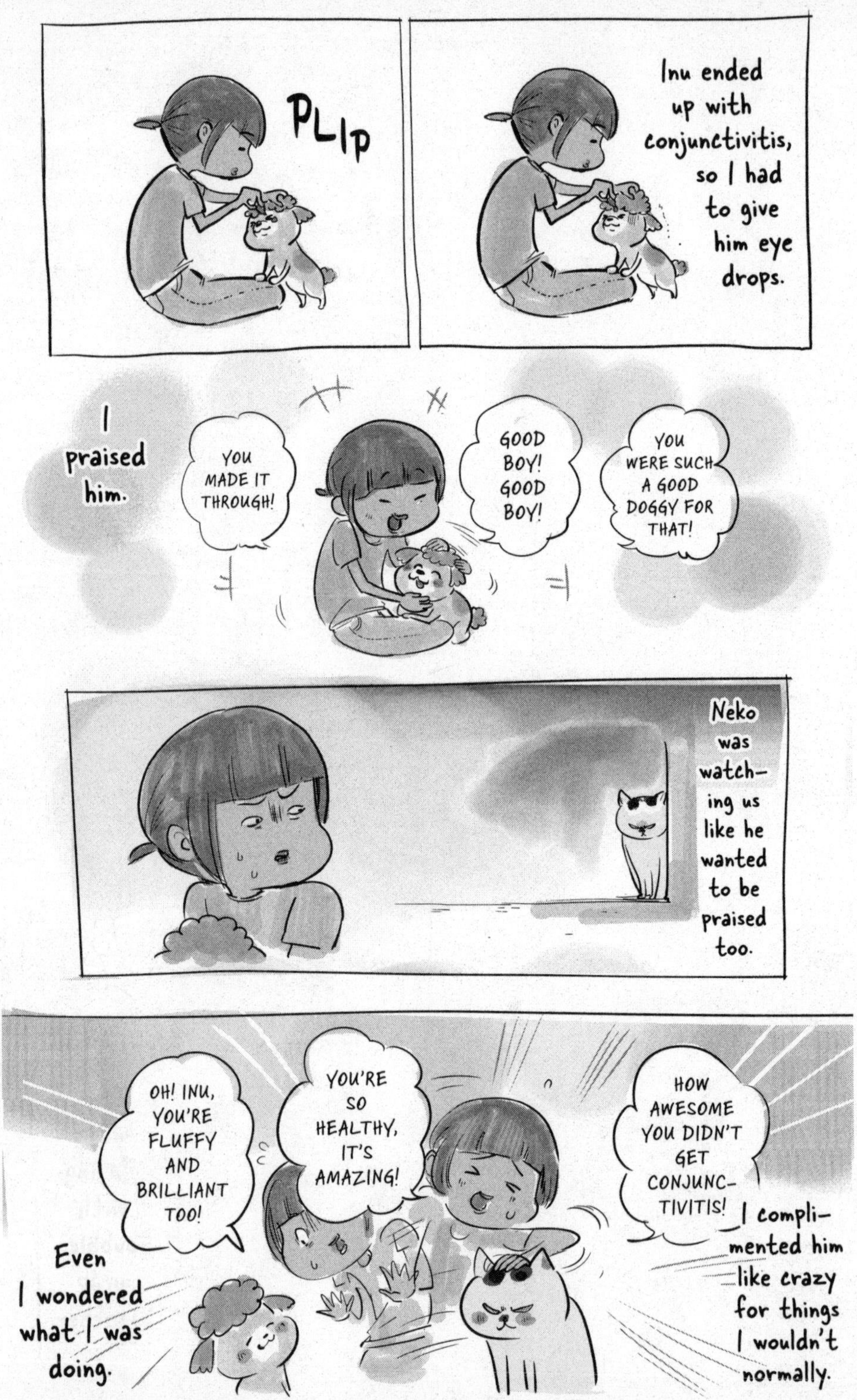

Inu ended up with conjunctivitis, so I had to give him eye drops.
PLIP
YOU WERE SUCH A GOOD DOGGY FOR THAT!
GOOD BOY! GOOD BOY!
YOU MADE IT THROUGH!
I praised him.
Neko was watching us like he wanted to be praised too.
HOW AWESOME YOU DIDN'T GET CONJUNCTIVITIS!
I complimented him like crazy for things I wouldn't normally.
YOU'RE SO HEALTHY, IT'S AMAZING!
OH! INU, YOU'RE FLUFFY AND BRILLIANT TOO!
Even I wondered what I was doing.

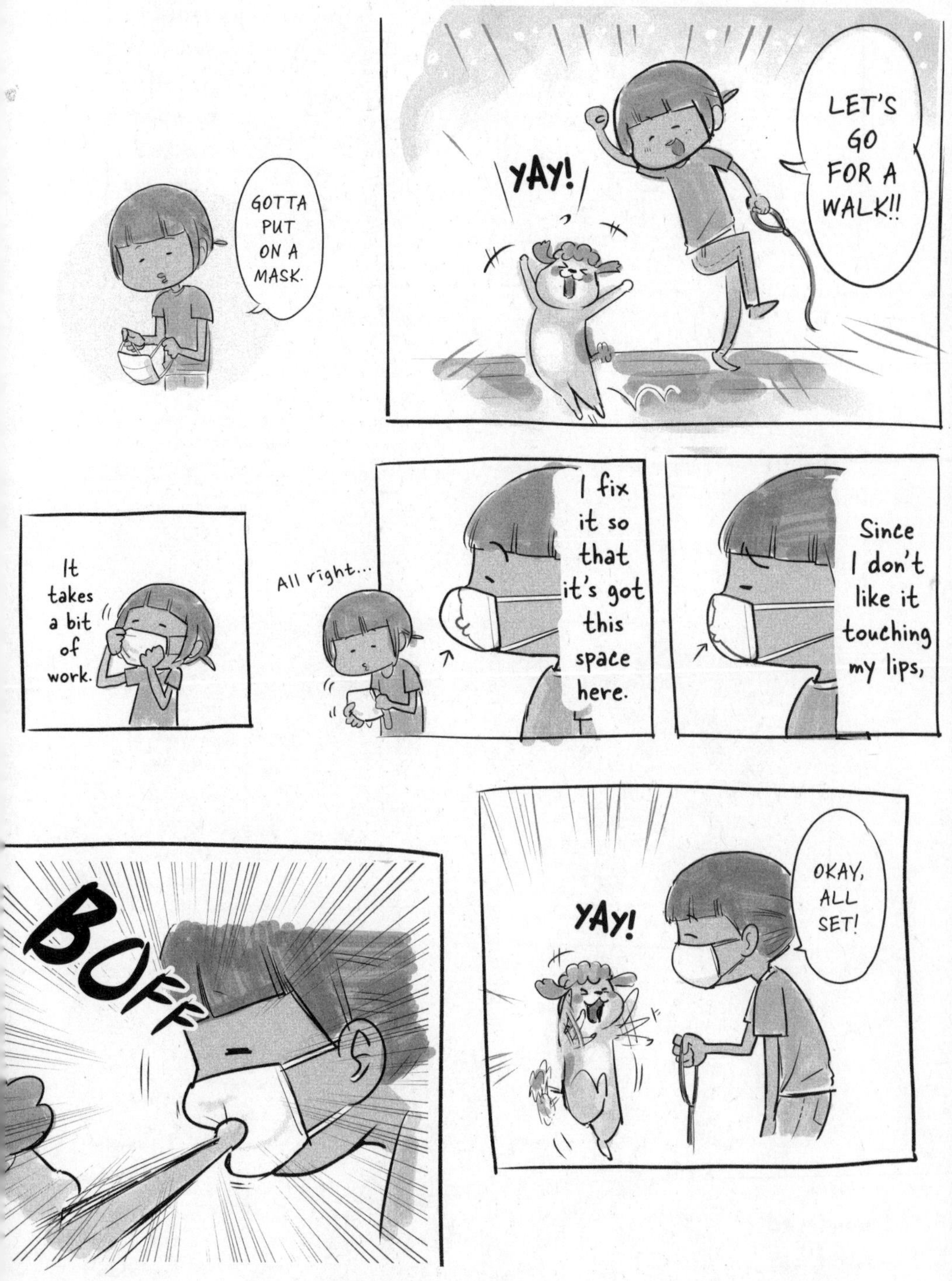
LET'S GO FOR A WALK!!
YAY!
GOTTA PUT ON A MASK.
Since I don't like it touching my lips,
I fix it so that it's got this space here.
All right...
It takes a bit of work.
OKAY, ALL SET!
YAY!
BOFF

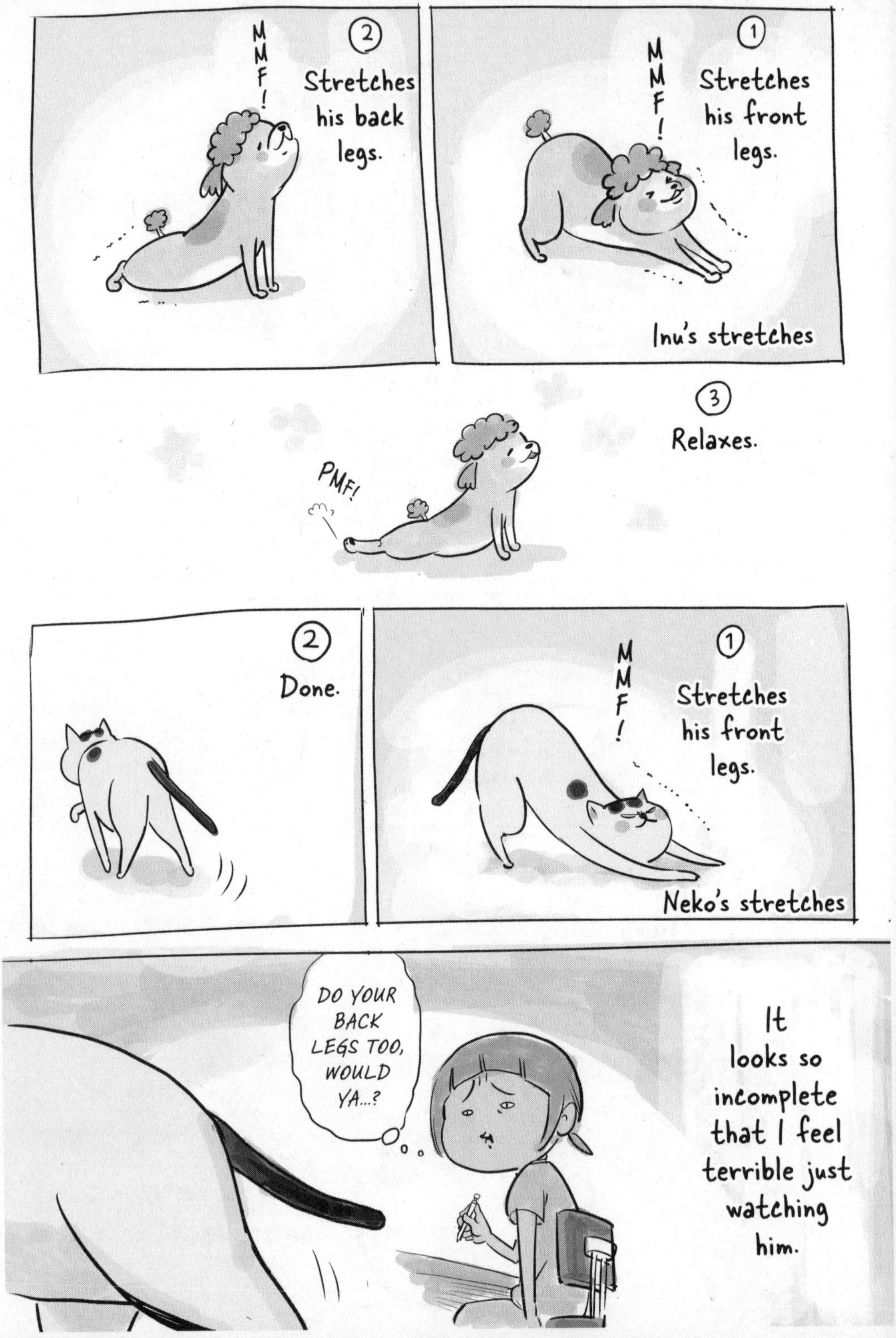

1
Stretches his front legs.
MMF!
Inu's stretches
2
Stretches his back legs.
MMF!
3
Relaxes.
PMF!
1
Stretches his front legs.
MMF!
Neko's stretches
2
Done.
It looks so incomplete that I feel terrible just watching him.
DO YOUR BACK LEGS TOO, WOULD YA...?

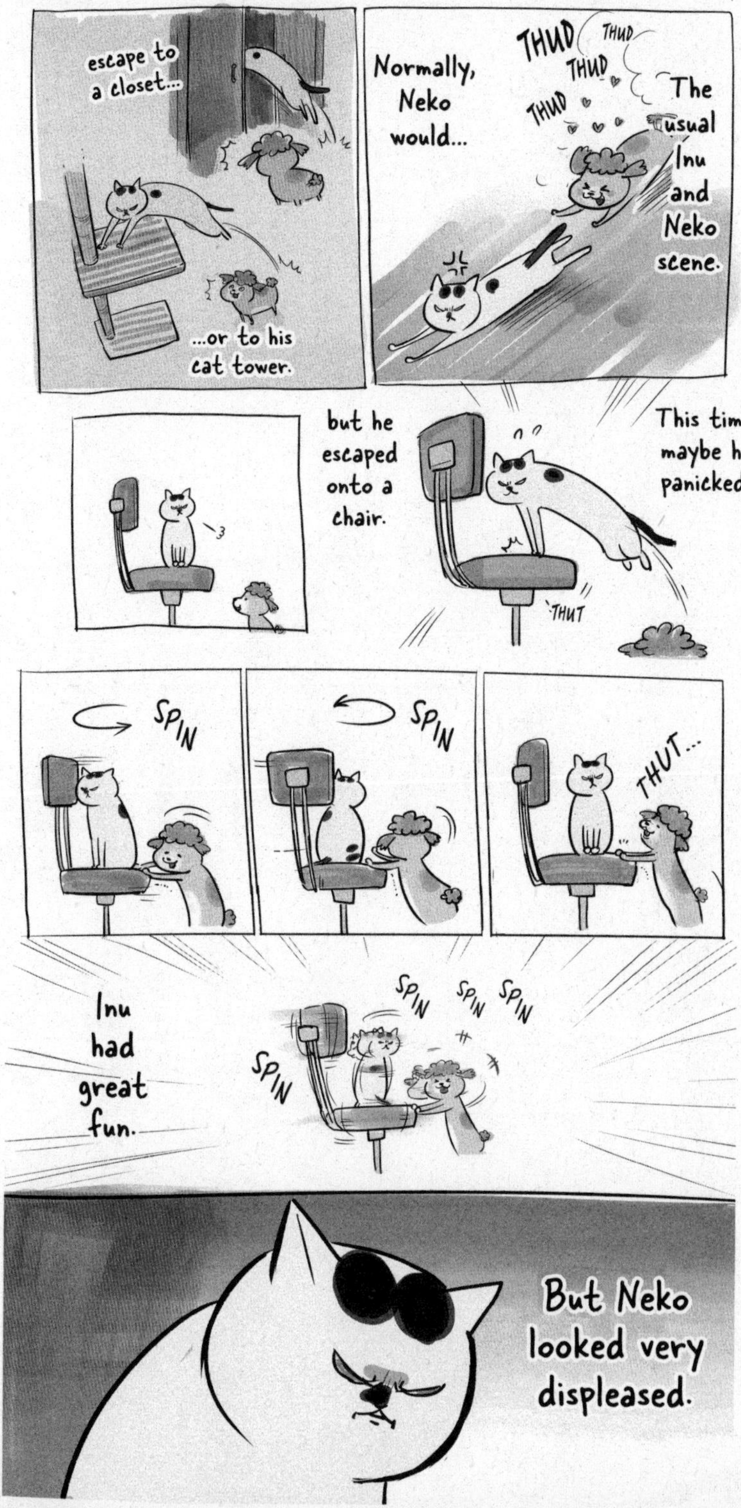
THUD THUD THUD THUD
The usual Inu and Neko scene.
Normally, Neko would...
escape to a closet...
...or to his cat tower.
This time, maybe he panicked,
but he escaped onto a chair.
THUT
THUT...
SPIN
SPIN
SPIN SPIN SPIN
SPIN
Inu had great fun.
But Neko looked very displeased.

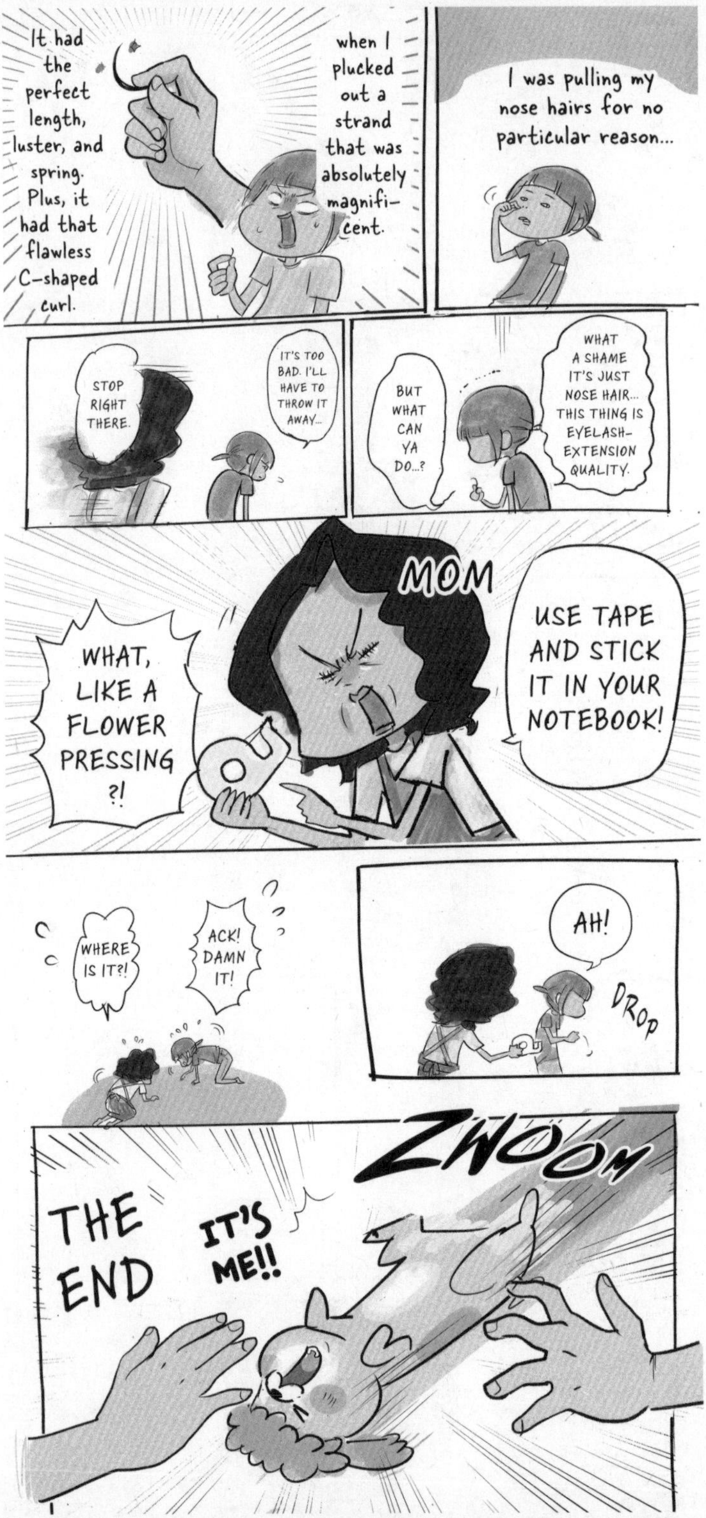
I was pulling my nose hairs for no particular reason...
when I plucked out a strand that was absolutely magnifi-cent.
It had the perfect length, luster, and spring. Plus, it had that flawless C-shaped curl.
WHAT A SHAME IT'S JUST NOSE HAIR... THIS THING IS EYELASH-EXTENSION QUALITY.
BUT WHAT CAN YA DO...?
IT'S TOO BAD. I'LL HAVE TO THROW IT AWAY...
STOP RIGHT THERE.
MOM
USE TAPE AND STICK IT IN YOUR NOTEBOOK!
WHAT, LIKE A FLOWER PRESSING?!
AH!
DROP
ACK! DAMN IT!
WHERE IS IT?!
ZWOOM
IT'S ME!!
THE END

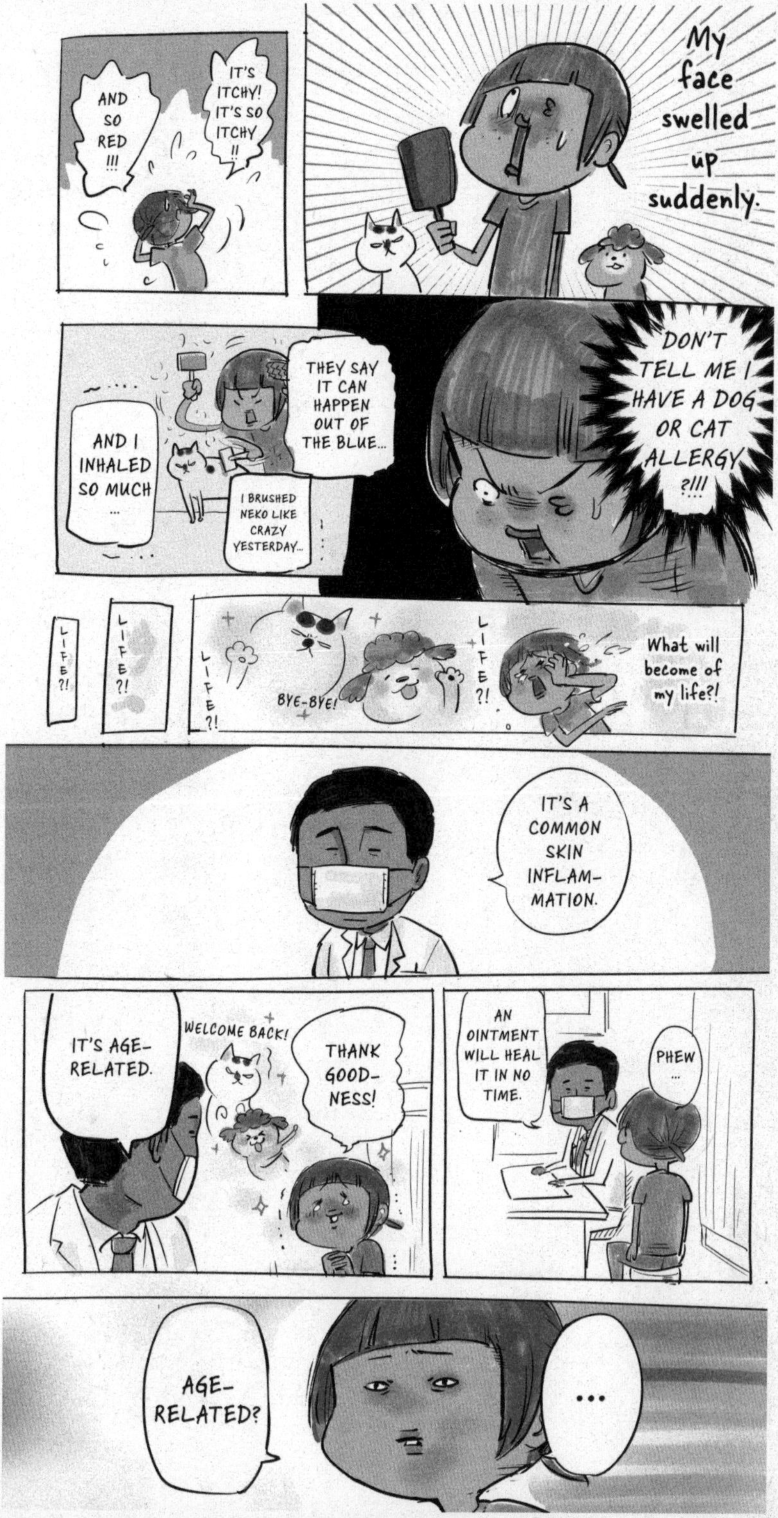
My face swelled up suddenly.
IT'S ITCHY! IT'S SO ITCHY !!
AND SO RED !!!
DON'T TELL ME I HAVE A DOG OR CAT ALLERGY ?!!!
THEY SAY IT CAN HAPPEN OUT OF THE BLUE...
I BRUSHED NEKO LIKE CRAZY YESTERDAY...
AND I INHALED SO MUCH ...
What will become of my life?!
LIFE ?!
BYE-BYE!
LIFE ?!
LIFE ?!
LIFE ?!
IT'S A COMMON SKIN INFLAM-MATION.
AN OINTMENT WILL HEAL IT IN NO TIME.
PHEW ...
THANK GOODNESS!
WELCOME BACK!
IT'S AGE-RELATED.
...
AGE-RELATED?

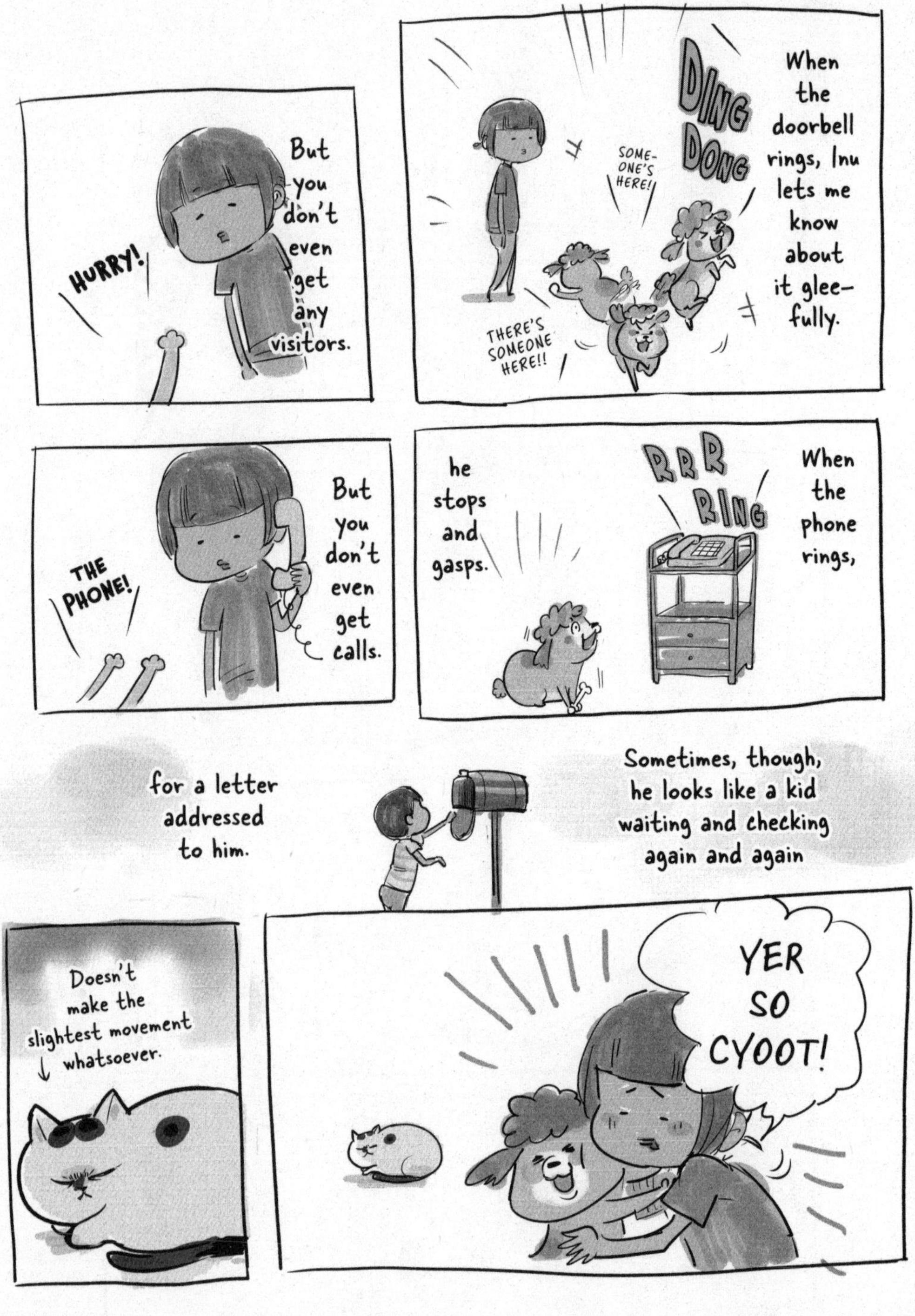

When the doorbell rings, Inu lets me know about it glee-fully.
DING DONG
SOME-ONE'S HERE!!
THERE'S SOMEONE HERE!!
But you don't even get any visitors.
HURRY!
When the phone rings,
RRR RING
he stops and gasps.
But you don't even get calls.
THE PHONE!
Sometimes, though, he looks like a kid waiting and checking again and again
for a letter addressed to him.
YER SO CYOOT!
Doesn't make the slightest movement whatsoever.

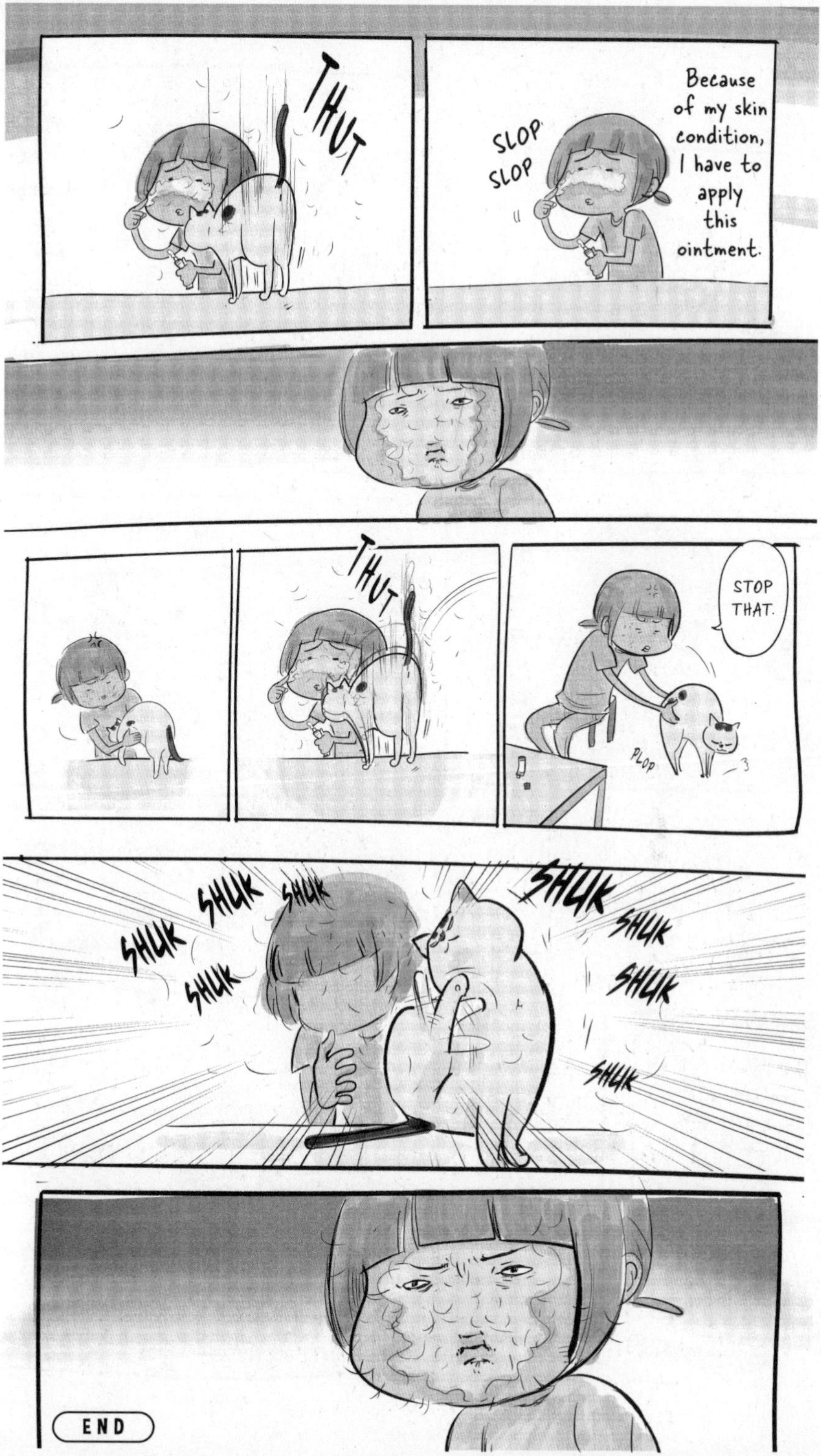

Because of my skin condition, I have to apply this ointment.
SLOP SLOP
THUT
STOP THAT.
PLOP
THUT
SHUK
SHUK
SHUK
SHUK
SHUK
SHUK
SHUK
SHUK
END

It's a butt! A butt! A dog butt!

Newly-Drawn 4-Panel Strip

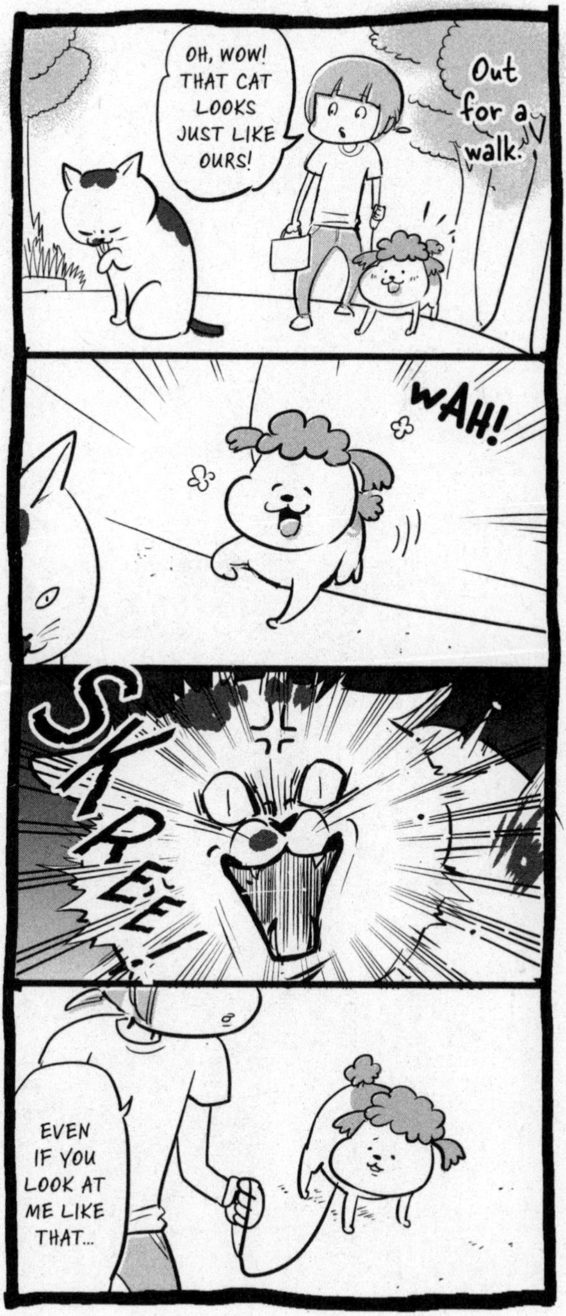
Out for a walk.
OH, WOW! THAT CAT LOOKS JUST LIKE OURS!
WAH!
SKREEE!
EVEN IF YOU LOOK AT ME LIKE THAT...

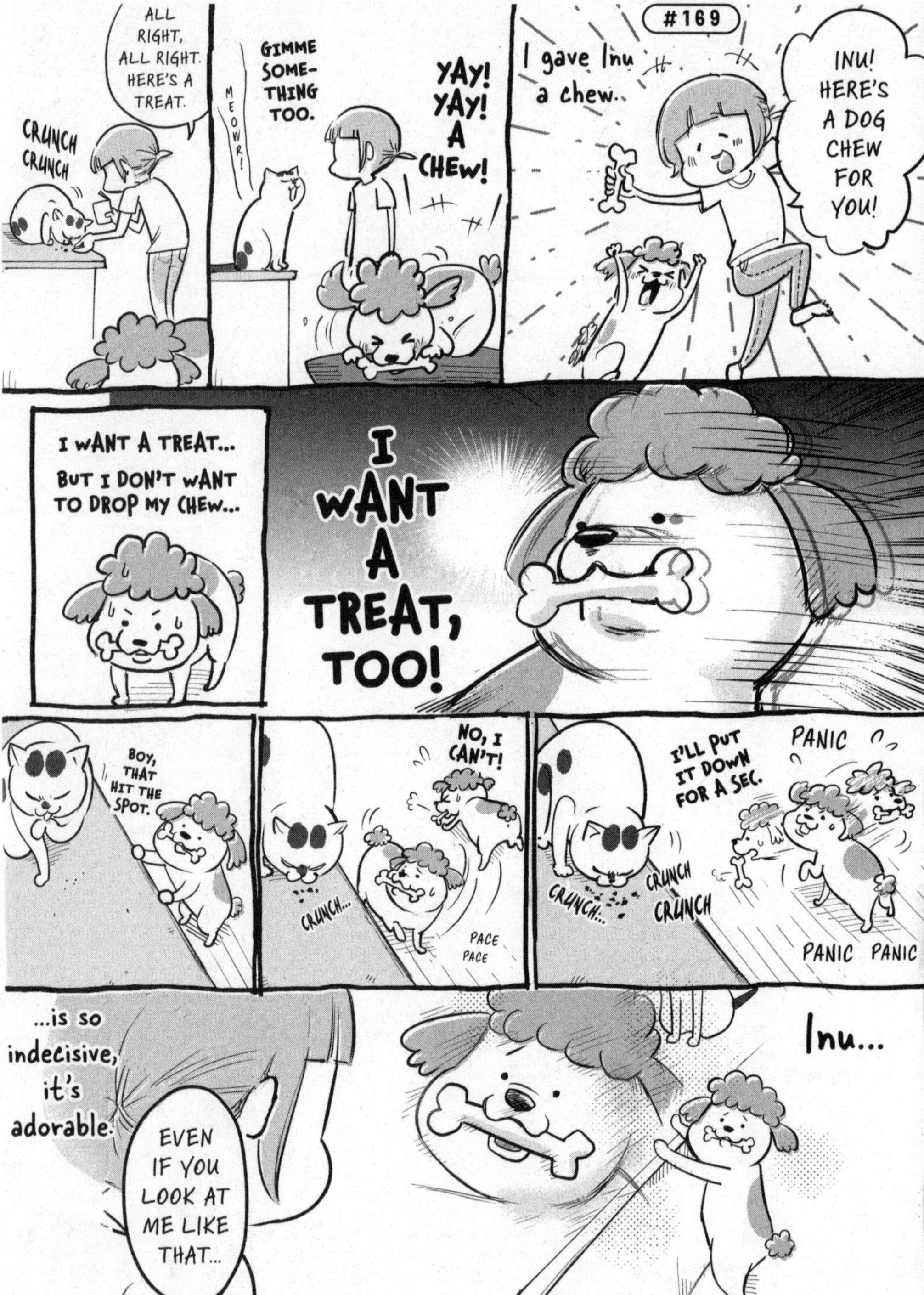
#169
I gave Inu a chew..
INU! HERE'S A DOG CHEW FOR YOU!
YAY! YAY! A CHEW!
GIMME SOME-THING TOO.
MEOWR!
ALL RIGHT, ALL RIGHT. HERE'S A TREAT.
CRUNCH CRUNCH
I WANT A TREAT, TOO!
I WANT A TREAT...
BUT I DON'T WANT TO DROP MY CHEW...
PANIC
I'LL PUT IT DOWN FOR A SEC.
CRUNCH CRUNCH
CRUNCH...
PANIC PANIC
NO, I CAN'T!
CRUNCH...
PACE PACE
BOY, THAT HIT THE SPOT.
Inu...
...is so indecisive, it's adorable.
EVEN IF YOU LOOK AT ME LIKE THAT...

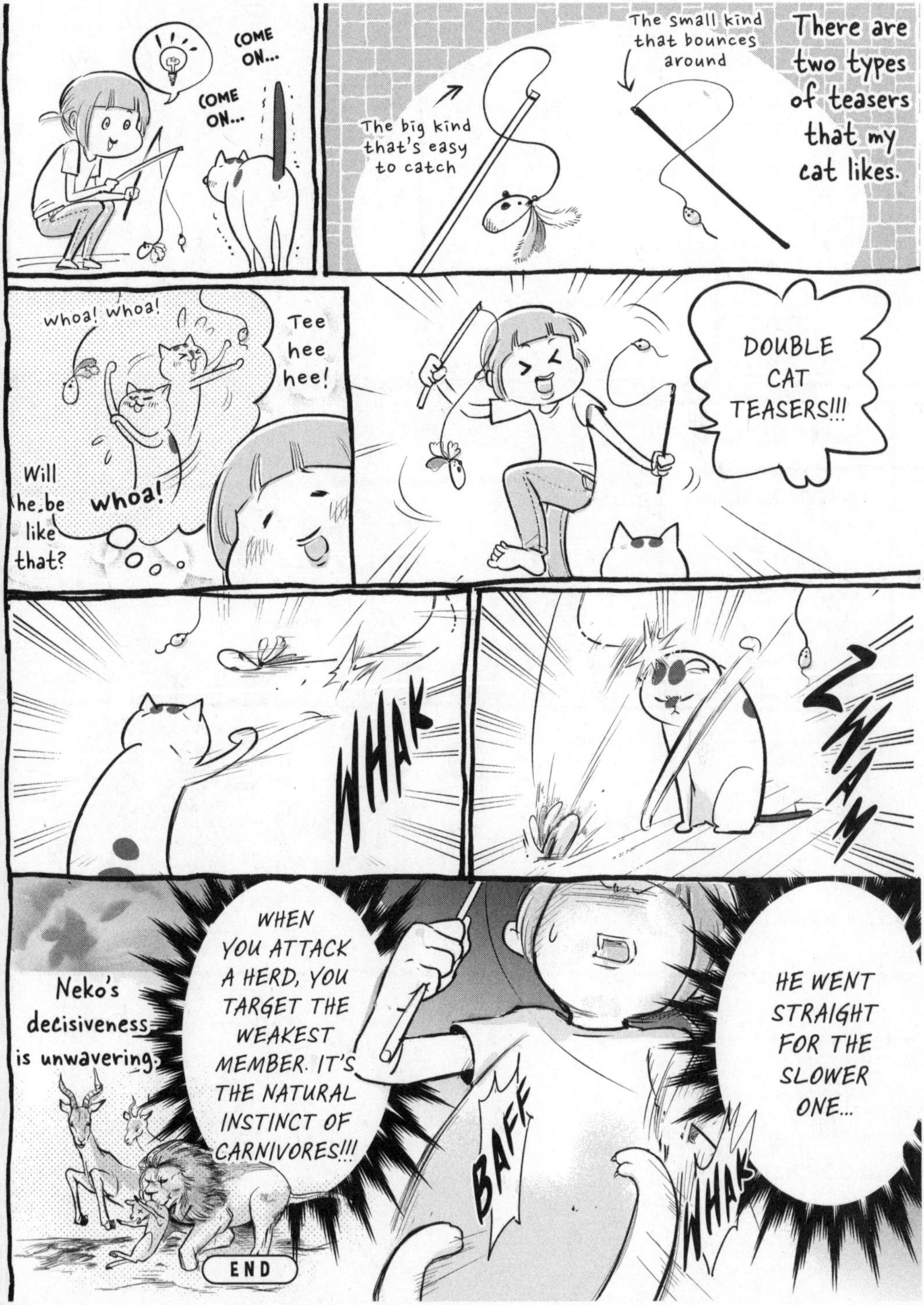
There are two types of teasers that my cat likes.
The small kind that bounces around
The big kind that's easy to catch
COME ON...
COME ON...
DOUBLE CAT TEASERS!!!
Tee hee hee!
whoa! whoa!
whoa!
Will he be like that?
ZWAM
WHAK
HE WENT STRAIGHT FOR THE SLOWER ONE...
WHAK
BAFF
WHEN YOU ATTACK A HERD, YOU TARGET THE WEAKEST MEMBER. IT'S THE NATURAL INSTINCT OF CARNIVORES!!!
Neko's decisiveness is unwavering.
END

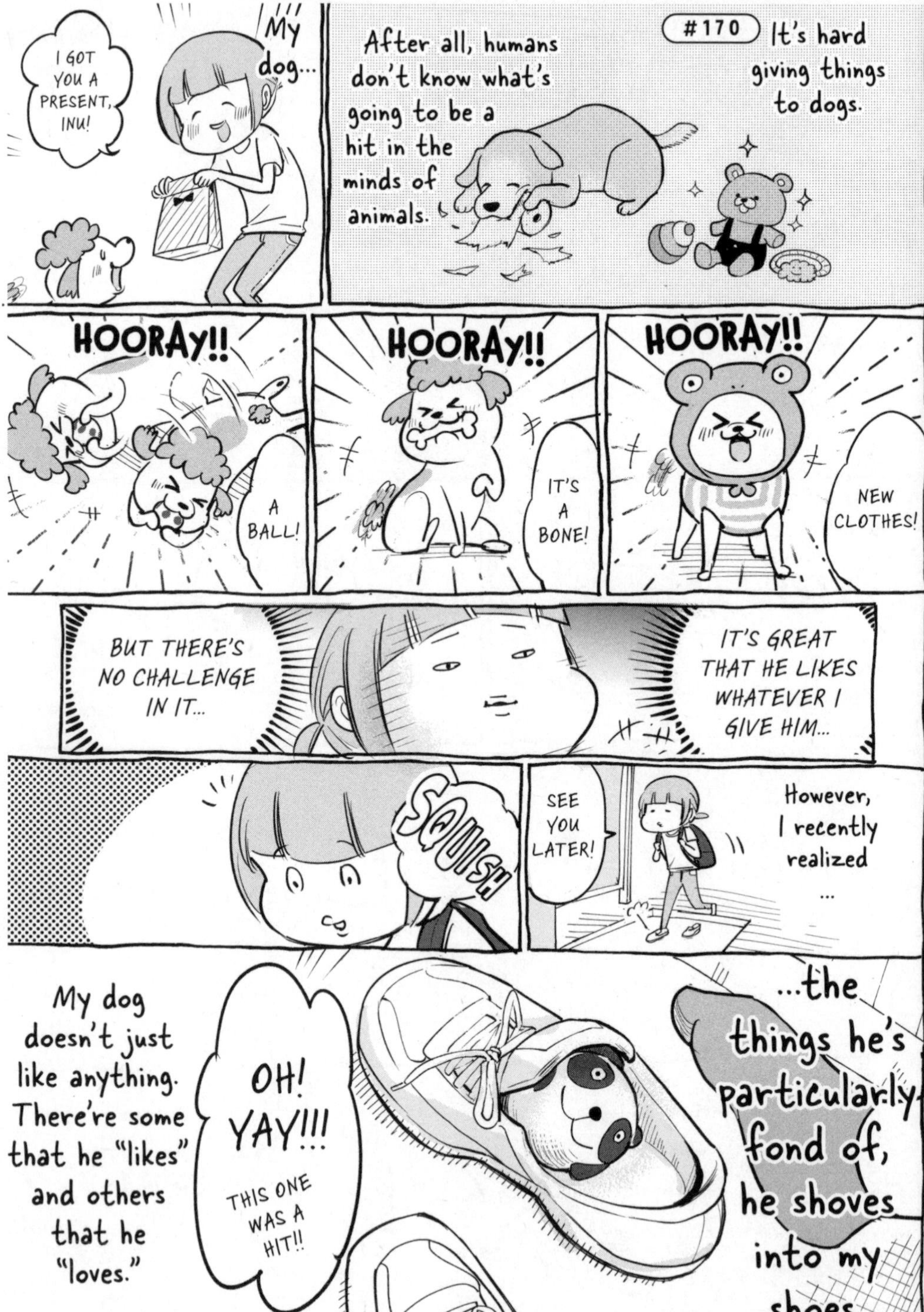
#170 It's hard giving things to dogs.
After all, humans don't know what's going to be a hit in the minds of animals.
My dog...
I GOT YOU A PRESENT, INU!
HOORAY!!
NEW CLOTHES!
HOORAY!!
IT'S A BONE!
HOORAY!!
A BALL!
IT'S GREAT THAT HE LIKES WHATEVER I GIVE HIM...
BUT THERE'S NO CHALLENGE IN IT...
However, I recently realized ...
SEE YOU LATER!
SQUISH
...the things he's particularly fond of, he shoves into my shoes.
OH! YAY!!!
THIS ONE WAS A HIT!!
My dog doesn't just like anything. There're some that he "likes" and others that he "loves."

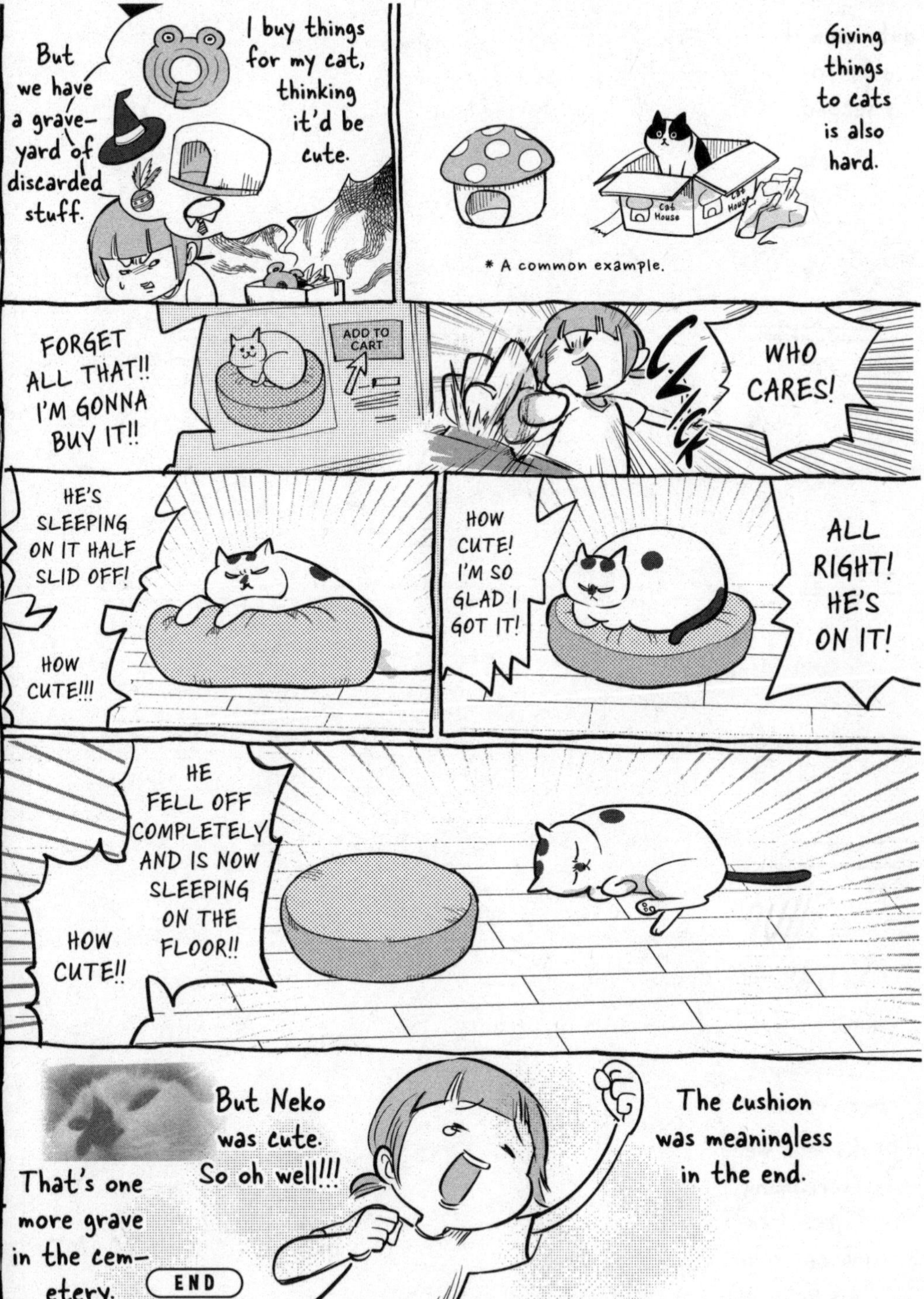
But we have a grave-yard of discarded stuff.
I buy things for my cat, thinking it'd be cute.
Giving things to cats is also hard.
Cat House
Cat House
* A common example.
FORGET ALL THAT!! I'M GONNA BUY IT!!
ADD TO CART
CLICK
WHO CARES!
HE'S SLEEPING ON IT HALF SLID OFF!
HOW CUTE!!!
ALL RIGHT! HE'S ON IT!
HOW CUTE! I'M SO GLAD I GOT IT!
HE FELL OFF COMPLETELY AND IS NOW SLEEPING ON THE FLOOR!!
HOW CUTE!!
The cushion was meaningless in the end.
But Neko was cute. So oh well!!!
That's one more grave in the cem-etery.
END

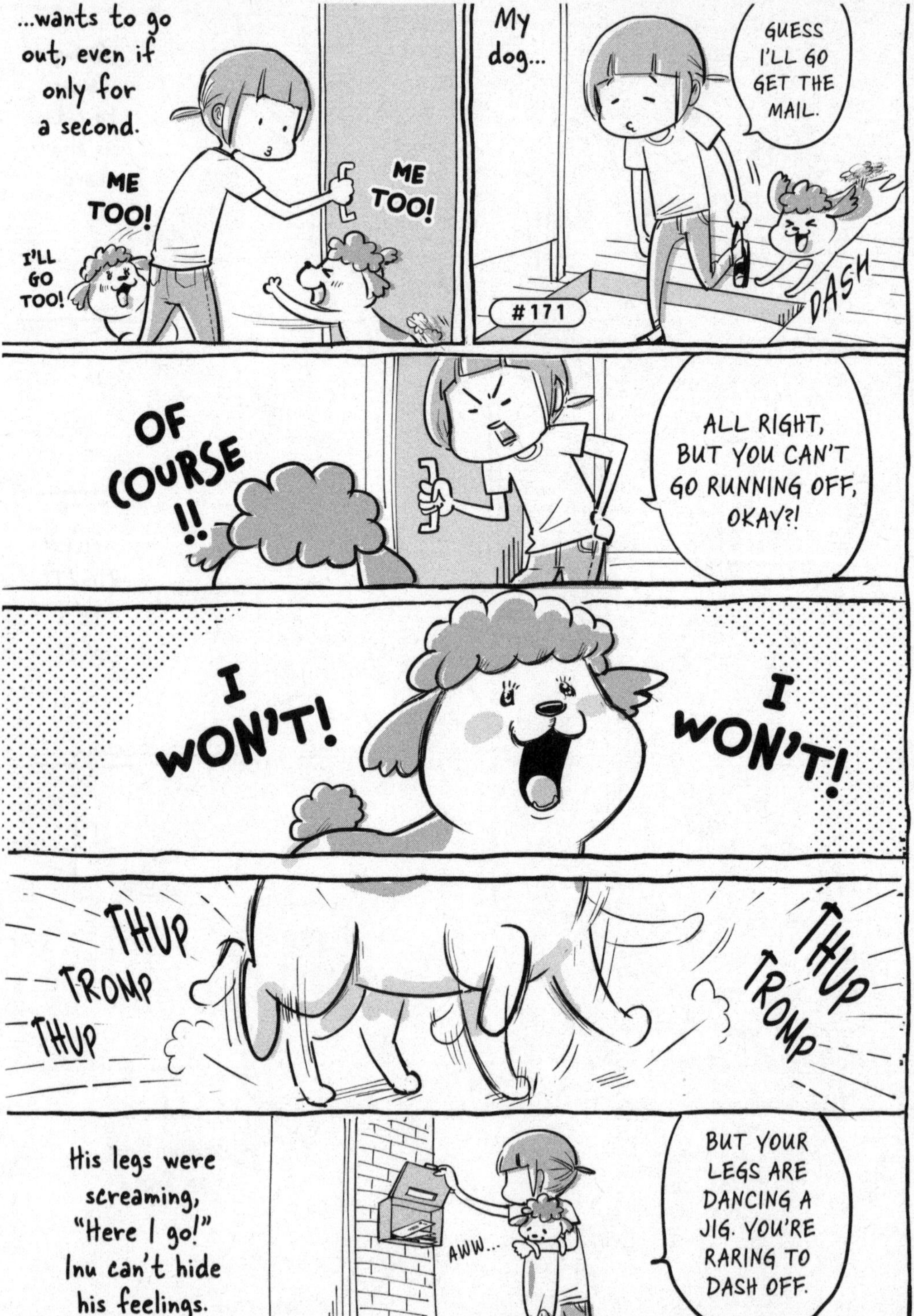

#171
GUESS I'LL GO GET THE MAIL.
My dog...
DASH
...wants to go out, even if only for a second.
ME TOO!
ME TOO!
I'LL GO TOO!
ALL RIGHT, BUT YOU CAN'T GO RUNNING OFF, OKAY?!
OF COURSE!!
I WON'T!
I WON'T!
THUP
TROMP
THUP
TROMP
THUP
BUT YOUR LEGS ARE DANCING A JIG. YOU'RE RARING TO DASH OFF.
AWW...
His legs were screaming, "Here I go!" Inu can't hide his feelings.

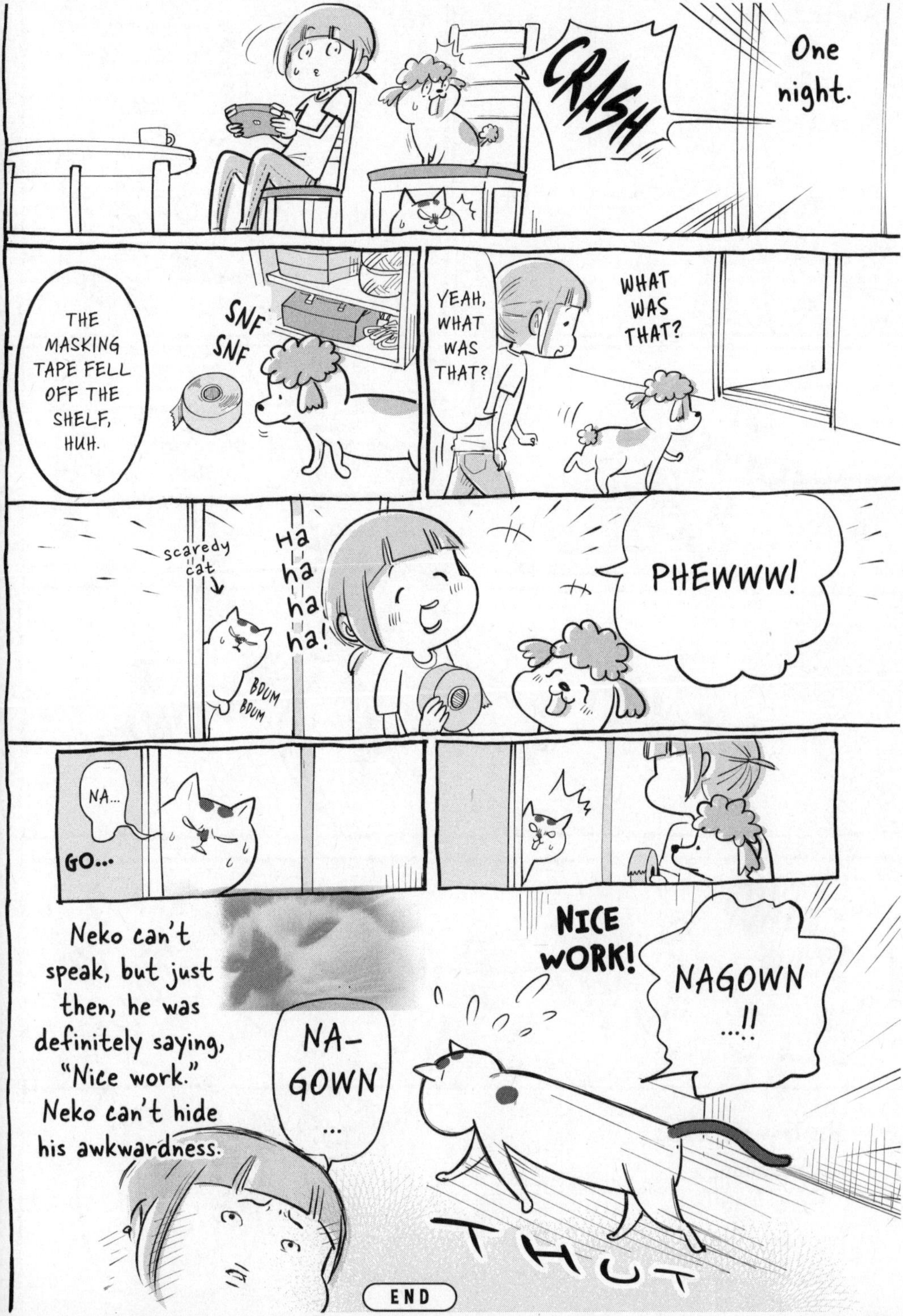
One night.
CRASH
WHAT WAS THAT?
YEAH, WHAT WAS THAT?
SNF SNF
THE MASKING TAPE FELL OFF THE SHELF, HUH.
PHEWWW!
Ha ha ha ha!
scaredy cat
BDUM BDUM
NA...
GO...
NAGOWN ...!!
NICE WORK!
NA-GOWN ...
Neko can't speak, but just then, he was definitely saying, "Nice work." Neko can't hide his awkwardness.
THUT
END

A sudden and unexpected display of friendship.

Newly-Drawn 4-Panel Strip

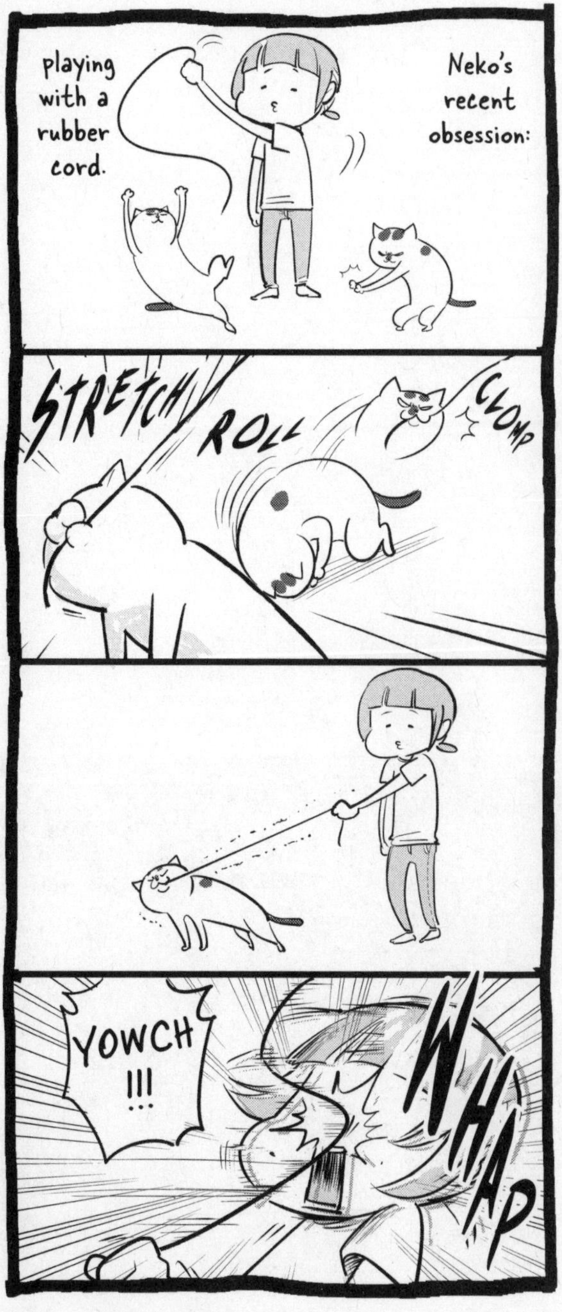
Neko's recent obsession:
playing with a rubber cord.
CLOMP
ROLL
STRETCH
WHAP
YOWCH!!!...

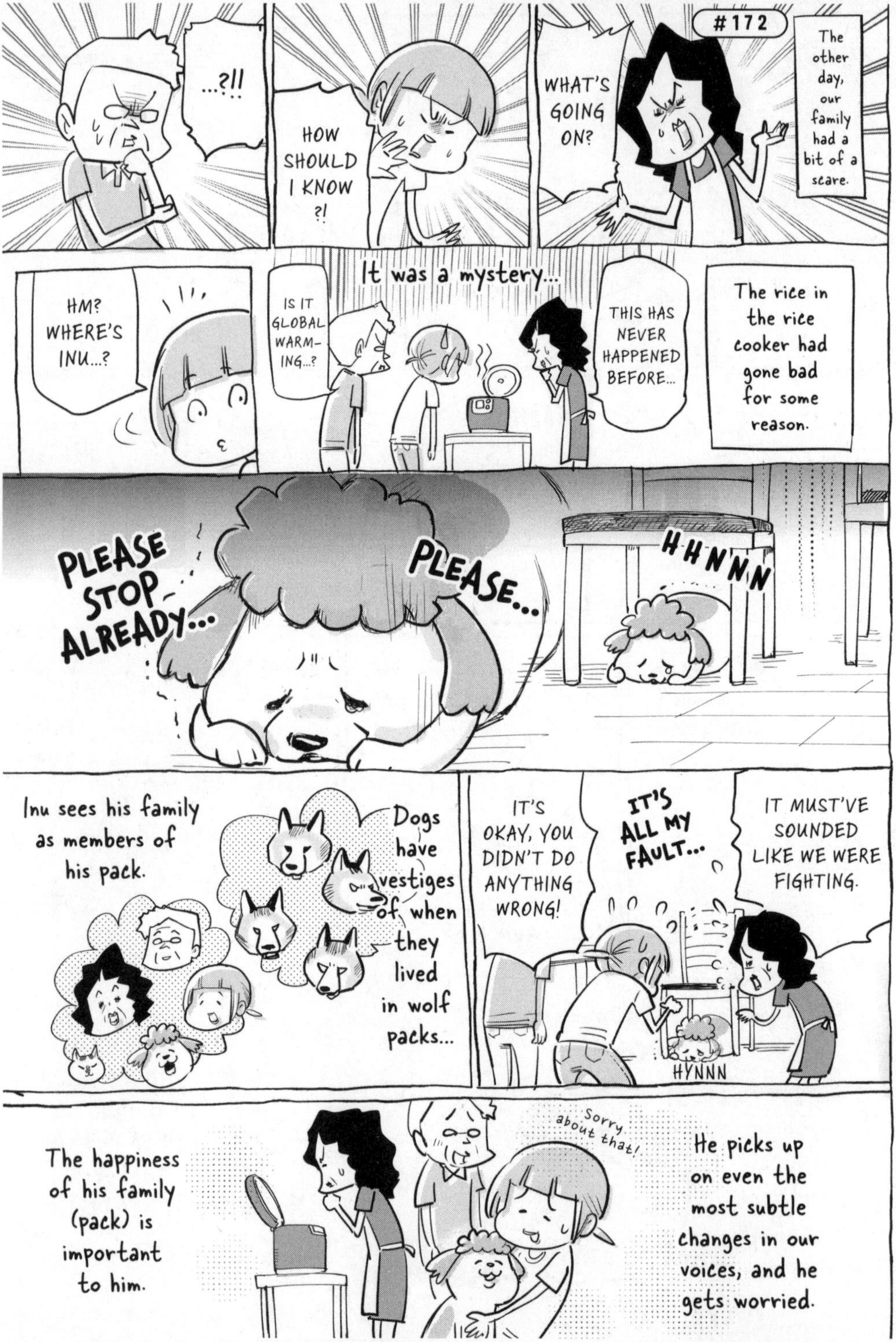

#172
The other day, our family had a bit of a scare.
WHAT'S GOING ON?
HOW SHOULD I KNOW ?!
...?!!
The rice in the rice cooker had gone bad for some reason.
THIS HAS NEVER HAPPENED BEFORE...
It was a mystery...
IS IT GLOBAL WARM-ING...?
HM? WHERE'S INU...?
HHNNN
PLEASE...
PLEASE STOP ALREADY...
IT MUST'VE SOUNDED LIKE WE WERE FIGHTING.
IT'S ALL MY FAULT...
IT'S OKAY, YOU DIDN'T DO ANYTHING WRONG!
HYNNN
Dogs have vestiges of when they lived in wolf packs...
Inu sees his family as members of his pack.
He picks up on even the most subtle changes in our voices, and he gets worried.
Sorry about that!
The happiness of his family (pack) is important to him.

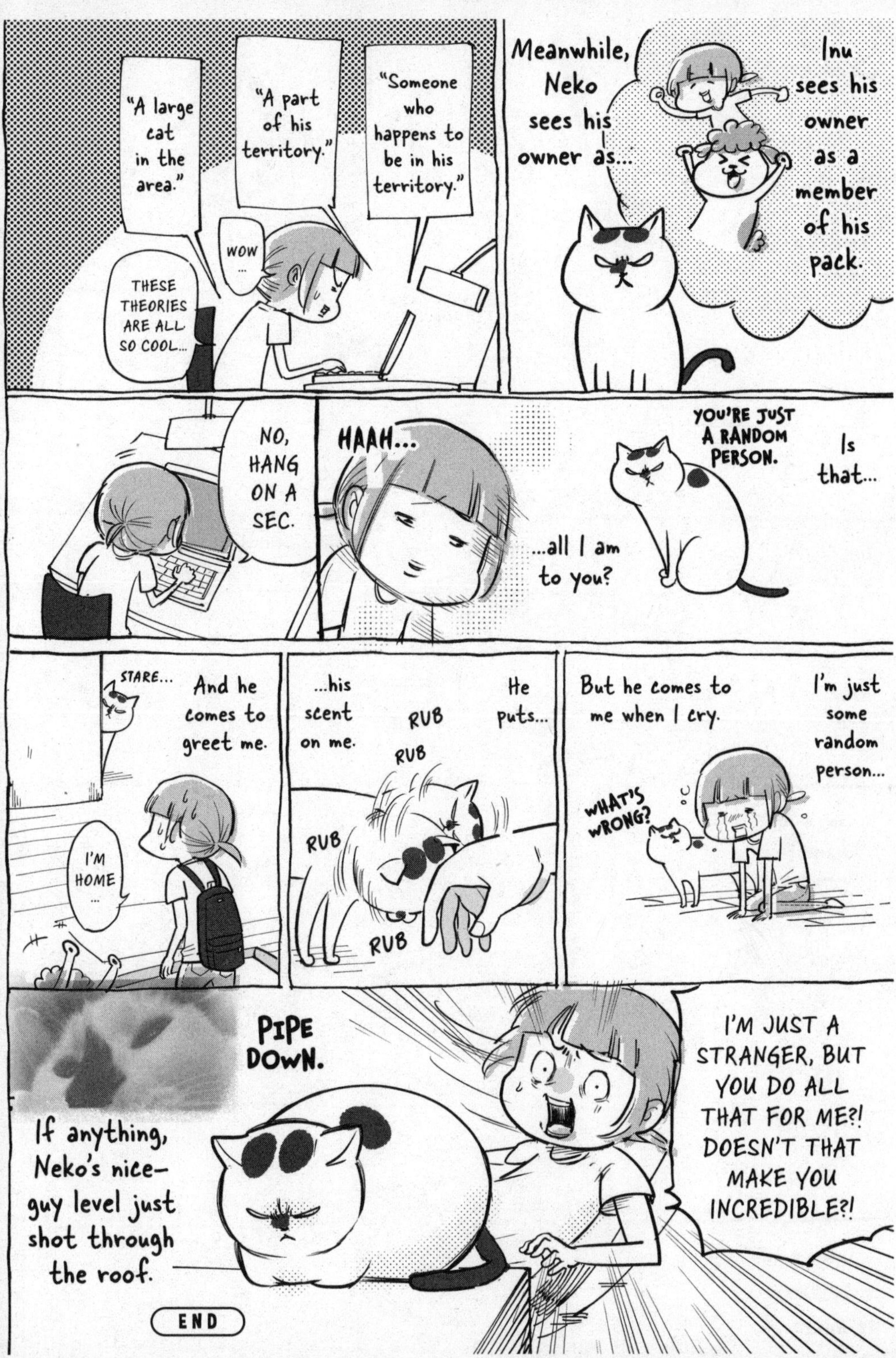
Inu sees his owner as a member of his pack.
Meanwhile, Neko sees his owner as...
"Someone who happens to be in his territory."
"A part of his territory."
"A large cat in the area."
WOW...
THESE THEORIES ARE ALL SO COOL...
Is that...
YOU'RE JUST A RANDOM PERSON.
...all I am to you?
HAAH...
NO, HANG ON A SEC.
I'm just some random person...
But he comes to me when I cry.
WHAT'S WRONG?
He puts...
...his scent on me.
RUB
RUB
RUB
RUB
And he comes to greet me.
STARE...
I'M HOME...
I'M JUST A STRANGER, BUT YOU DO ALL THAT FOR ME?! DOESN'T THAT MAKE YOU INCREDIBLE?!
PIPE DOWN.
If anything, Neko's nice-guy level just shot through the roof.
END

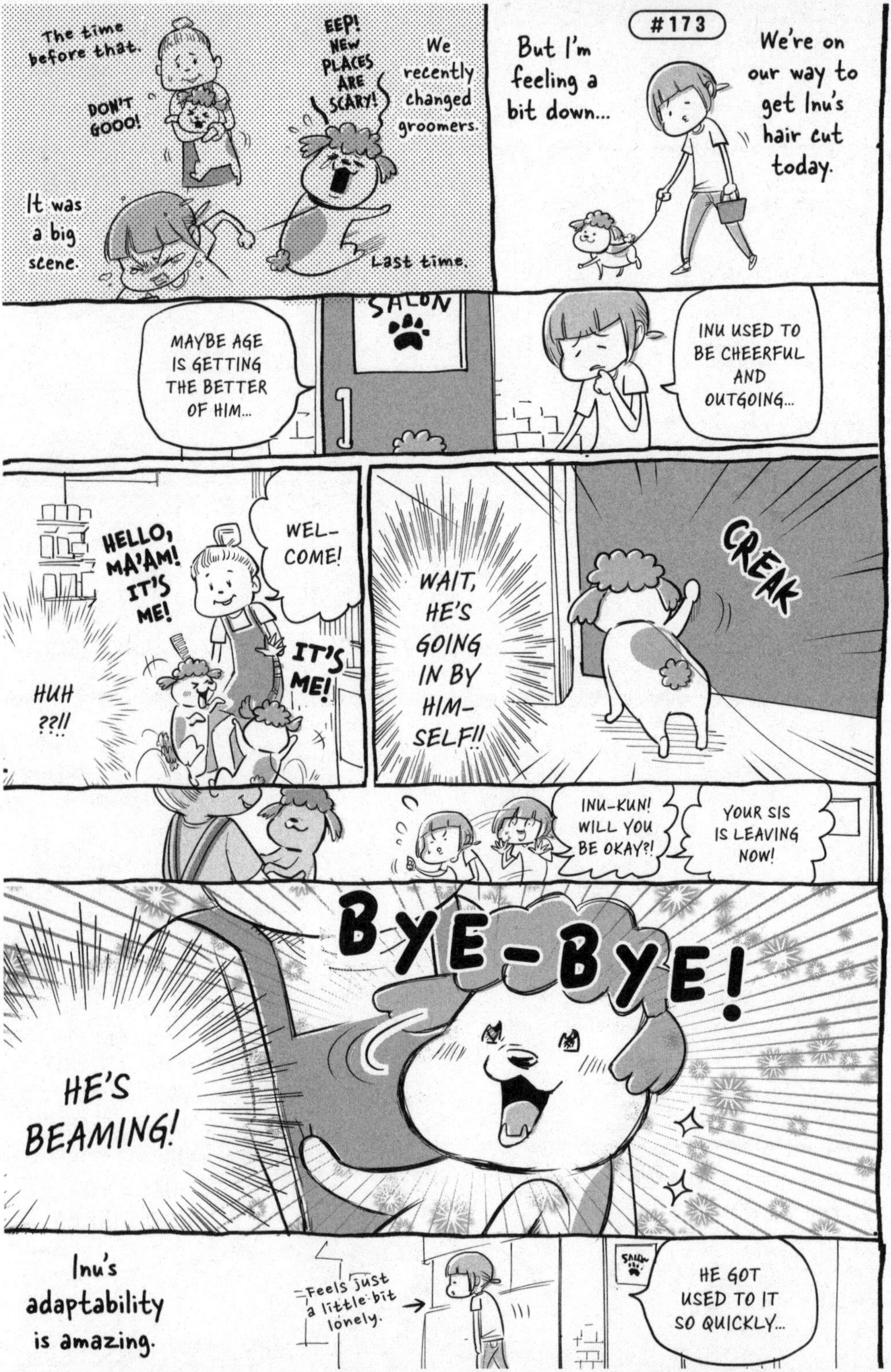
#173
We're on our way to get Inu's hair cut today.
But I'm feeling a bit down...
We recently changed groomers.
EEP! NEW PLACES ARE SCARY!
Last time.
The time before that.
DON'T GOOO!
It was a big scene.
INU USED TO BE CHEERFUL AND OUTGOING...
SALON
MAYBE AGE IS GETTING THE BETTER OF HIM...
CREAK
WAIT, HE'S GOING IN BY HIMSELF!!
WEL-COME!
HELLO, MA'AM! IT'S ME!
IT'S ME!
HUH ??!!
YOUR SIS IS LEAVING NOW!
INU-KUN! WILL YOU BE OKAY?!
BYE-BYE!
HE'S BEAMING!
HE GOT USED TO IT SO QUICKLY...
SALON
Feels just a little bit lonely.
Inu's adaptability is amazing.

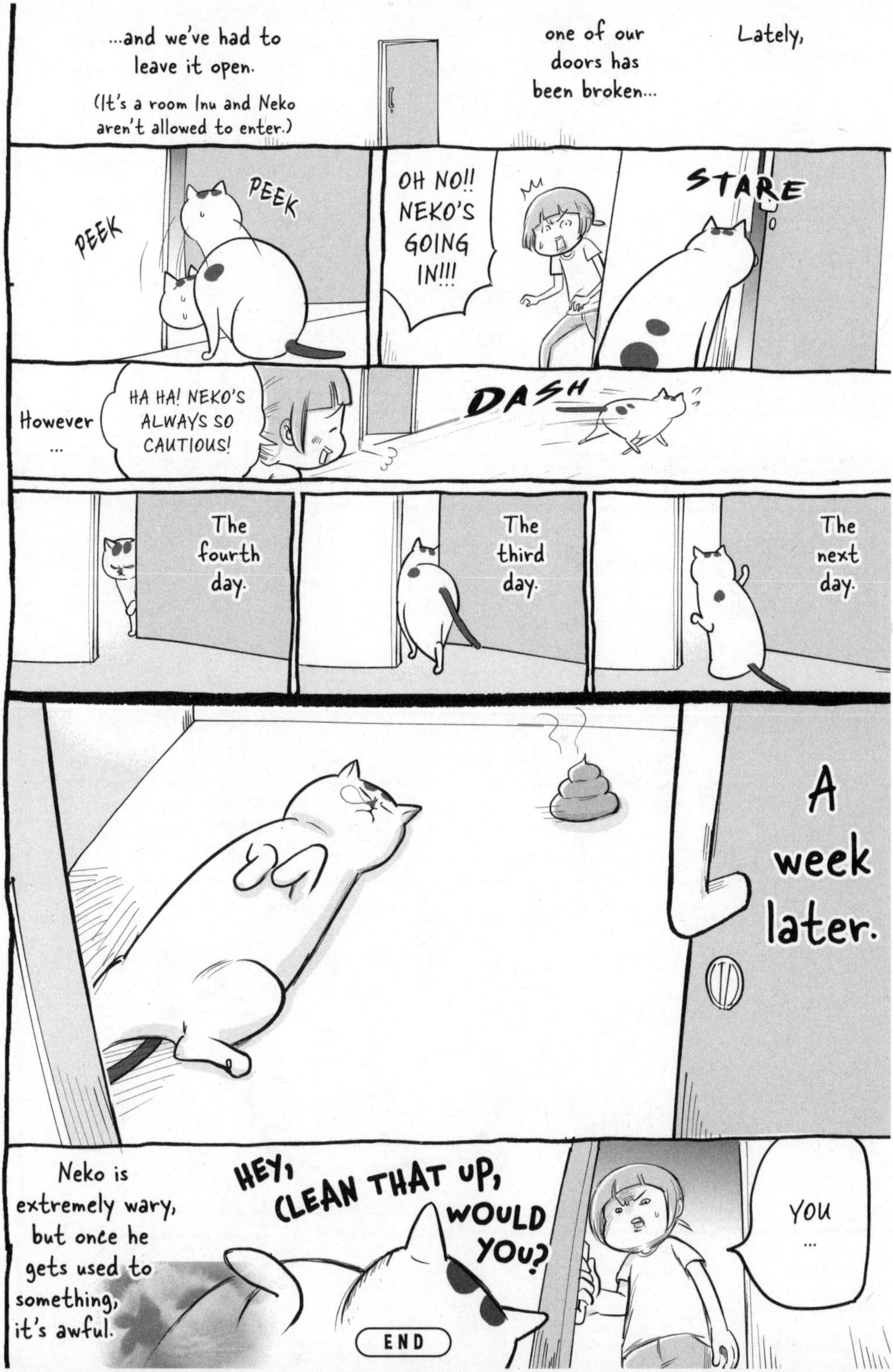
Lately,
one of our doors has been broken...
...and we've had to leave it open.
(It's a room Inu and Neko aren't allowed to enter.)
STARE
OH NO!! NEKO'S GOING IN!!!
PEEK
PEEK
DASH
HA HA! NEKO'S ALWAYS SO CAUTIOUS!
However ...
The next day.
The third day.
The fourth day.
A week later.
YOU ...
HEY, CLEAN THAT UP, WOULD YOU?
Neko is extremely wary, but once he gets used to something, it's awful.
END

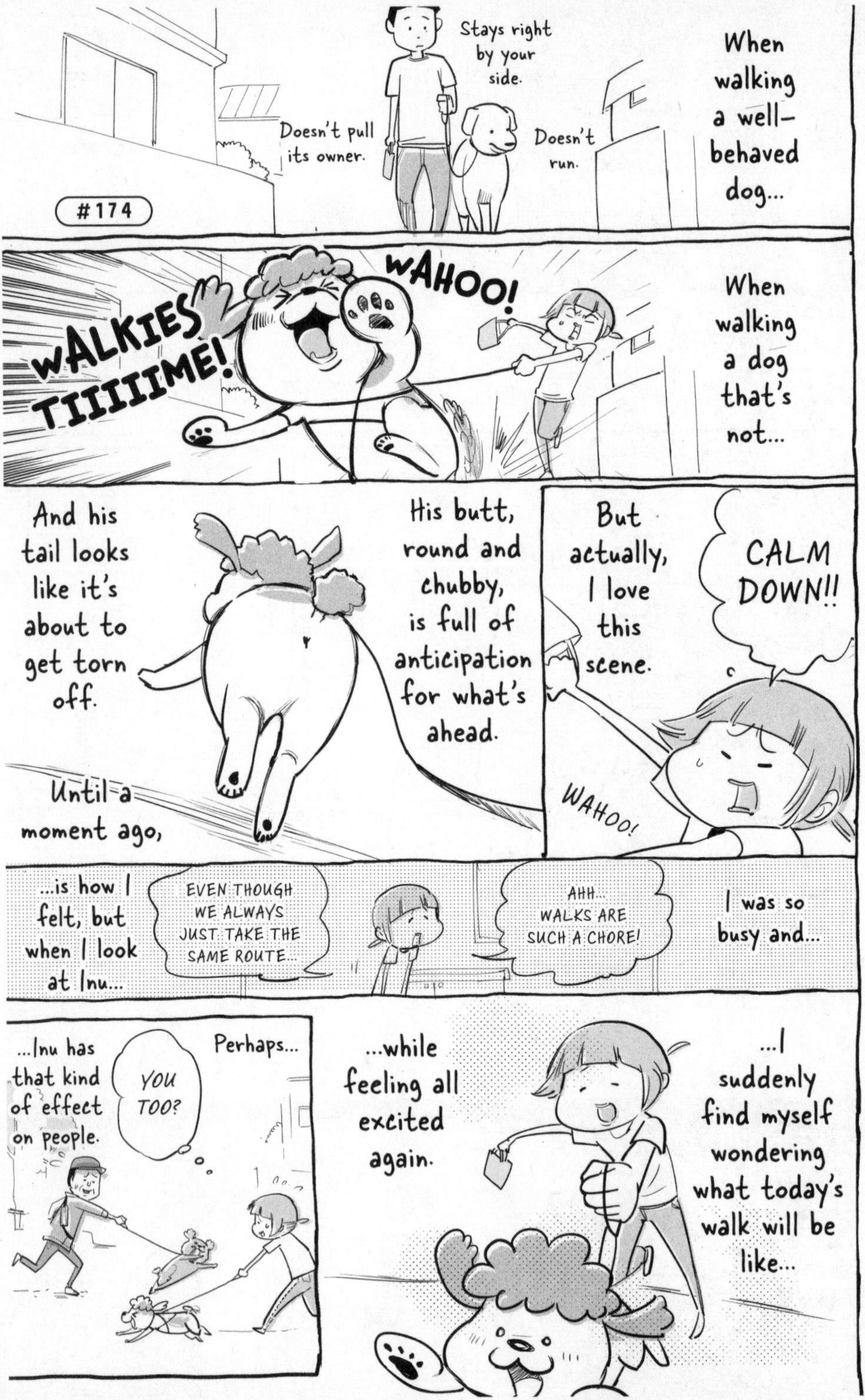
When walking a well-behaved dog...
Stays right by your side.
Doesn't run.
Doesn't pull its owner.
#174
When walking a dog that's not...
WAHOO!
WALKIES TIIIIIME!
CALM DOWN!!
But actually, I love this scene.
WAHOO!
His butt, round and chubby, is full of anticipation for what's ahead.
And his tail looks like it's about to get torn off.
Until a moment ago,
I was so busy and...
AHH... WALKS ARE SUCH A CHORE!
EVEN THOUGH WE ALWAYS JUST TAKE THE SAME ROUTE...
...is how I felt, but when I look at Inu...
...I suddenly find myself wondering what today's walk will be like...
...while feeling all excited again.
Perhaps...
YOU TOO?
...Inu has that kind of effect on people.

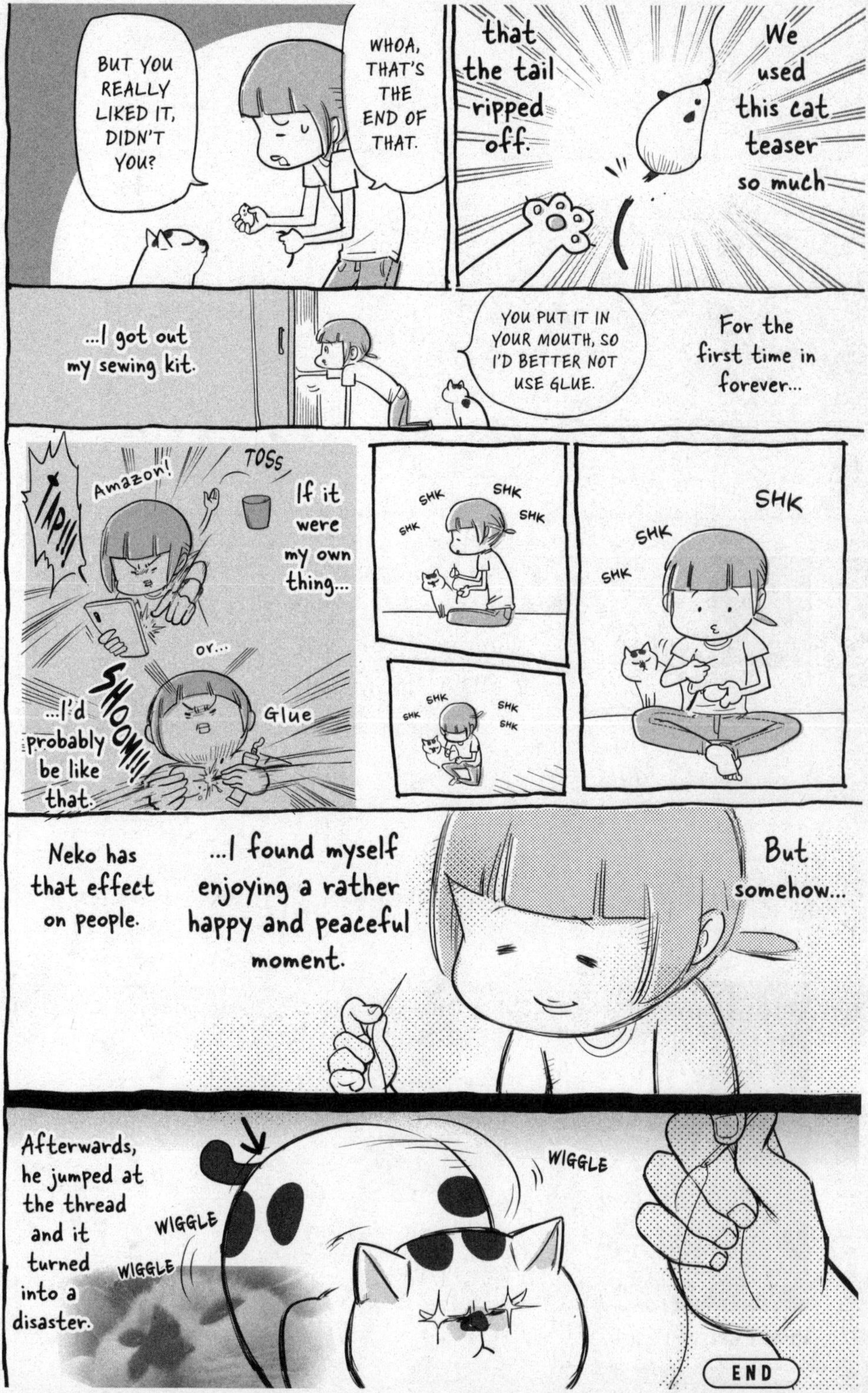
We used this cat teaser so much
that the tail ripped off.
WHOA, THAT'S THE END OF THAT.
BUT YOU REALLY LIKED IT, DIDN'T YOU?
For the first time in forever...
YOU PUT IT IN YOUR MOUTH, SO I'D BETTER NOT USE GLUE.
...I got out my sewing kit.
SHK
SHK
SHK
SHK
SHK
SHK
SHK
SHK
SHK
SHK
SHK
If it were my own thing...
TOSS
Amazon!
TAP!!!
or...
SHOOM!!!
Glue
...I'd probably be like that.
But somehow...
...I found myself enjoying a rather happy and peaceful moment.
Neko has that effect on people.
WIGGLE
WIGGLE
WIGGLE
Afterwards, he jumped at the thread and it turned into a disaster.
END

An art critic's gaze.

Newly-Drawn 4-Panel Strip

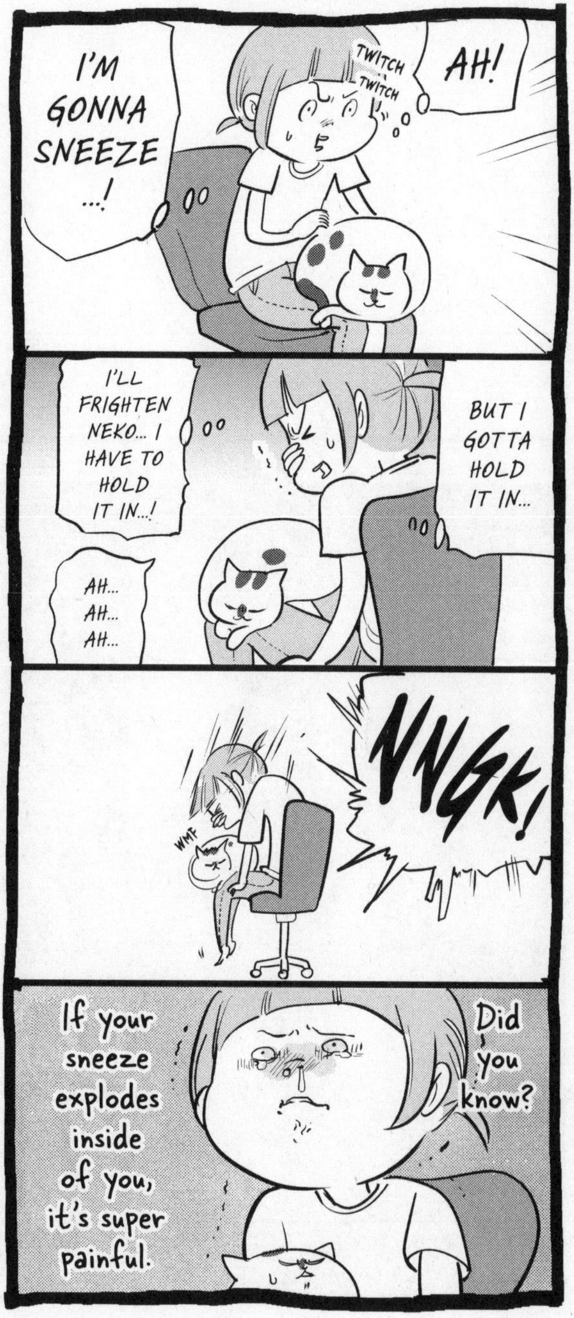

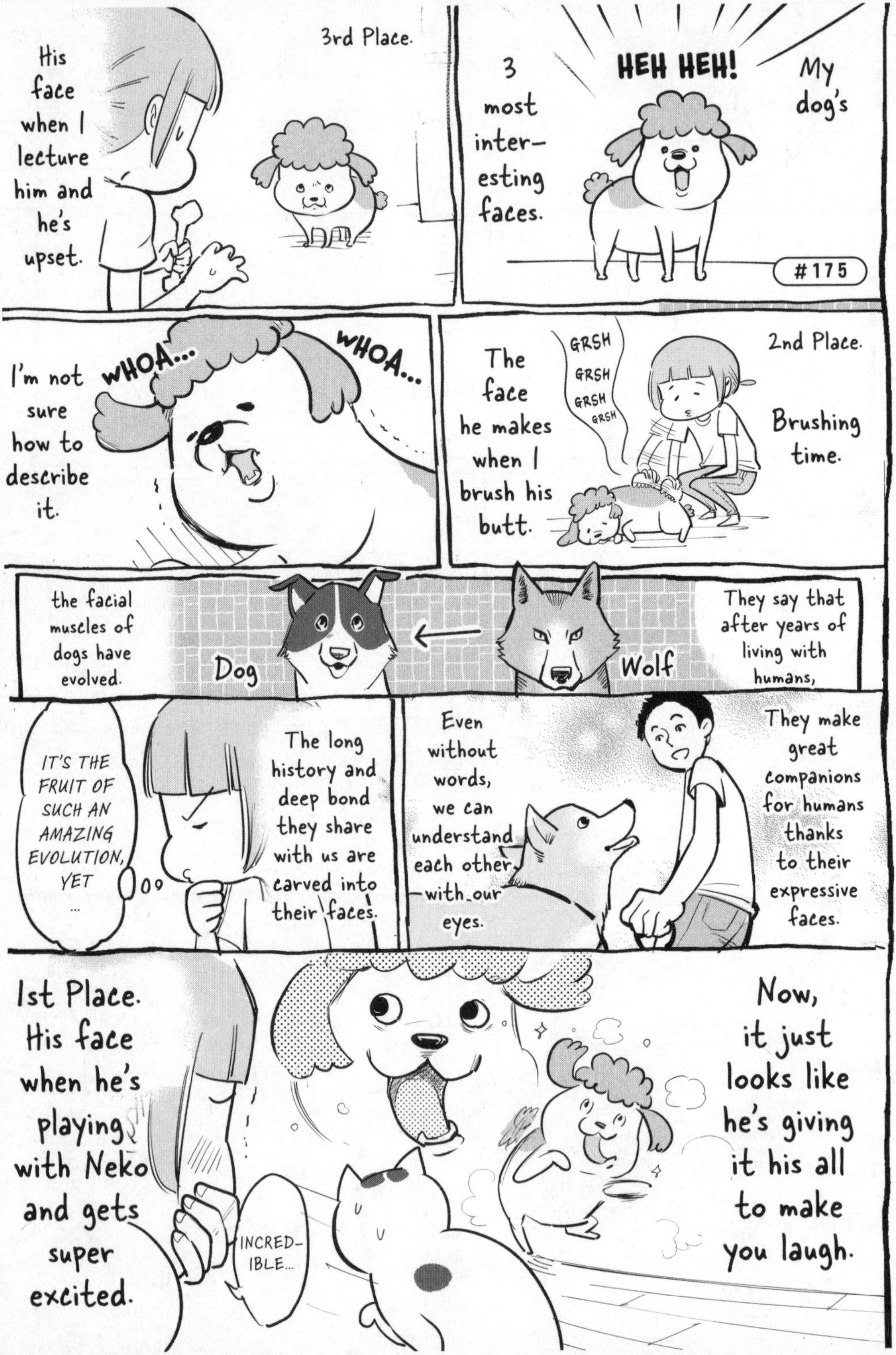

My dog's
HEH HEH!
3 most interesting faces.
#175
3rd Place.
His face when I lecture him and he's upset.
2nd Place.
Brushing time.
The face he makes when I brush his butt.
GRSH GRSH GRSH GRSH
WHOA...
WHOA...
I'm not sure how to describe it.
They say that after years of living with humans,
Wolf
Dog
the facial muscles of dogs have evolved.
They make great companions for humans thanks to their expressive faces.
Even without words, we can understand each other with our eyes.
The long history and deep bond they share with us are carved into their faces.
IT'S THE FRUIT OF SUCH AN AMAZING EVOLUTION, YET ...
Now, it just looks like he's giving it his all to make you laugh.
1st Place. His face when he's playing with Neko and gets super excited.
INCRED-IBLE...

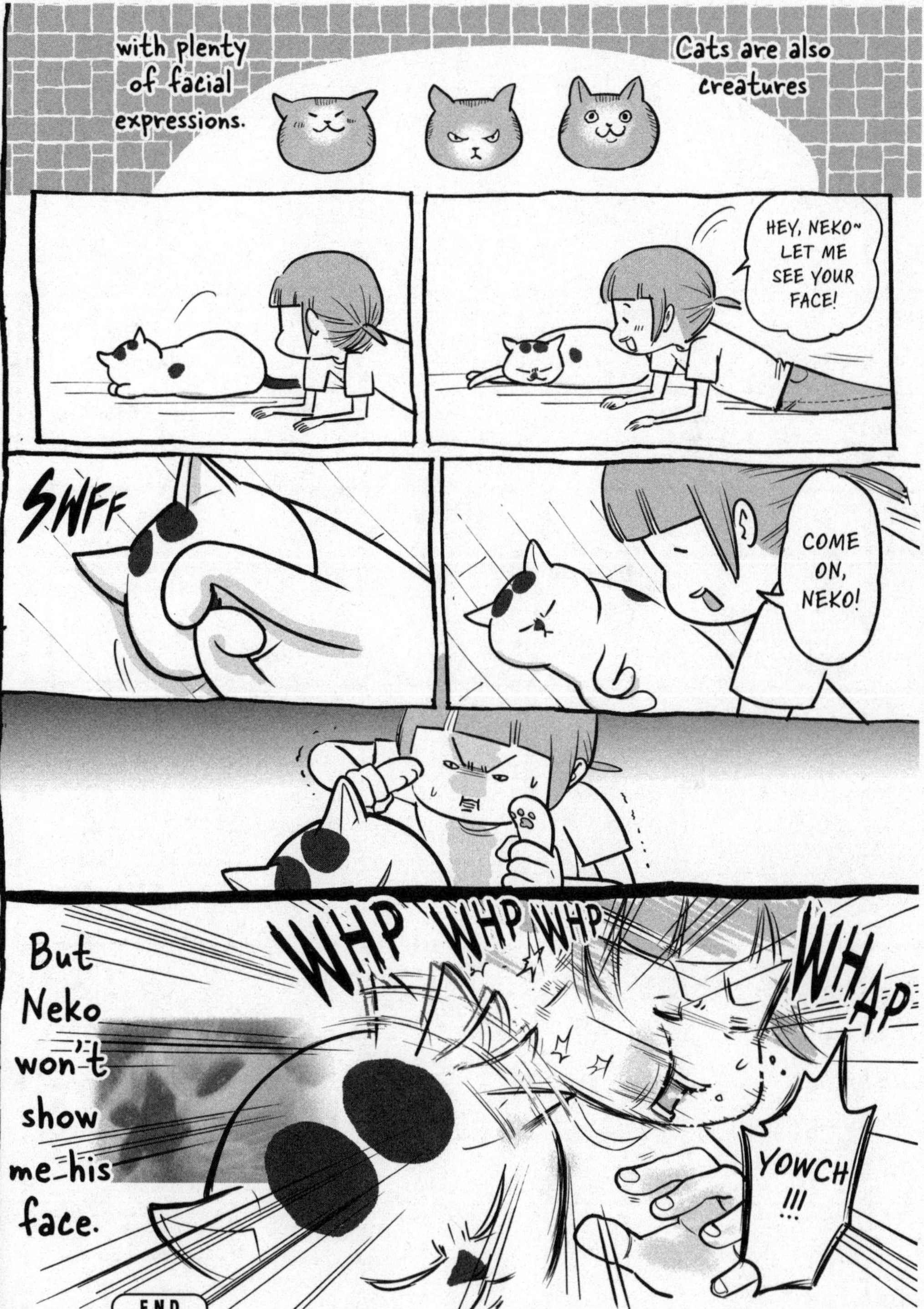
Cats are also creatures
with plenty of facial expressions.
HEY, NEKO~ LET ME SEE YOUR FACE!
COME ON, NEKO!
SWFF
WHP WHP WHP
WHAP
YOWCH !!!
But Neko won't show me his face.
END

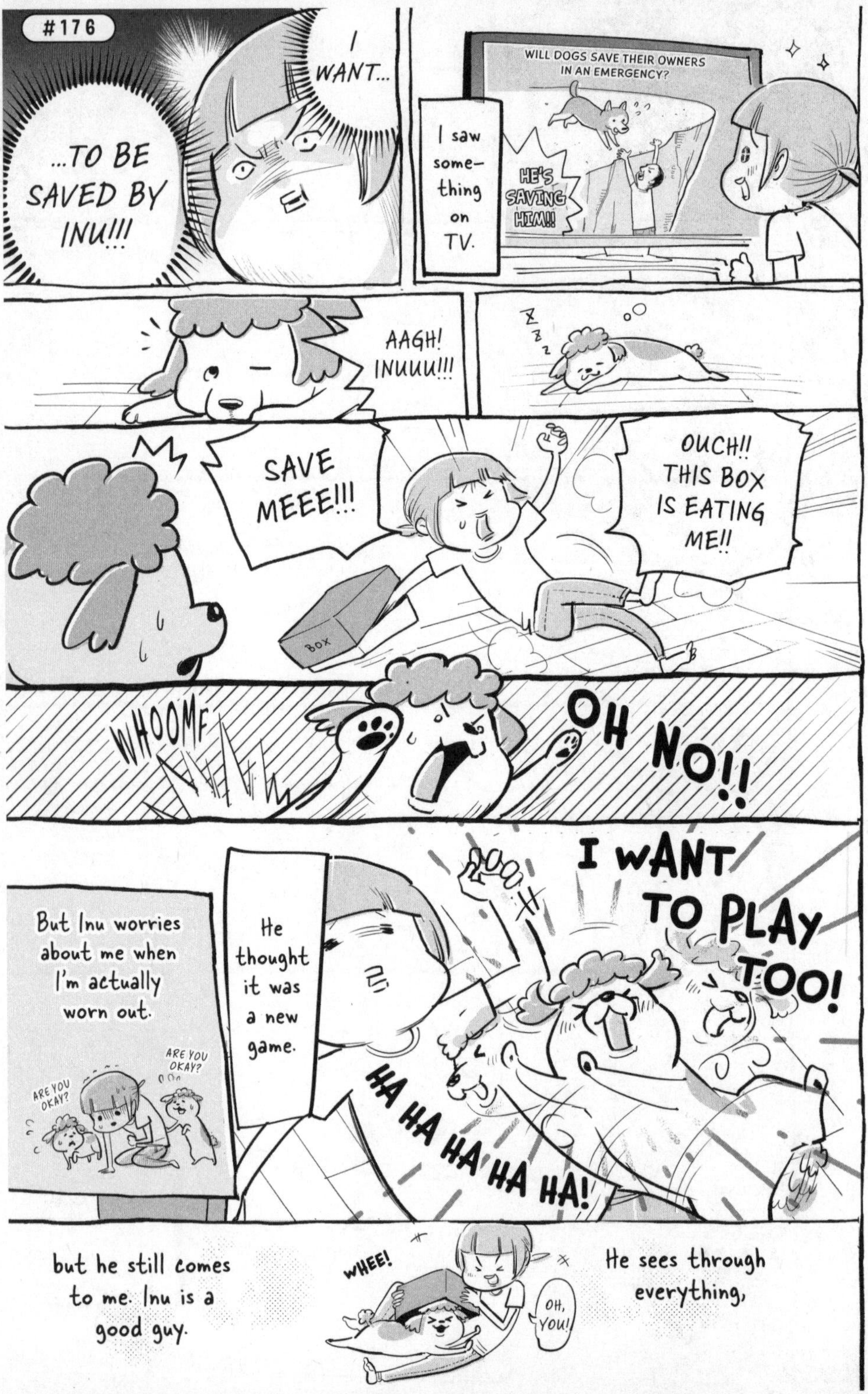
#176
I saw something on TV.
WILL DOGS SAVE THEIR OWNERS IN AN EMERGENCY?
HE'S SAVING HIM!!
I WANT...
...TO BE SAVED BY INU!!!
Z Z Z
AAGH! INUUU!!!
OUCH!! THIS BOX IS EATING ME!!
SAVE MEEE!!!
BOX
OH NO!!
WHOOMF
I WANT TO PLAY TOO!
HA HA HA HA HA HA!
He thought it was a new game.
But Inu worries about me when I'm actually worn out.
ARE YOU OKAY?
ARE YOU OKAY?
He sees through everything,
OH, YOU!
WHEE!
but he still comes to me. Inu is a good guy.

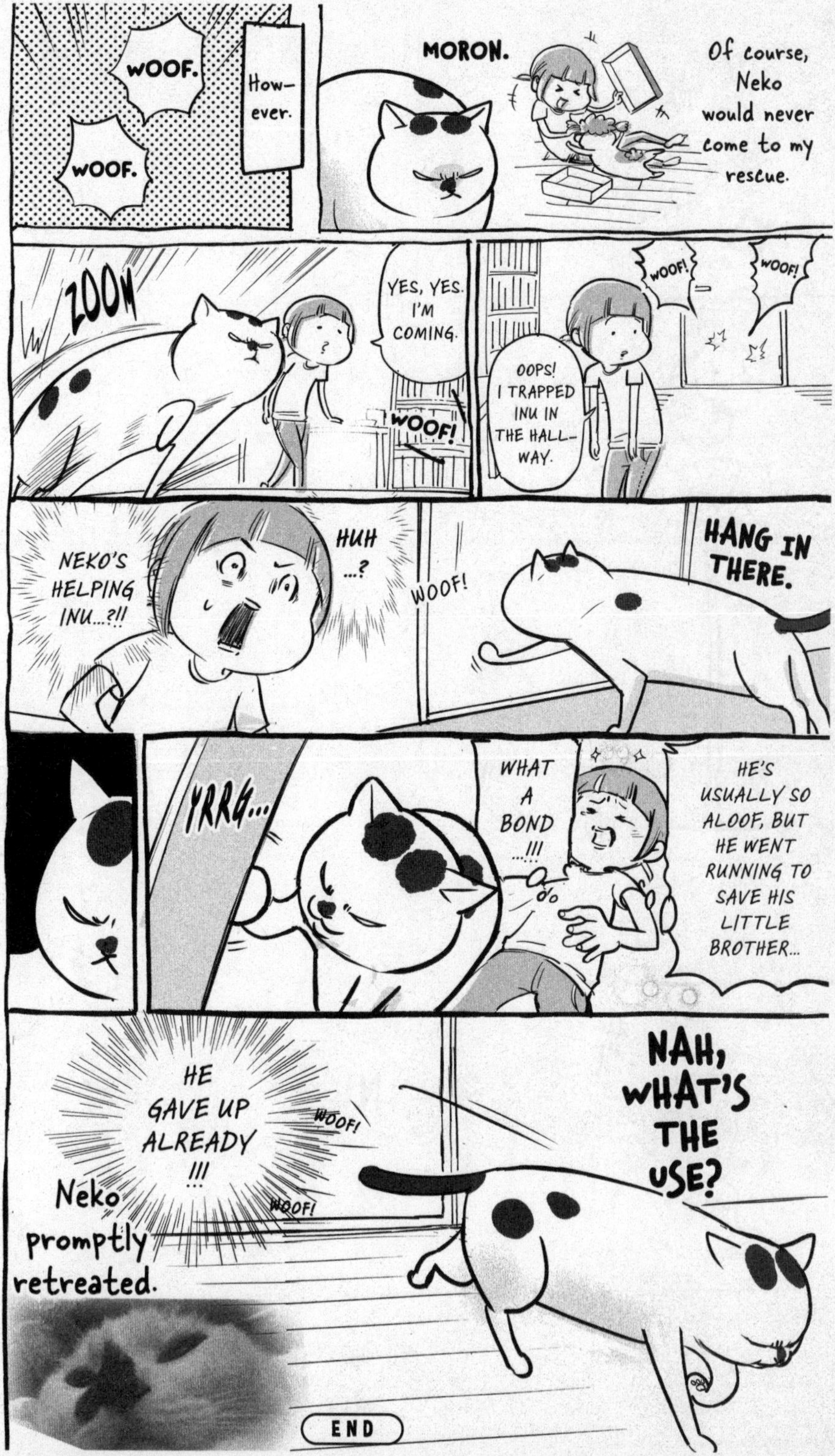
Of course, Neko would never come to my rescue.
MORON.
However.
WOOF.
WOOF.
WOOF!
WOOF!
OOPS! I TRAPPED INU IN THE HALLWAY.
YES, YES. I'M COMING.
WOOF!
ZOOM
HANG IN THERE.
WOOF!
HUH ...?
NEKO'S HELPING INU...?!!
HE'S USUALLY SO ALOOF, BUT HE WENT RUNNING TO SAVE HIS LITTLE BROTHER...
WHAT A BOND ...!!!
YRRG...
NAH, WHAT'S THE USE?
WOOF!
HE GAVE UP ALREADY !!!
WOOF!
Neko promptly retreated.
END

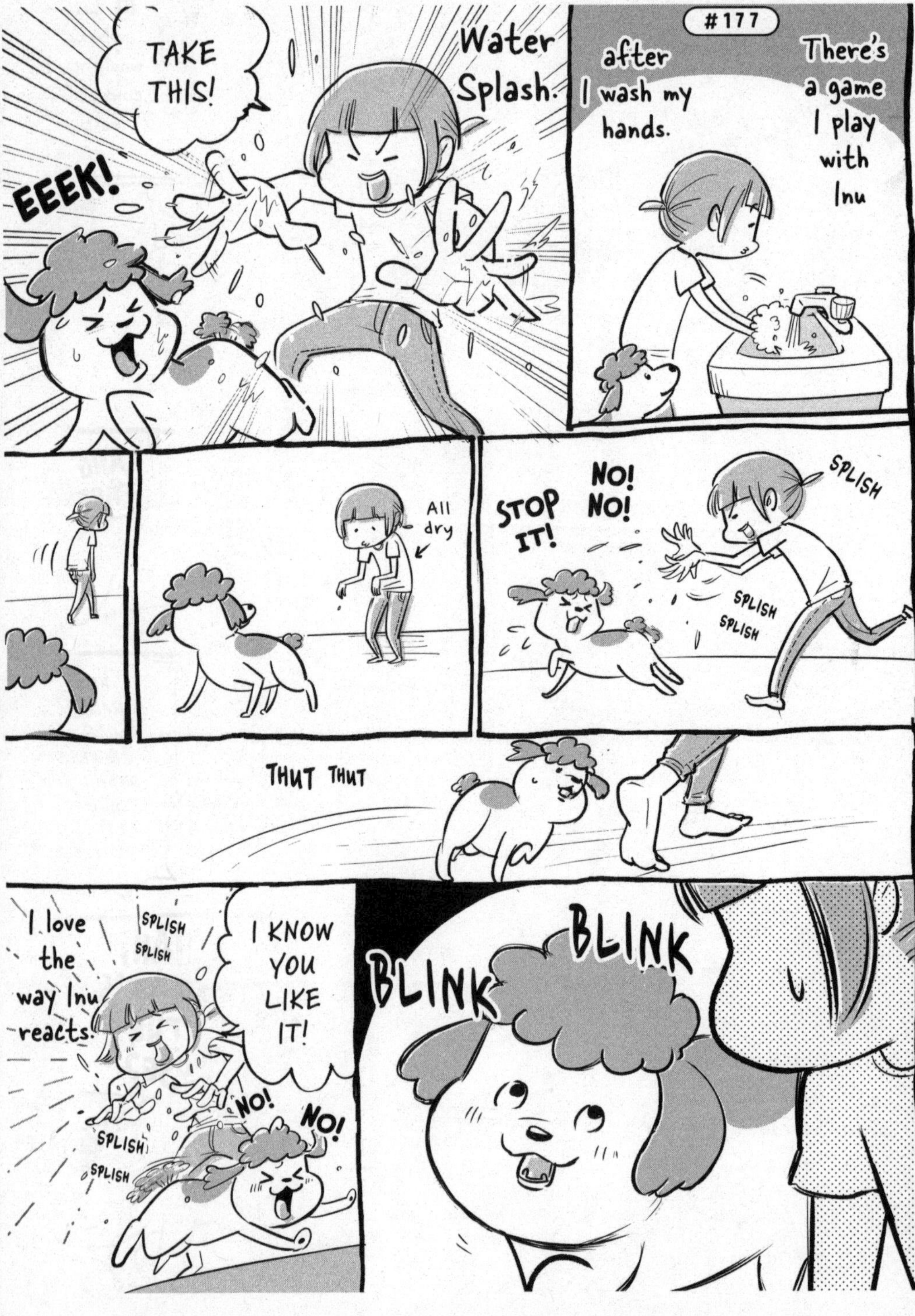
#177
There's a game I play with Inu
after I wash my hands.
Water Splash.
TAKE THIS!
EEEK!
SPLISH
NO! NO!
STOP IT!
SPLISH
SPLISH
All dry
THUT THUT
BLINK
BLINK
I KNOW YOU LIKE IT!
I love the way Inu reacts.
SPLISH
SPLISH
NO!
NO!
SPLISH
SPLISH

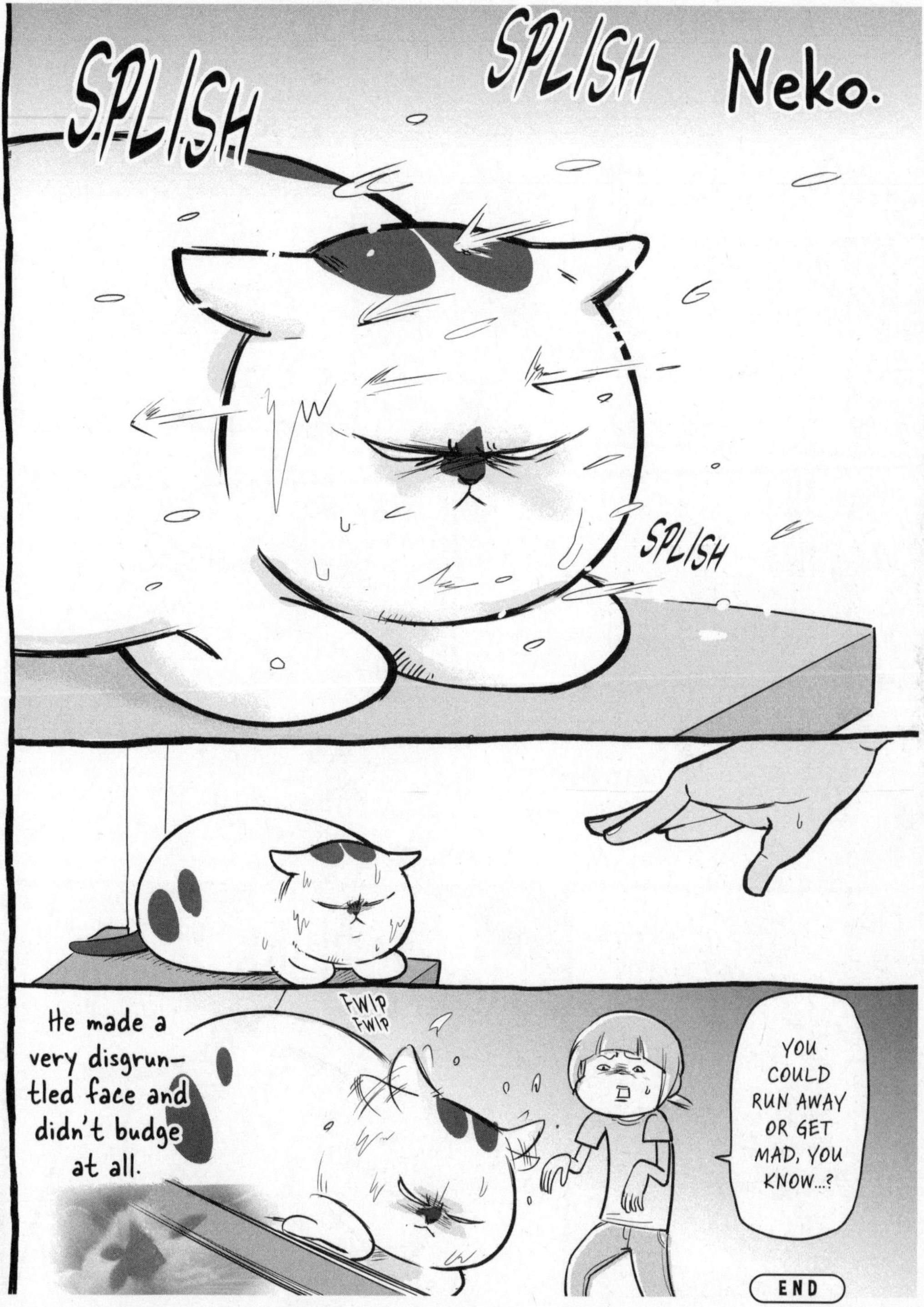
Neko.
SPLISH
SPLISH
SPLISH
YOU COULD RUN AWAY OR GET MAD, YOU KNOW...?
FWIP FWIP
He made a very disgrun-tled face and didn't budge at all.
END

Neko watching over with indifferent eyes.

Newly-Drawn 4-Panel Strip

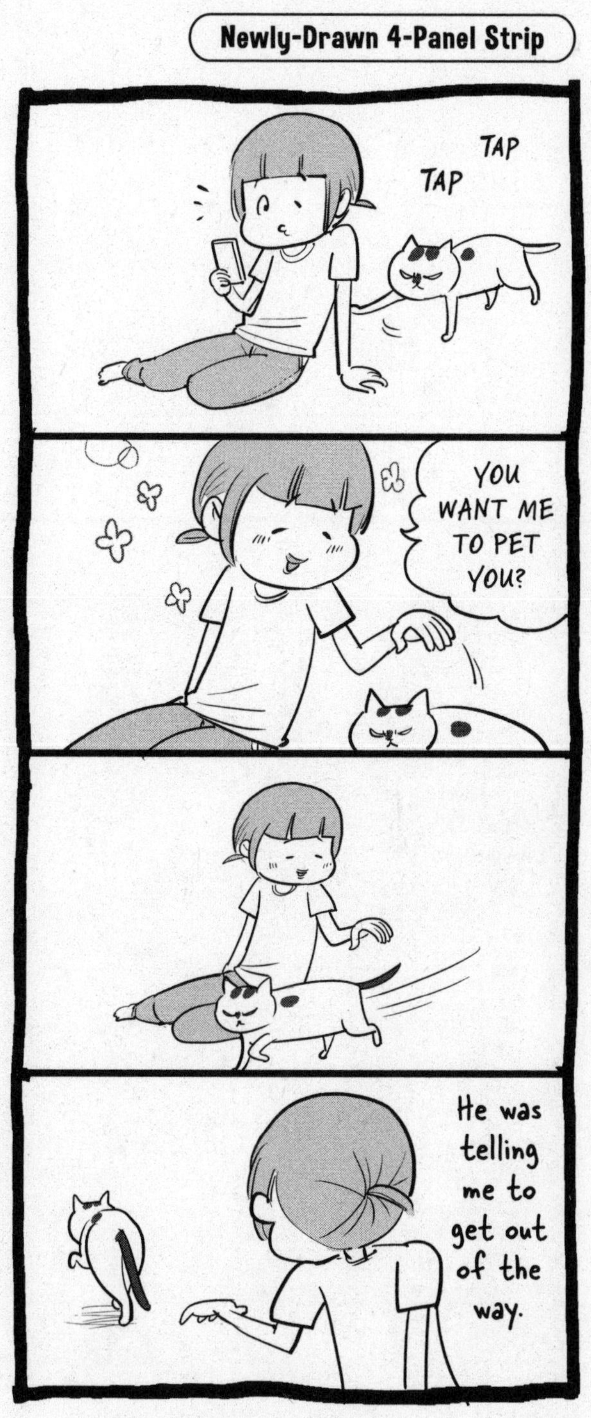
TAP
TAP
YOU WANT ME TO PET YOU?
He was telling me to get out of the way.

Bonus

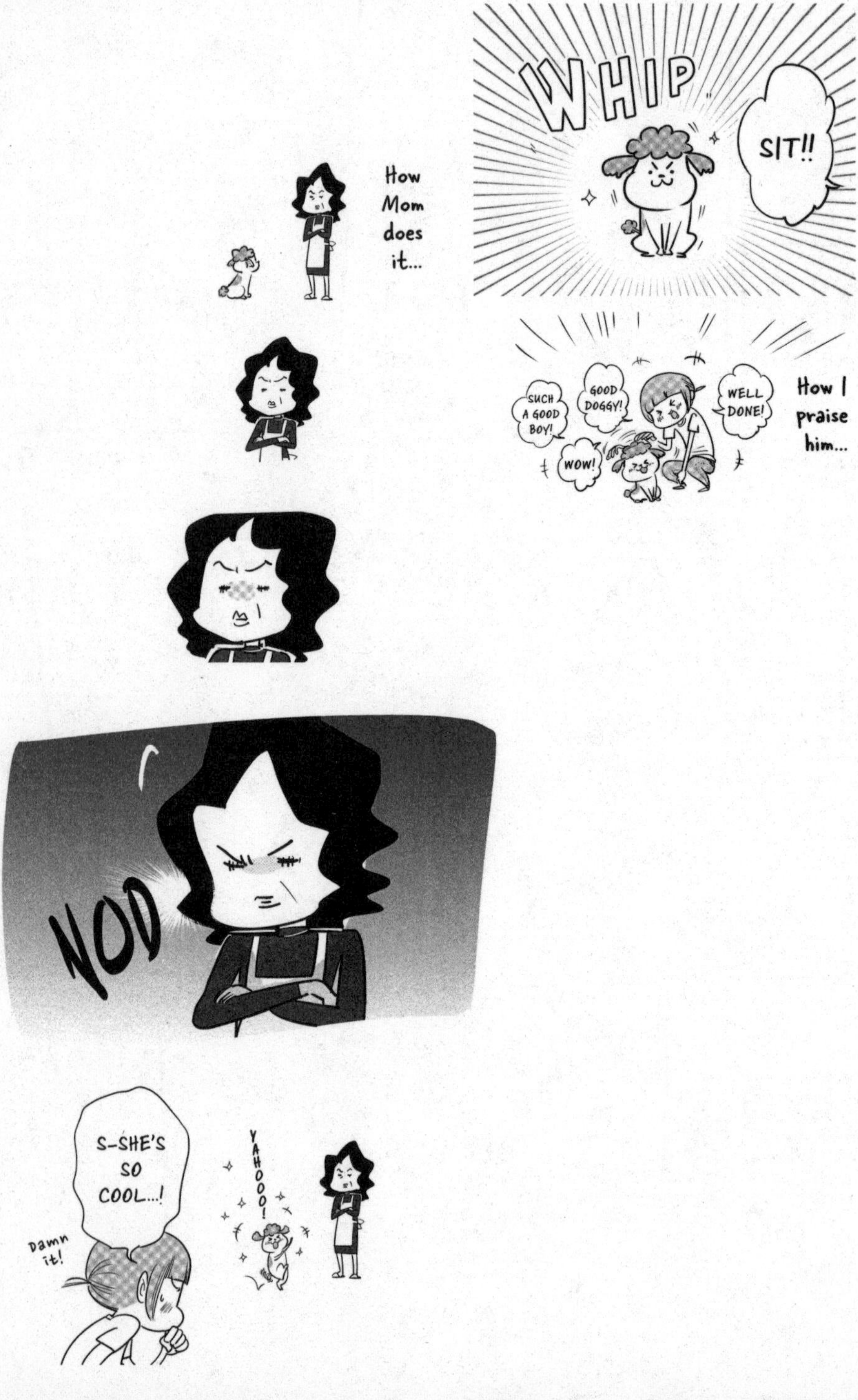
WHIP
SIT!!
How Mom does it...
How I praise him...
WELL DONE!
GOOD DOGGY!
SUCH A GOOD BOY!
WOW!
NOD
YAHOOOO!
S-SHE'S SO COOL...!
Damn it!

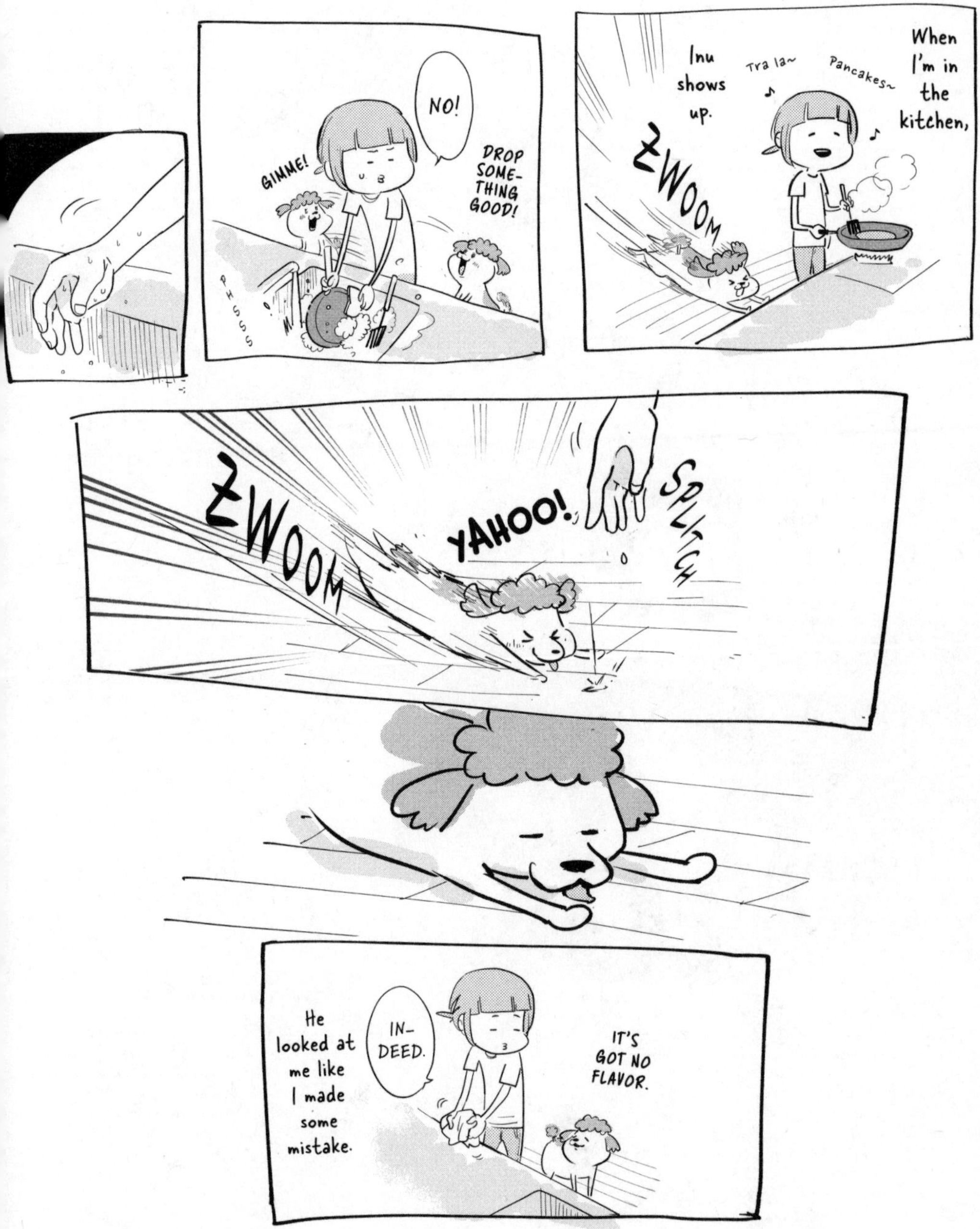
When I'm in the kitchen,
Pancakes~
Tra la~
Inu shows up.
ZWOOM
NO!
DROP SOMETHING GOOD!
GIMME!
PHSSS
SPLTCH
YAHOO!
ZWOOM
IT'S GOT NO FLAVOR.
IN-DEED.
He looked at me like I made some mistake.

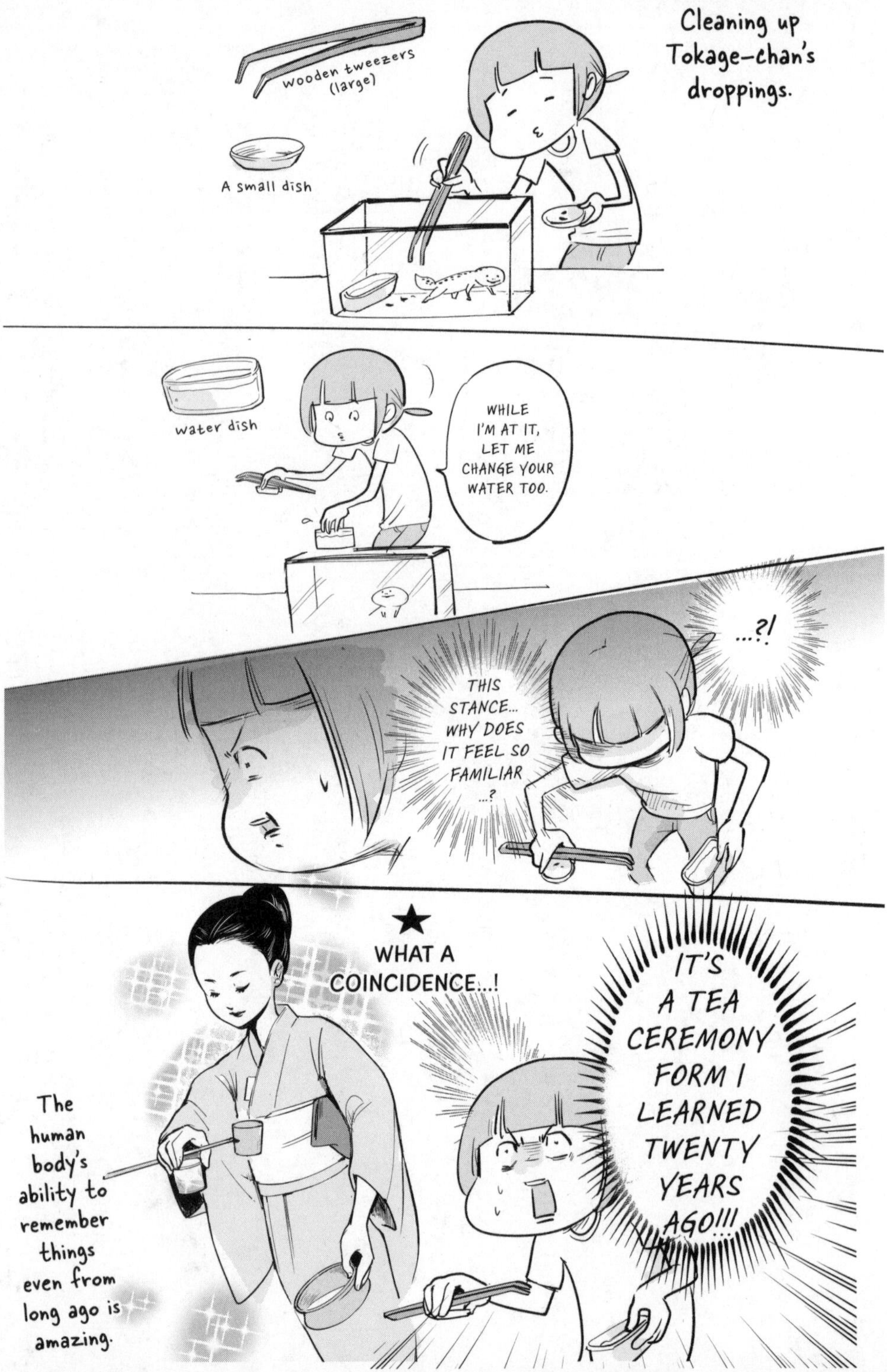
Cleaning up Tokage-chan's droppings.
wooden tweezers (large)
A small dish
water dish
WHILE I'M AT IT, LET ME CHANGE YOUR WATER TOO.
...?!
THIS STANCE... WHY DOES IT FEEL SO FAMILIAR ...?
IT'S A TEA CEREMONY FORM I LEARNED TWENTY YEARS AGO!!!
★ WHAT A COINCIDENCE...!
The human body's ability to remember things even from long ago is amazing.

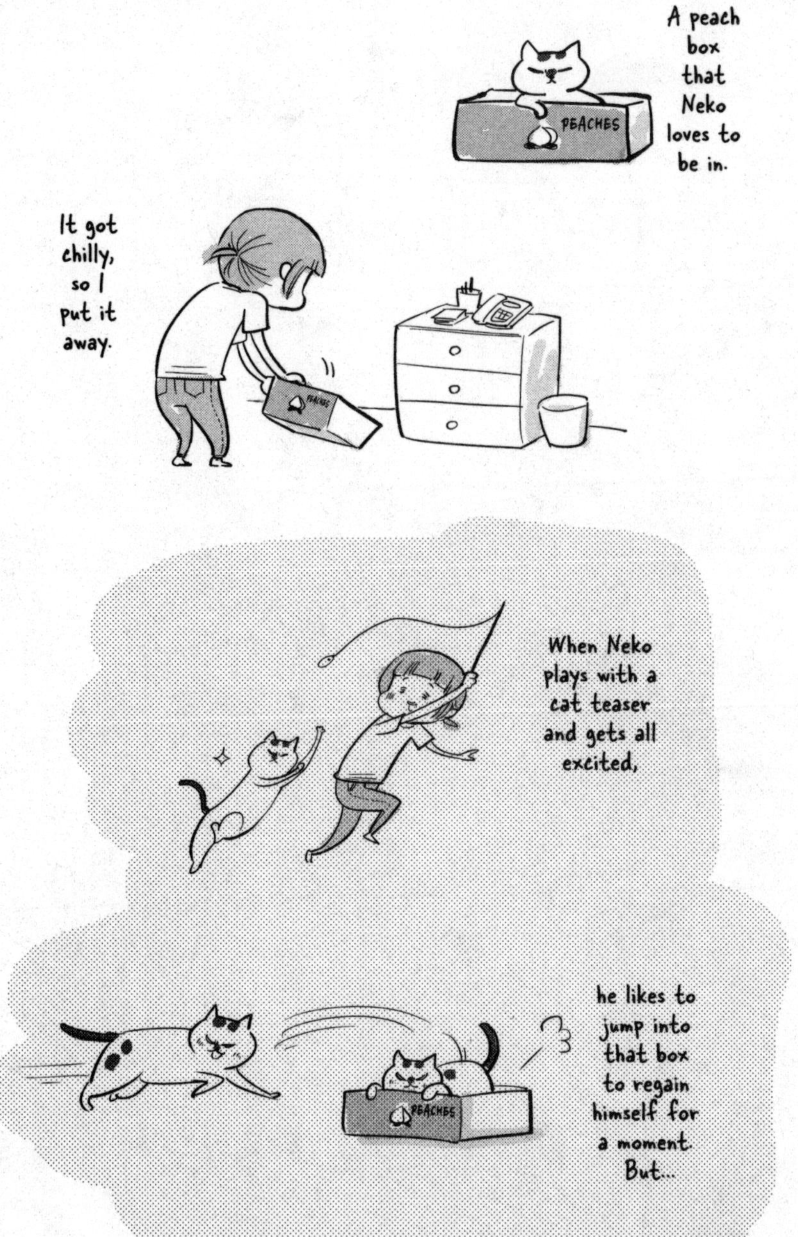
A peach box that Neko loves to be in.
PEACHES
It got chilly, so I put it away.
PEACHES
When Neko plays with a cat teaser and gets all excited,
he likes to jump into that box to regain himself for a moment. But...
PEACHES

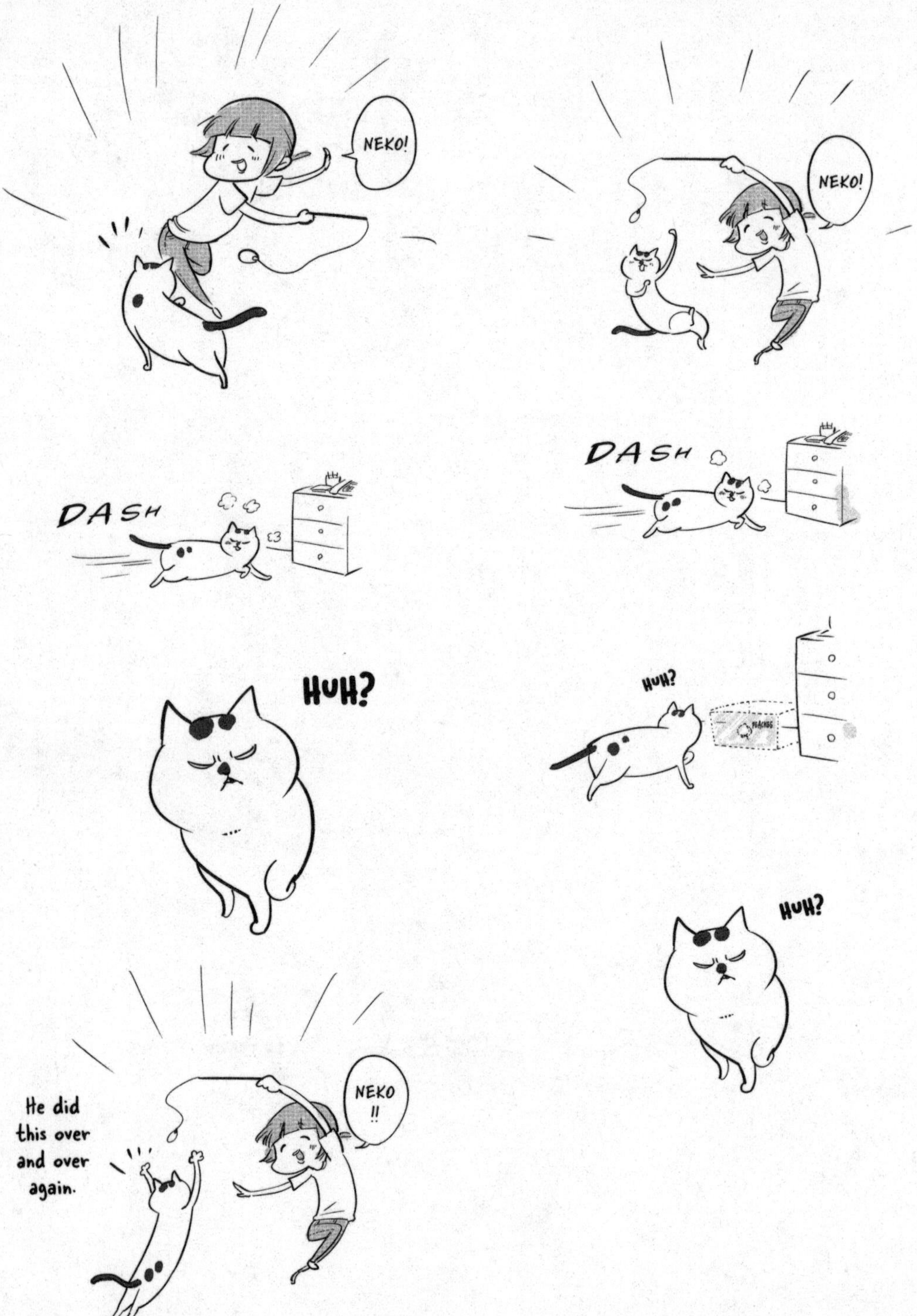
NEKO!
DASH
HUH?
HUH?
NEKO!
DASH
HUH?
NEKO !!
He did this over and over again.

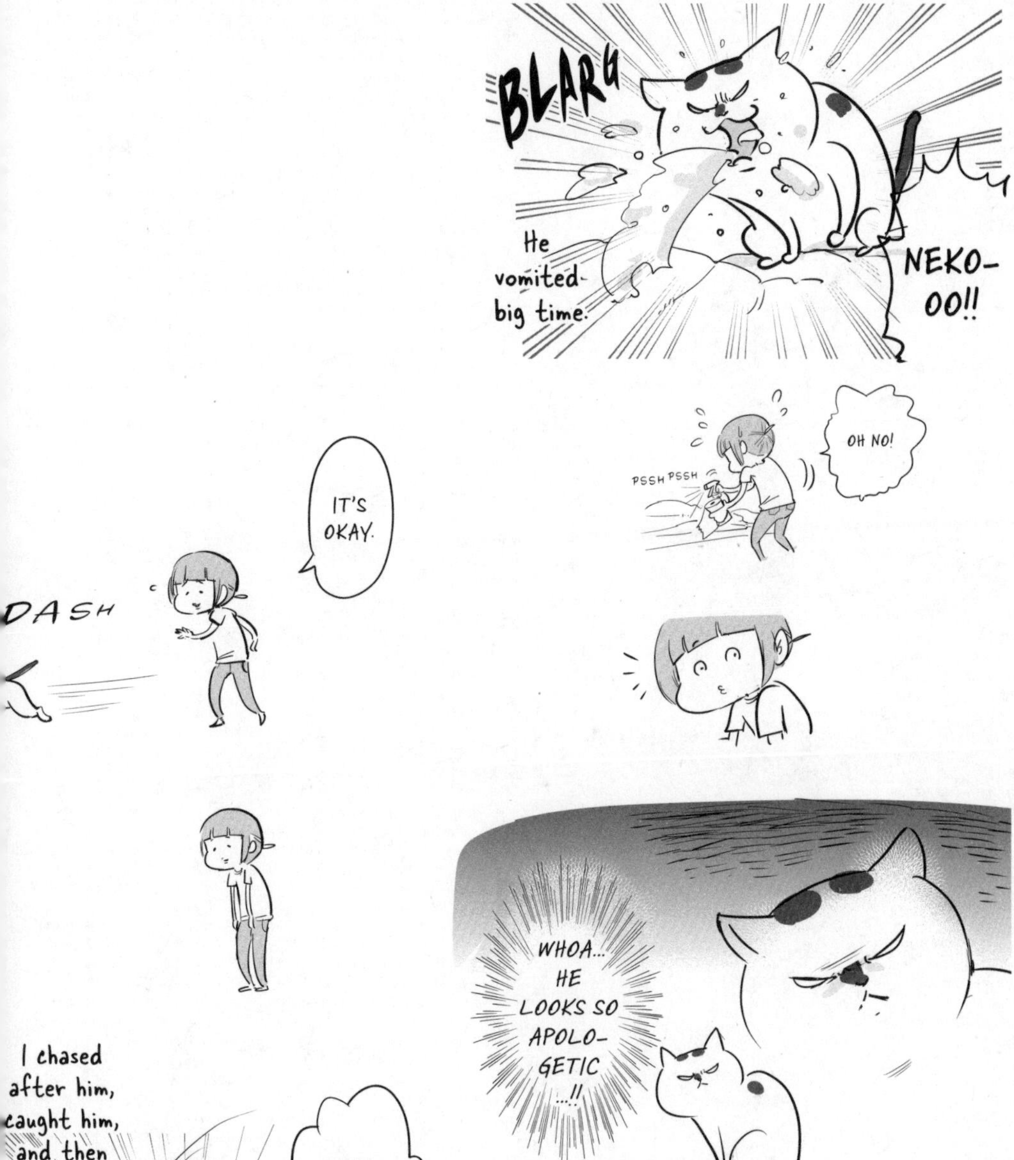
BLARG
NEKO-OO!!
He vomited big time.
OH NO!
PSSH PSSH
WHOA... HE LOOKS SO APOLOGETIC ...!!
A subtle expression only his owner can read.
IT'S OKAY.
DASH
IT'S OKAY!
I chased after him, caught him, and then comforted him.

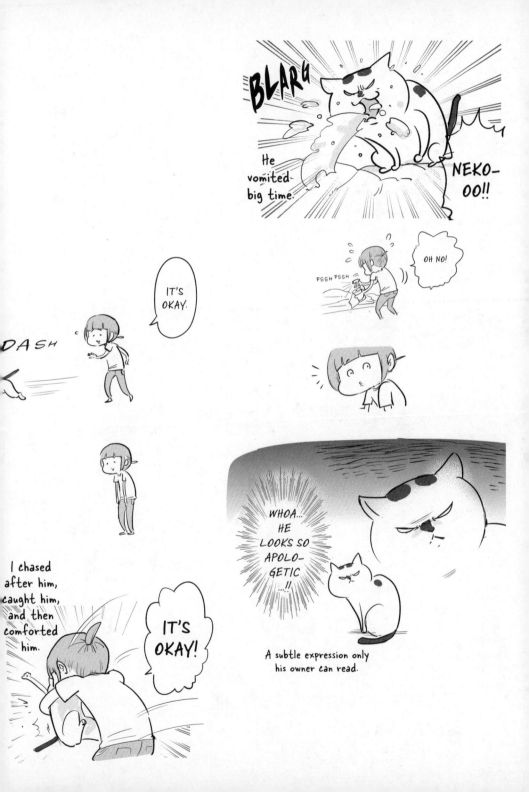

About an hour later...

IT'S OKAY.

Sorry about that.

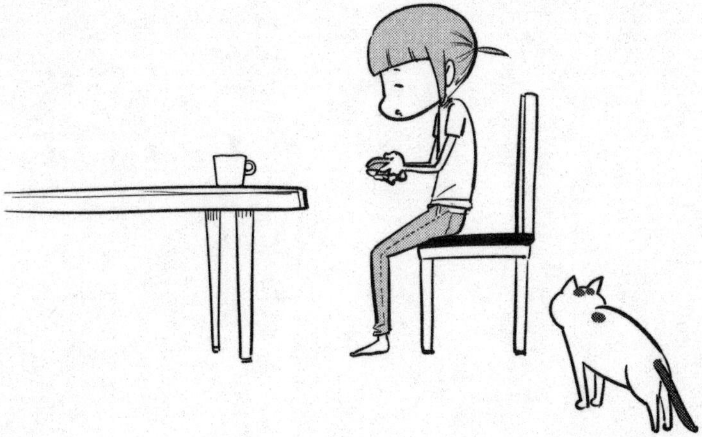

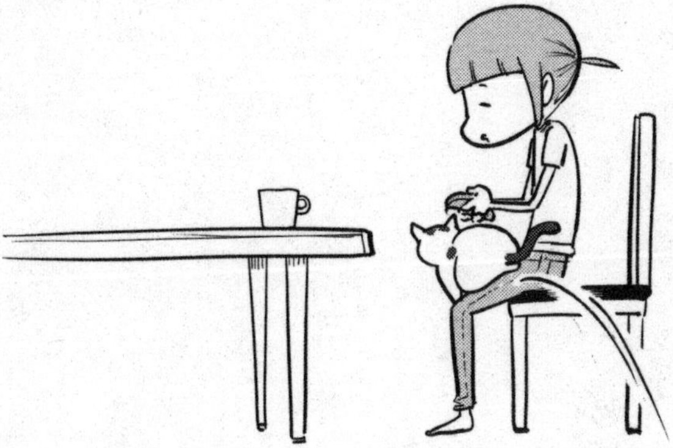

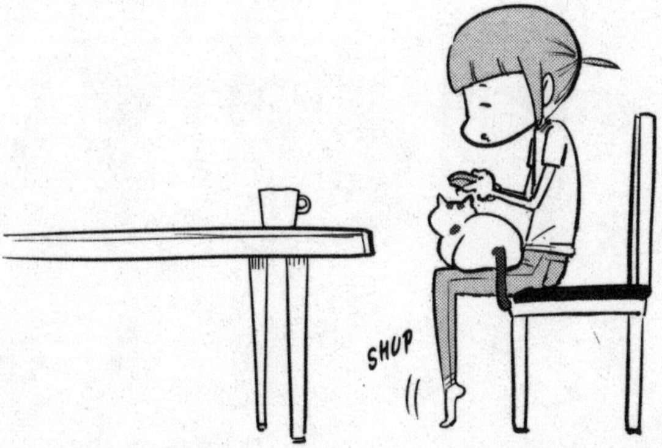
SHUP

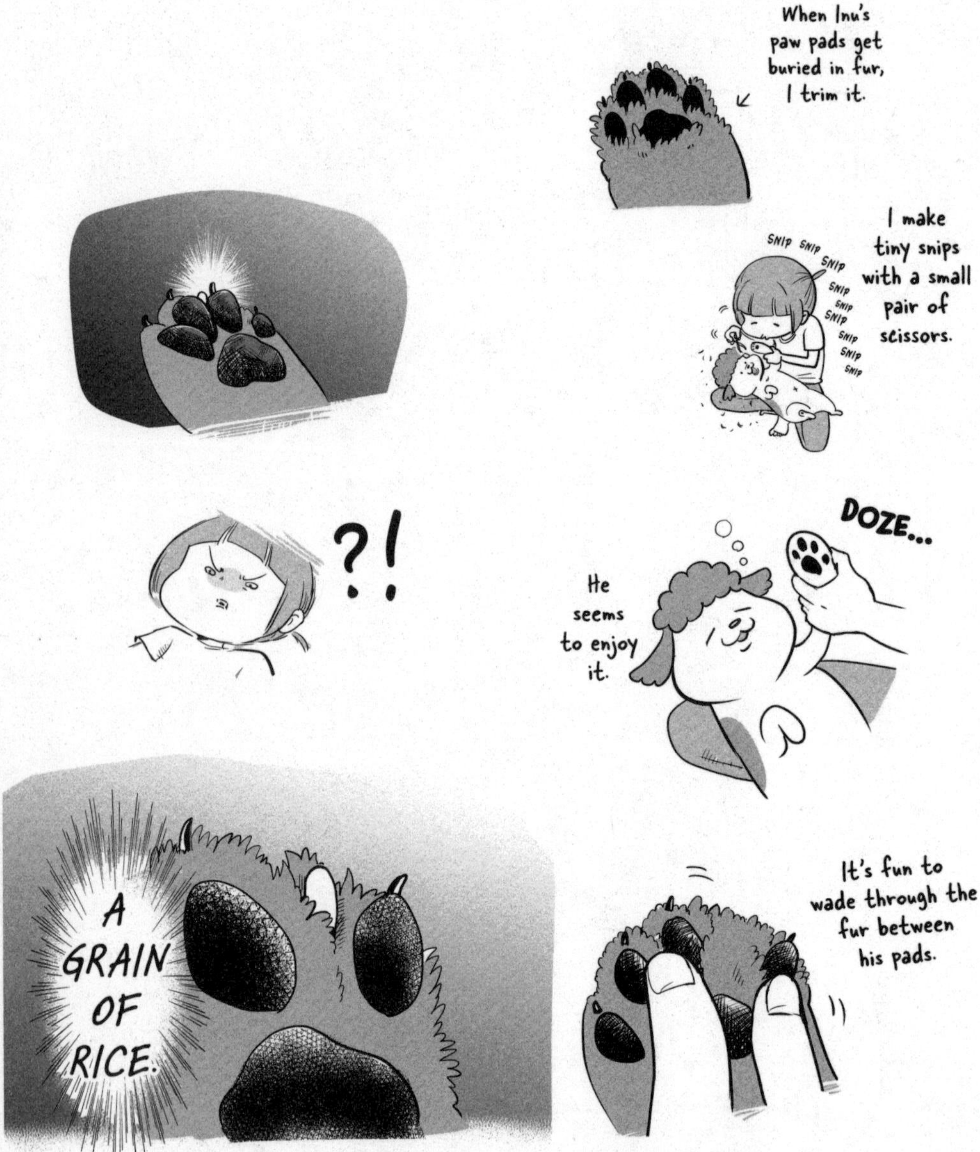
When Inu's paw pads get buried in fur, I trim it.
I make tiny snips with a small pair of scissors.
SNIP SNIP SNIP SNIP SNIP SNIP SNIP SNIP SNIP
DOZE...
He seems to enjoy it.
It's fun to wade through the fur between his pads.
?!
A GRAIN OF RICE.

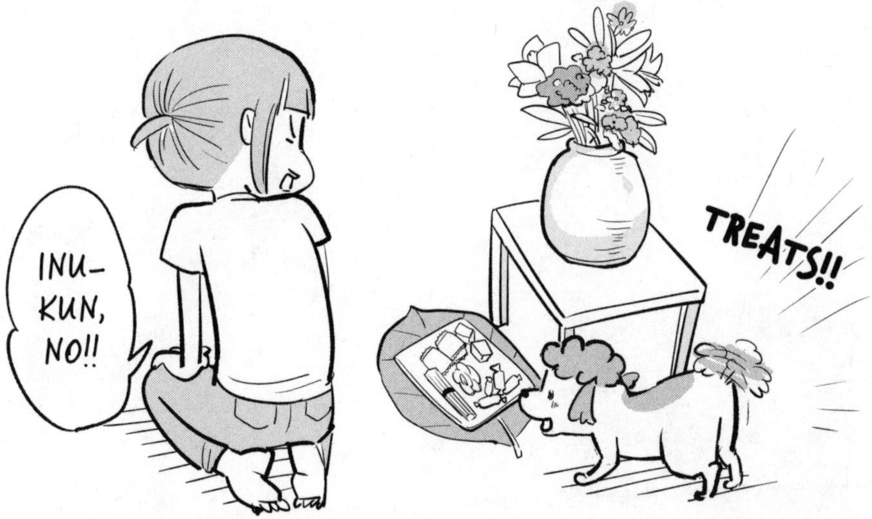
TREATS!!
INU-KUN, NO!!

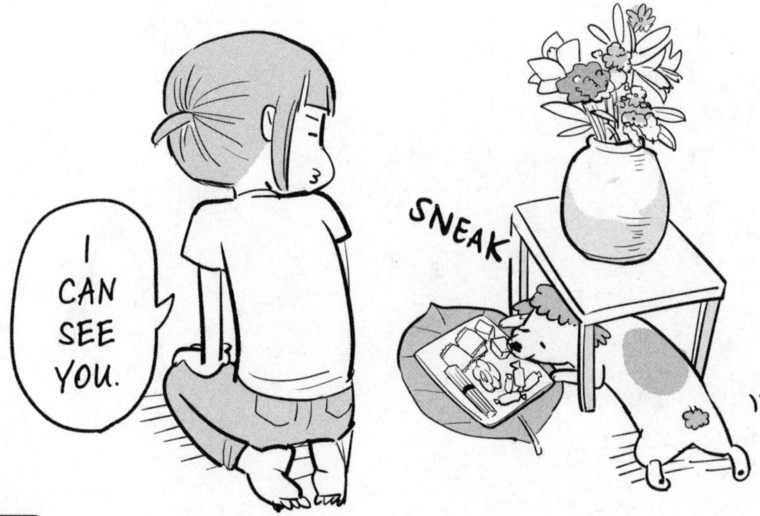
SNEAK
I CAN SEE YOU.

END

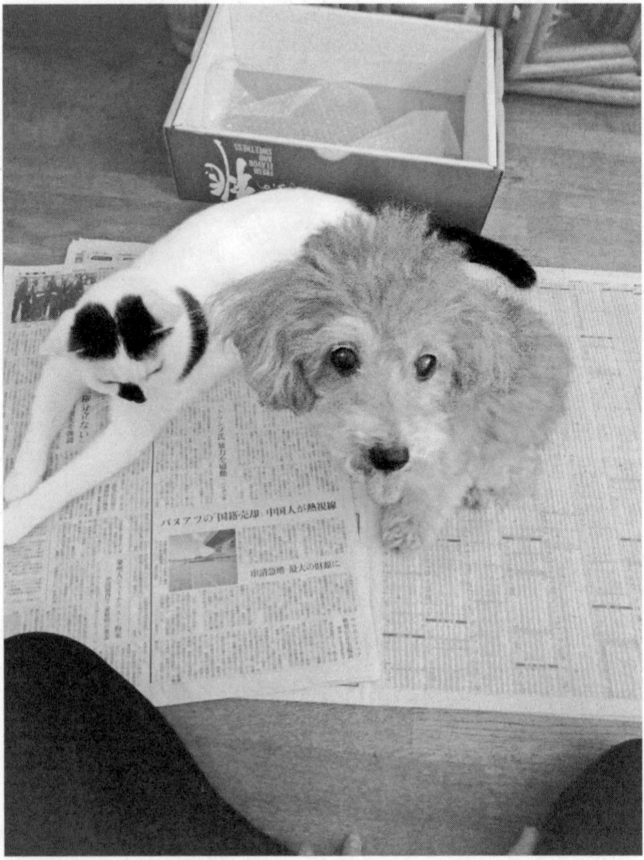
バヌアツの「国籍売却」中国人が熱視線
申請急増 最大の財源に

Illiterate.

Newly-Drawn 4-Panel Strip

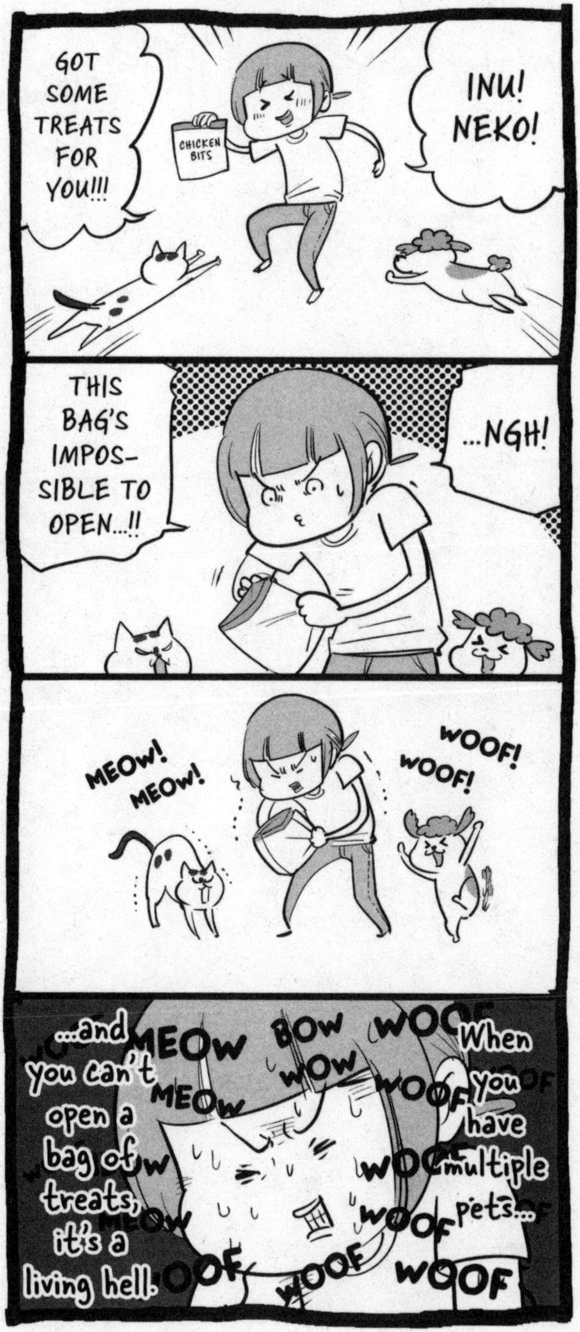

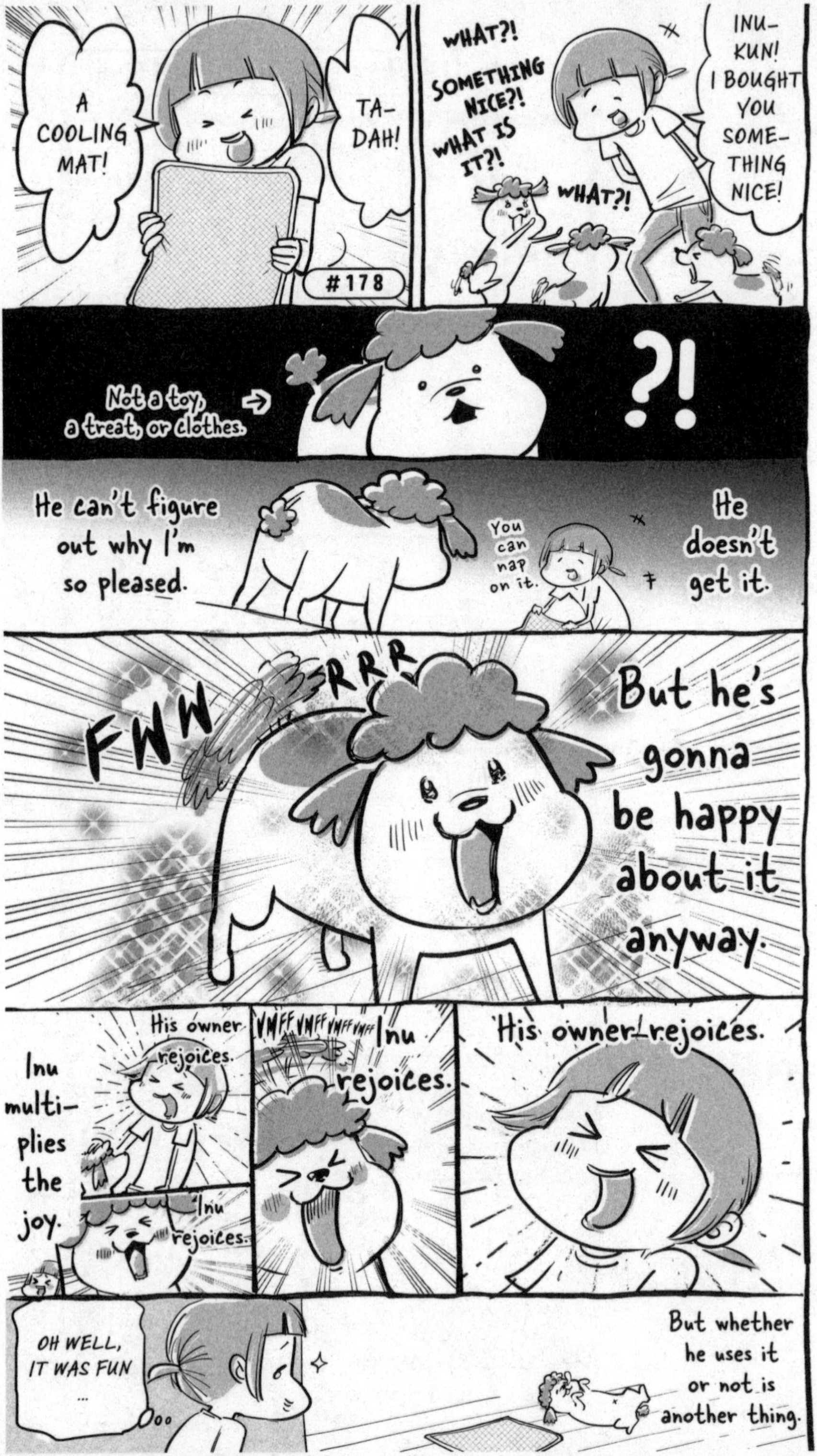
INU-KUN! I BOUGHT YOU SOMETHING NICE!
WHAT?! SOMETHING NICE?! WHAT IS IT?!
WHAT?!
TA-DAH!
A COOLING MAT!
#178
?!
Not a toy, a treat, or clothes.
He doesn't get it.
You can nap on it.
He can't figure out why I'm so pleased.
But he's gonna be happy about it anyway.
FWWRRR
His owner rejoices.
VMFF VMFF VMFF VMFF
Inu rejoices.
His owner rejoices.
Inu rejoices.
Inu multiplies the joy.
But whether he uses it or not is another thing.
OH WELL, IT WAS FUN ...

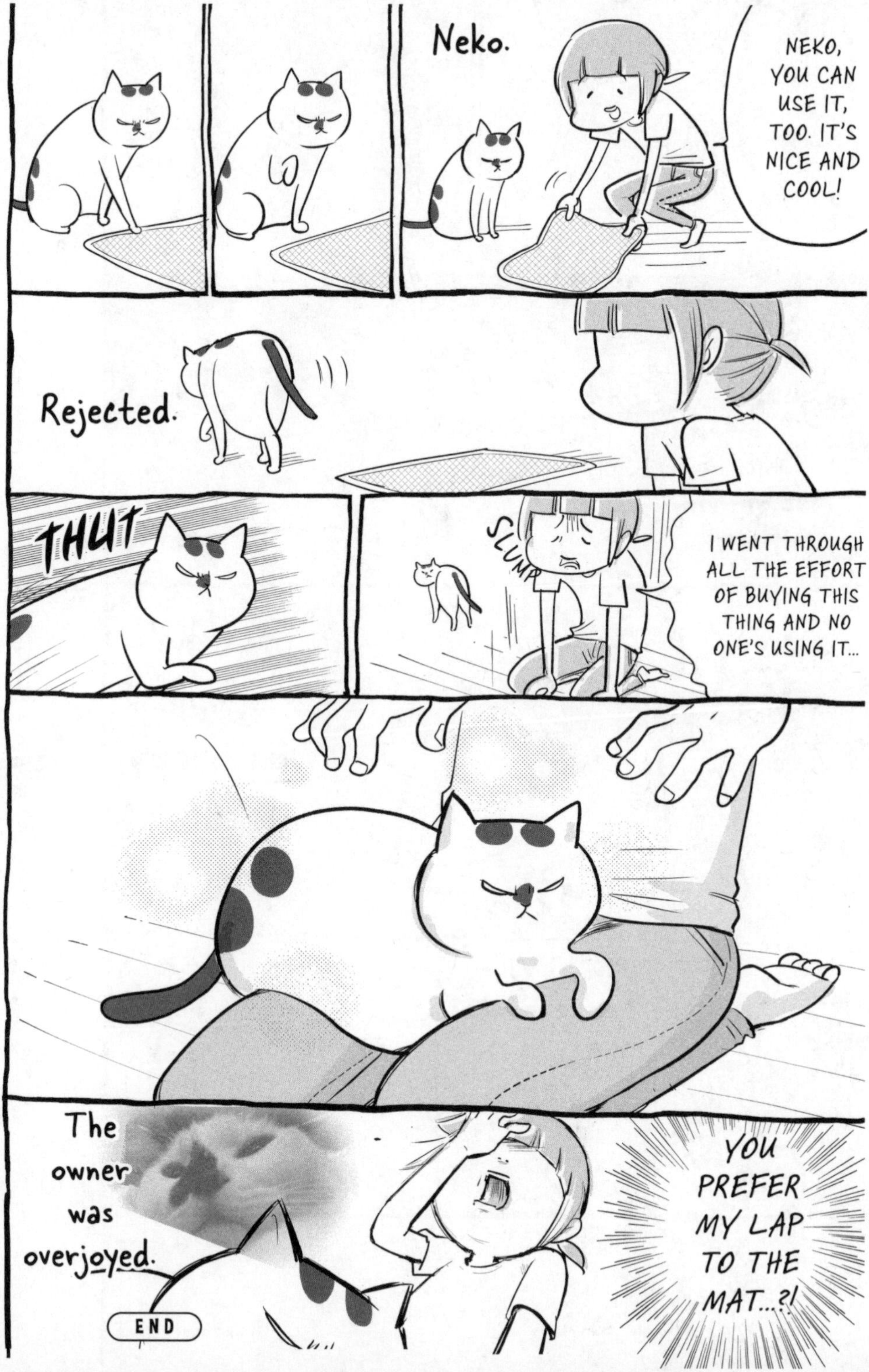
NEKO, YOU CAN USE IT, TOO. IT'S NICE AND COOL!
Neko.
Rejected.
I WENT THROUGH ALL THE EFFORT OF BUYING THIS THING AND NO ONE'S USING IT...
SLUMP
THUT
YOU PREFER MY LAP TO THE MAT...?!
The owner was overjoyed.
END

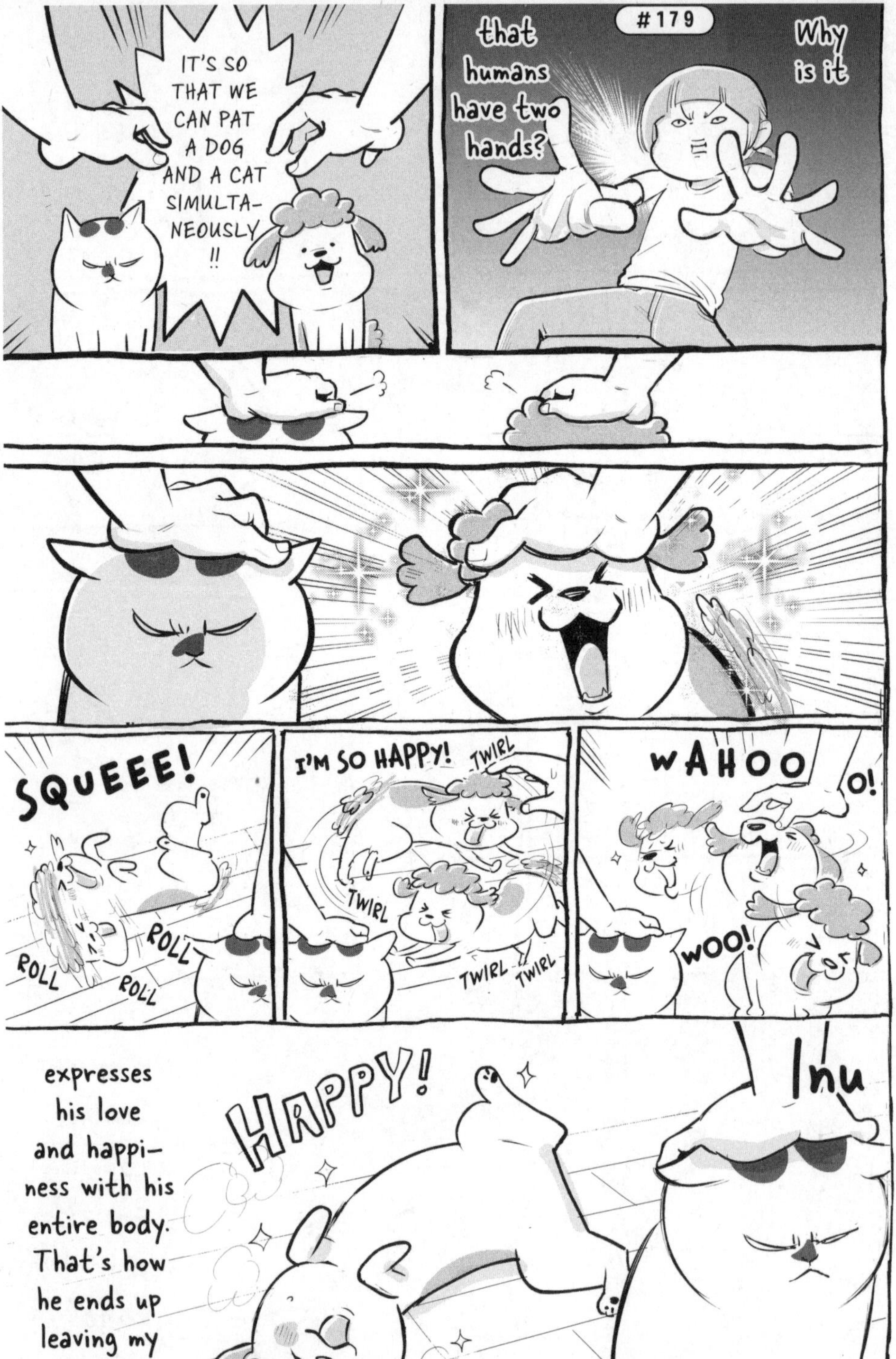
#179
Why is it
that humans have two hands?
IT'S SO THAT WE CAN PAT A DOG AND A CAT SIMULTANEOUSLY!!
WAHOO
O!
WOO!
I'M SO HAPPY!
TWIRL
TWIRL
TWIRL
TWIRL
SQUEEEE!
ROLL
ROLL
ROLL
Inu
HAPPY!
expresses his love and happiness with his entire body. That's how he ends up leaving my hand.

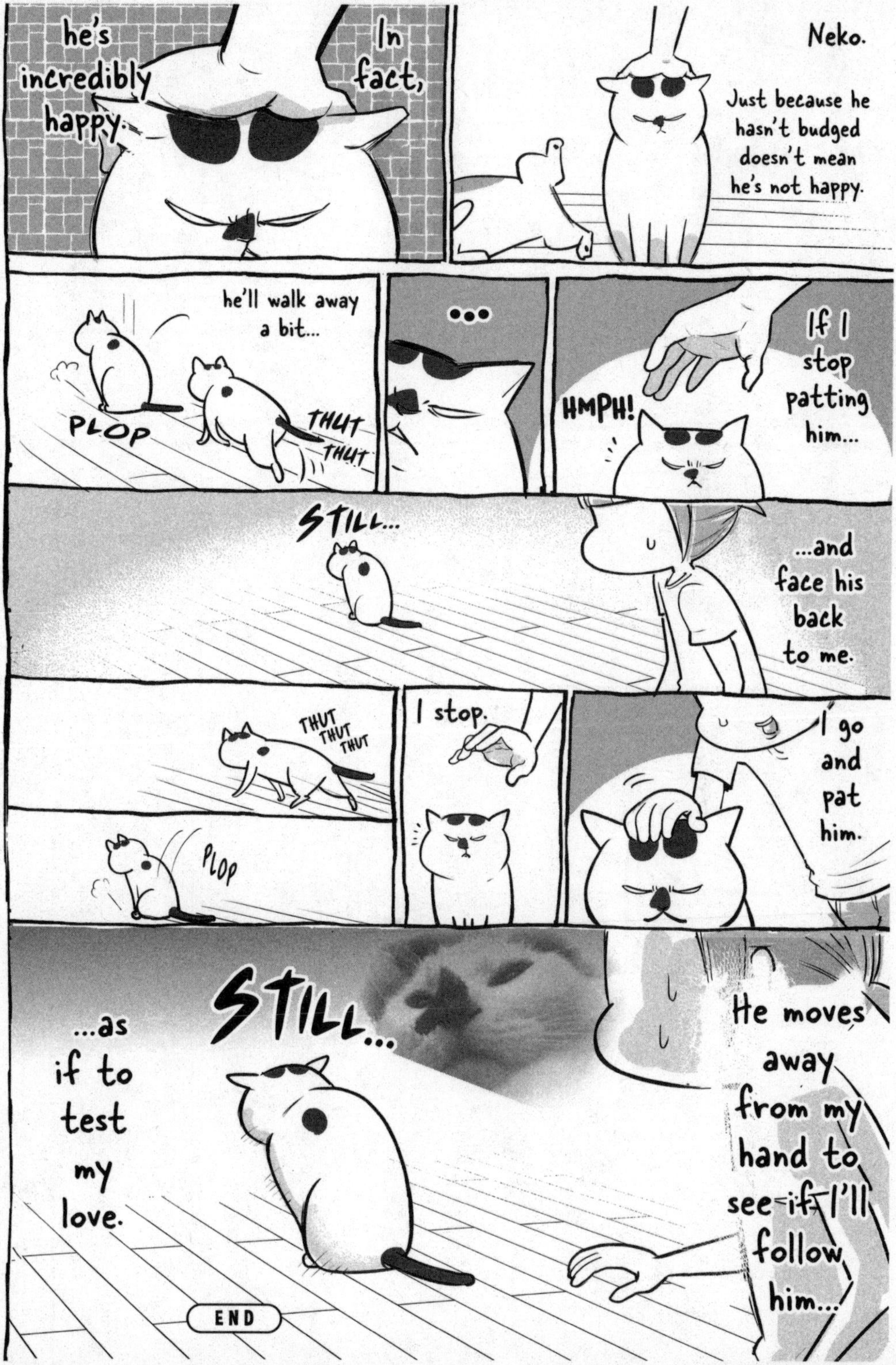
Neko.
Just because he hasn't budged doesn't mean he's not happy.
In fact,
he's incredibly happy.
If I stop patting him...
HMPH!
...
he'll walk away a bit...
THUT THUT
PLOP
...and face his back to me.
STILL...
I go and pat him.
I stop.
THUT THUT THUT
PLOP
He moves away from my hand to see if I'll follow him...
STILL...
...as if to test my love.
END

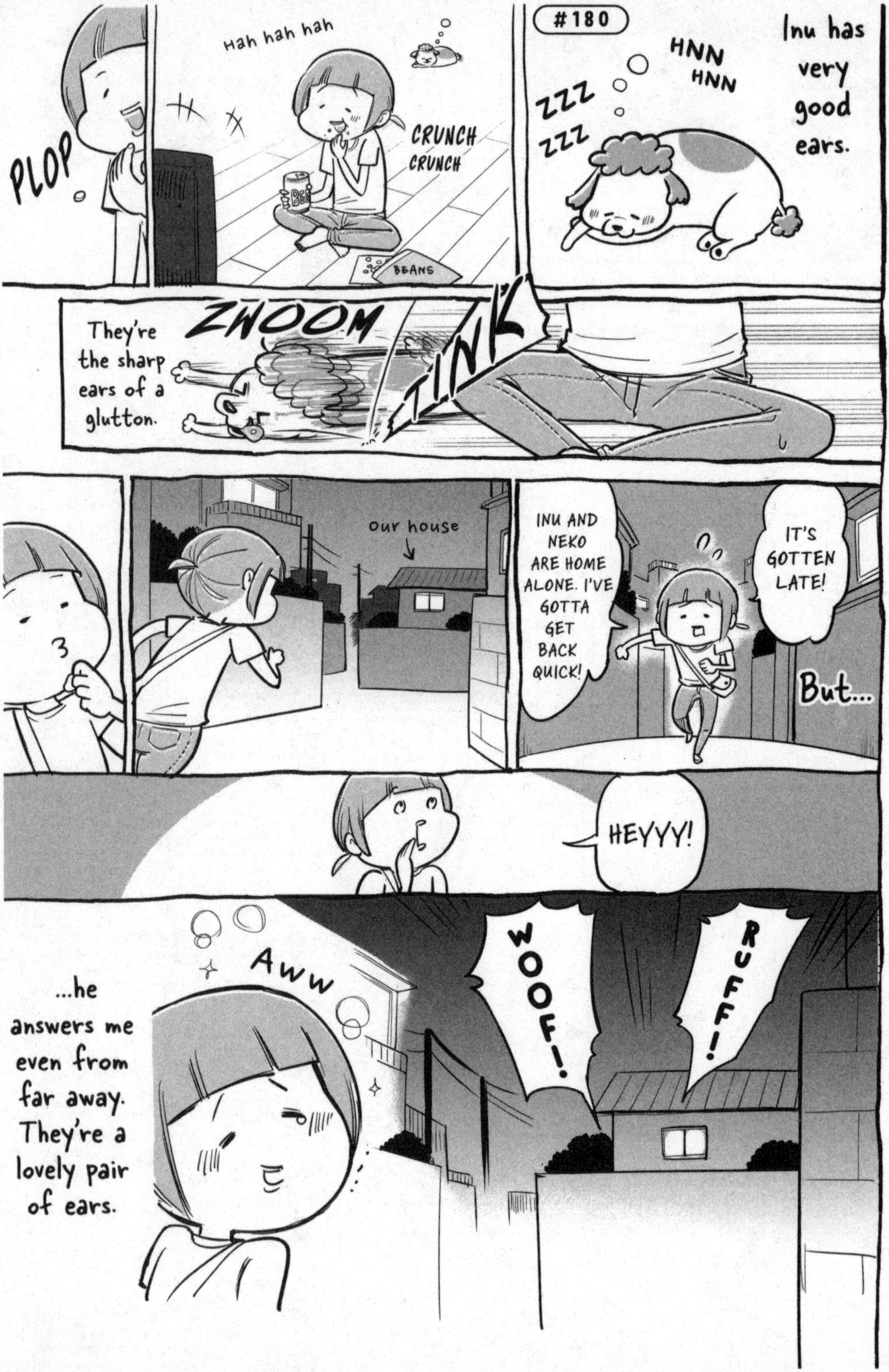
#180
Inu has very good ears.
HNN HNN
ZZZ ZZZ
Hah hah hah
CRUNCH CRUNCH
BEER
BEANS
PLOP
TINK
ZWOOM
They're the sharp ears of a glutton.
IT'S GOTTEN LATE!
INU AND NEKO ARE HOME ALONE. I'VE GOTTA GET BACK QUICK!
But...
our house
HEYYY!
RUFF!
WOOF!
Aww
...he answers me even from far away. They're a lovely pair of ears.

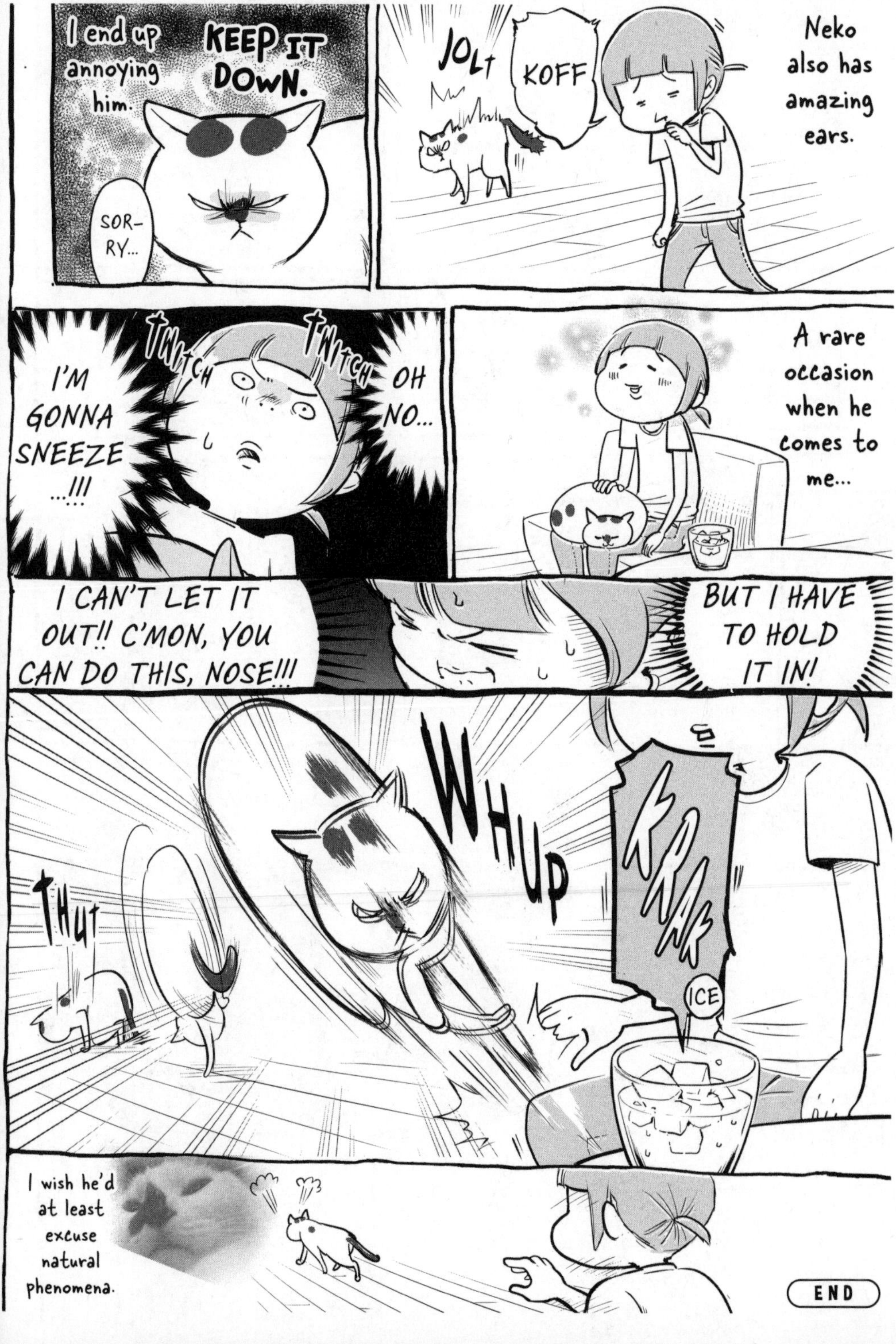
Neko also has amazing ears.
KOFF
JOLT
KEEP IT DOWN.
I end up annoying him.
SORRY...
A rare occasion when he comes to me...
OH NO...
TWITCH
TWITCH
I'M GONNA SNEEZE ...!!!
BUT I HAVE TO HOLD IT IN!
I CAN'T LET IT OUT!! C'MON, YOU CAN DO THIS, NOSE!!!
KRAK
ICE
WHUP
THUT
I wish he'd at least excuse natural phenomena.
END

What's with that position...?

Newly-Drawn 4-Panel Strip

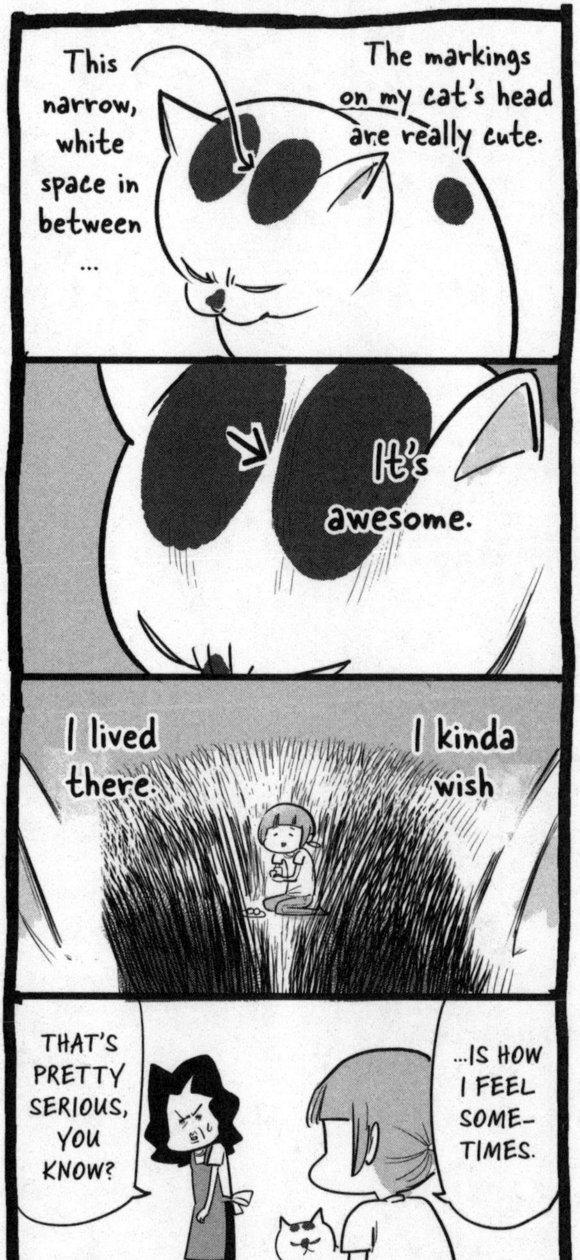

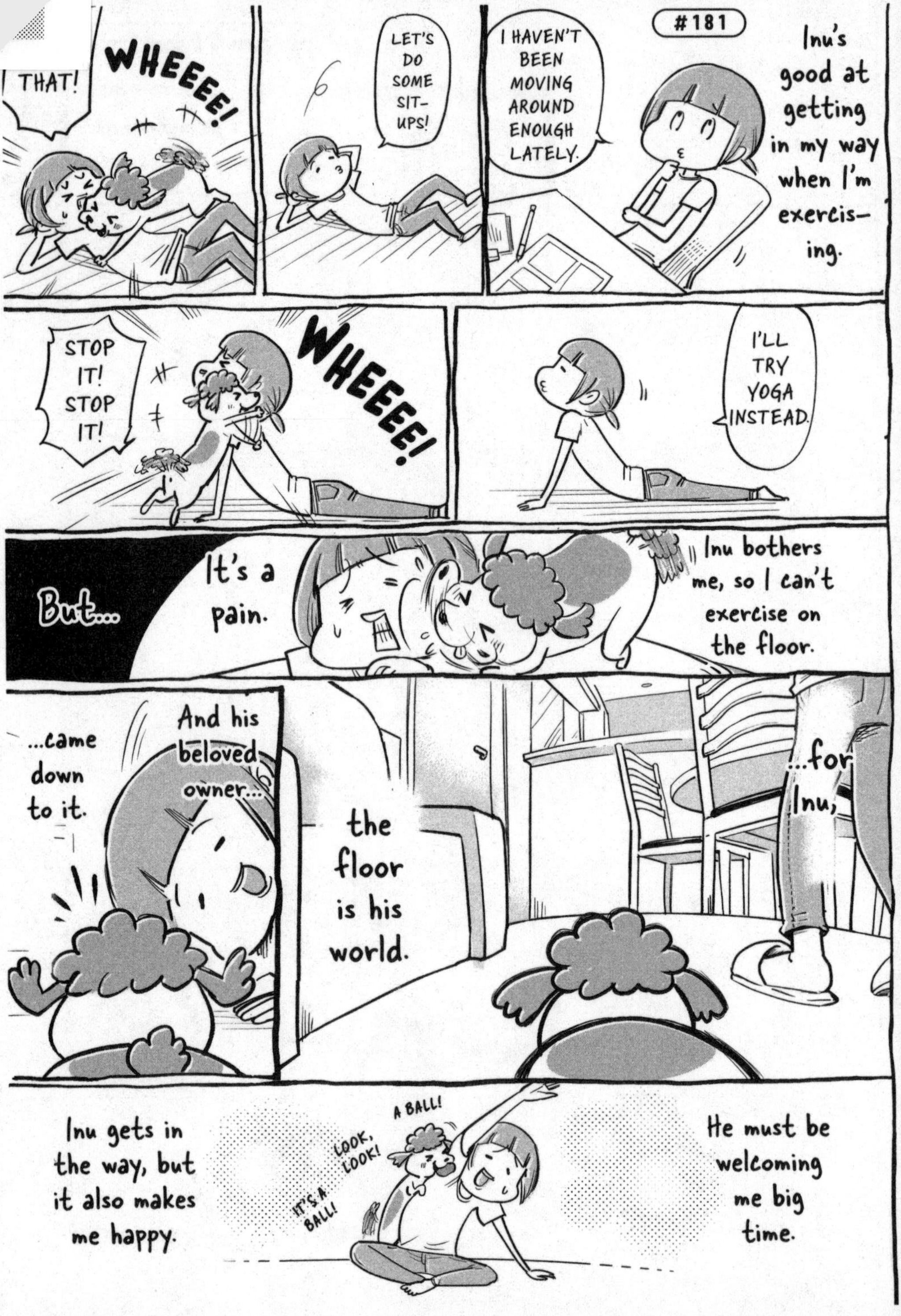
#181
Inu's good at getting in my way when I'm exercising.
I HAVEN'T BEEN MOVING AROUND ENOUGH LATELY.
LET'S DO SOME SIT-UPS!
WHEEEEE!
THAT!
I'LL TRY YOGA INSTEAD.
WHEEEEE!
STOP IT! STOP IT!
Inu bothers me, so I can't exercise on the floor.
It's a pain.
But...
...for Inu,
the floor is his world.
And his beloved owner...
...came down to it.
He must be welcoming me big time.
A BALL!
LOOK, LOOK!
IT'S A BALL!
Inu gets in the way, but it also makes me happy.

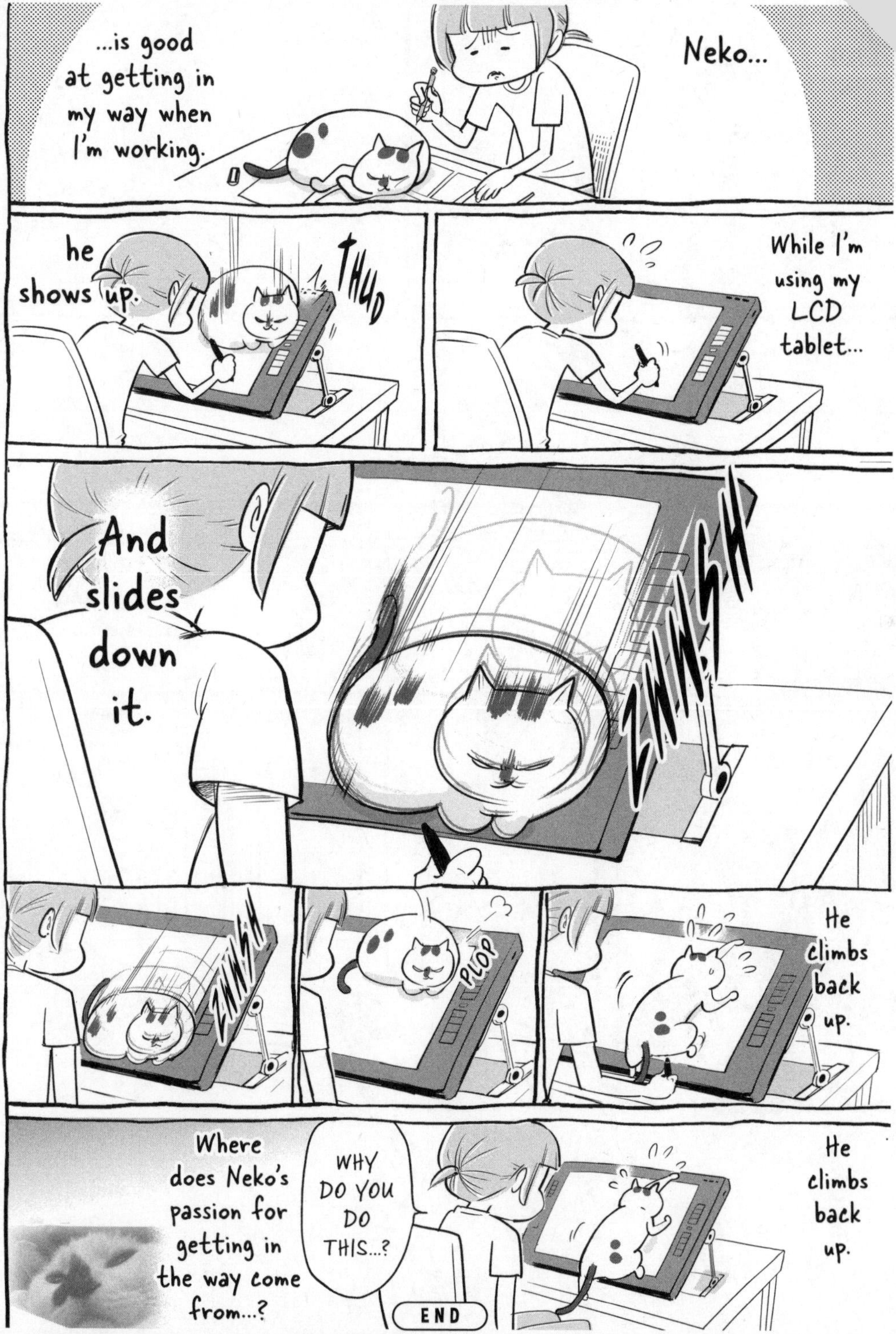
Neko...
...is good at getting in my way when I'm working.
While I'm using my LCD tablet...
he shows up.
THUD
And slides down it.
ZWISH
He climbs back up.
PLOP
ZWISH
He climbs back up.
WHY DO YOU DO THIS...?
Where does Neko's passion for getting in the way come from...?
END

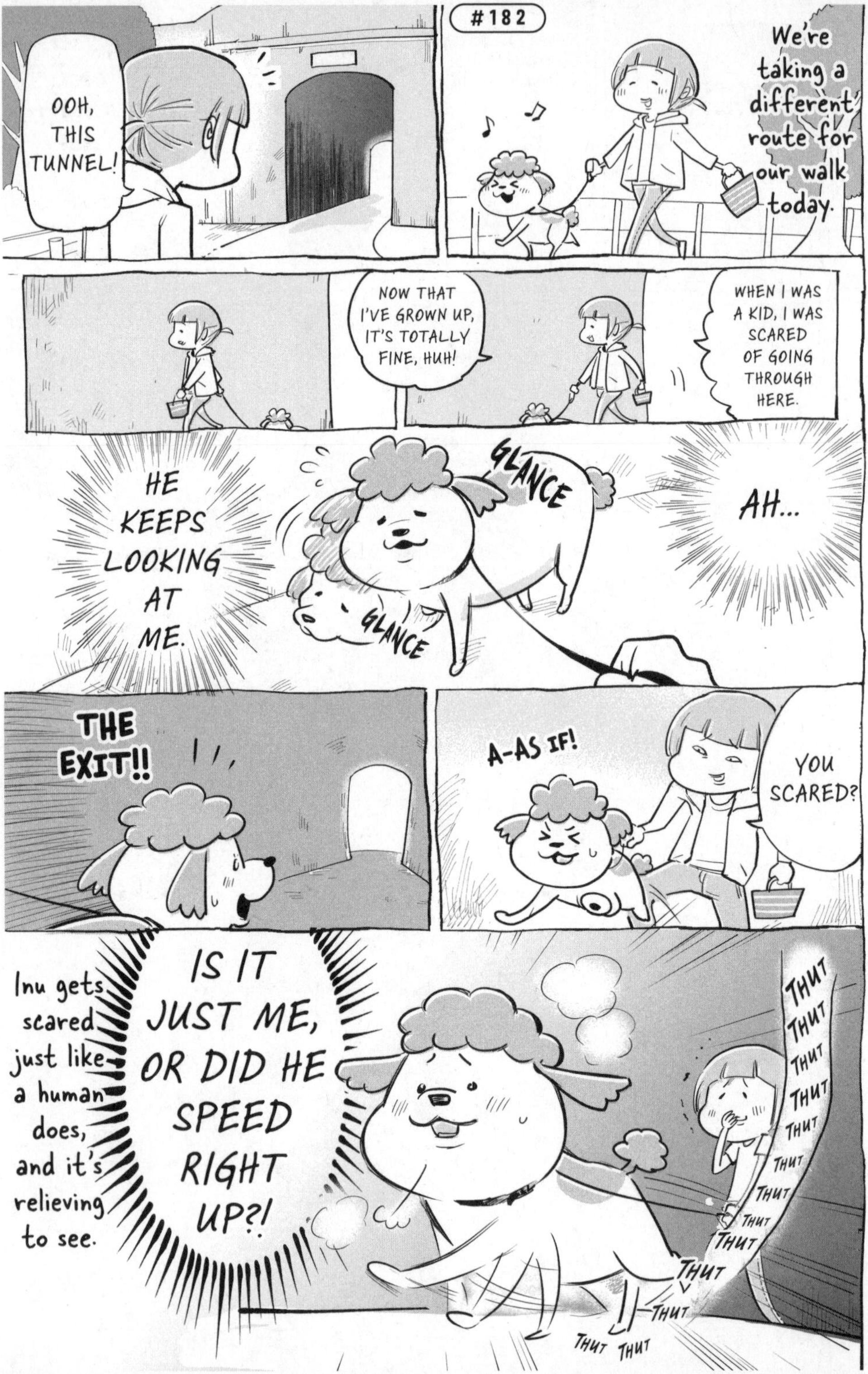
#182
We're taking a different route for our walk today.
OOH, THIS TUNNEL!
WHEN I WAS A KID, I WAS SCARED OF GOING THROUGH HERE.
NOW THAT I'VE GROWN UP, IT'S TOTALLY FINE, HUH!
AH...
GLANCE
HE KEEPS LOOKING AT ME.
GLANCE
YOU SCARED?
A-AS IF!
THE EXIT!!
THUT THUT THUT THUT THUT THUT THUT THUT THUT THUT THUT THUT THUT
IS IT JUST ME, OR DID HE SPEED RIGHT UP?!
Inu gets scared just like a human does, and it's relieving to see.

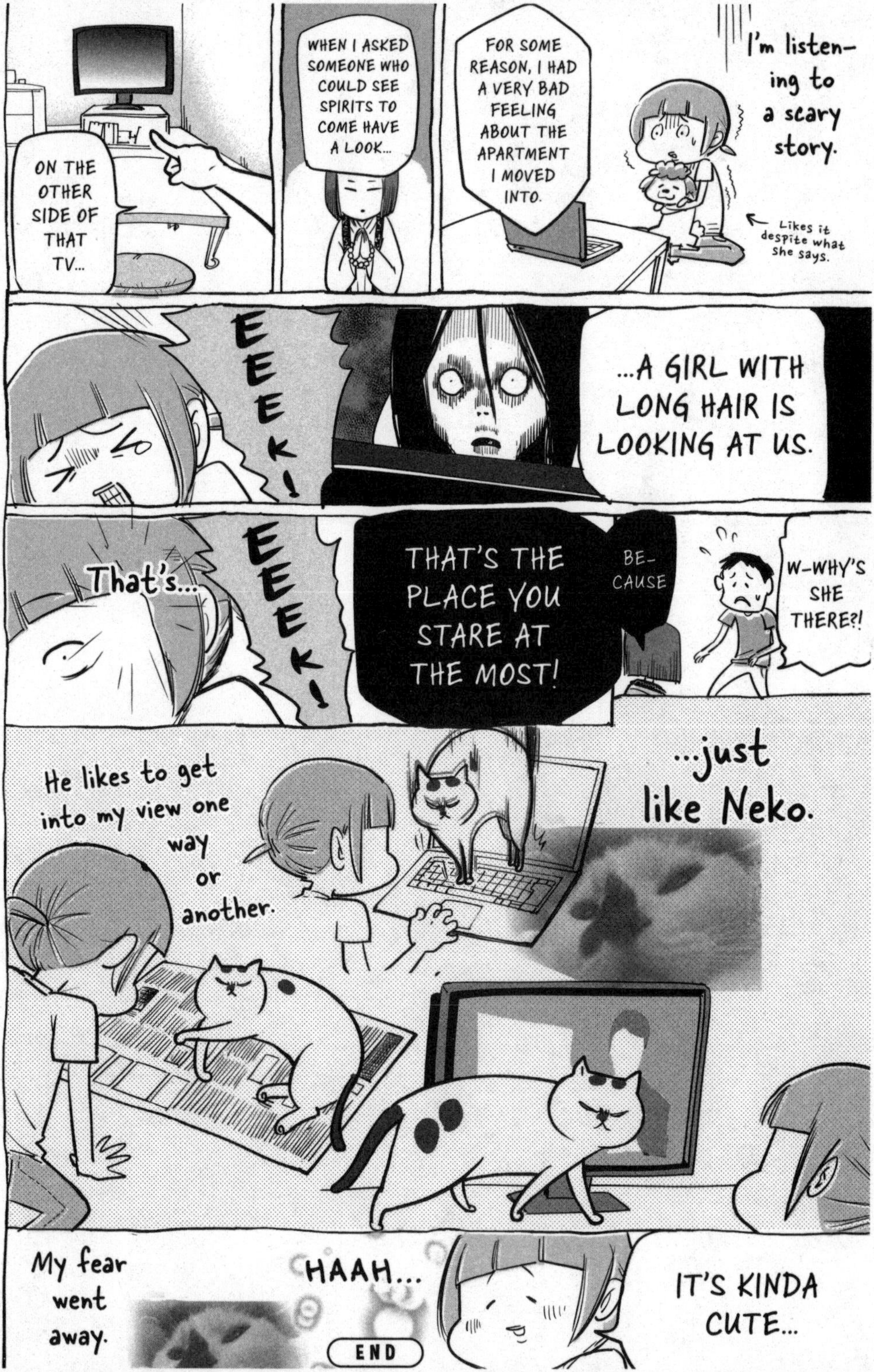
I'm listening to a scary story.
Likes it despite what she says.
FOR SOME REASON, I HAD A VERY BAD FEELING ABOUT THE APARTMENT I MOVED INTO.
WHEN I ASKED SOMEONE WHO COULD SEE SPIRITS TO COME HAVE A LOOK...
ON THE OTHER SIDE OF THAT TV...
...A GIRL WITH LONG HAIR IS LOOKING AT US.
EEEEK!
W-WHY'S SHE THERE?!
BECAUSE
THAT'S THE PLACE YOU STARE AT THE MOST!
EEEEK!
That's...
...just like Neko.
He likes to get into my view one way or another.
IT'S KINDA CUTE...
HAAH...
My fear went away.
END

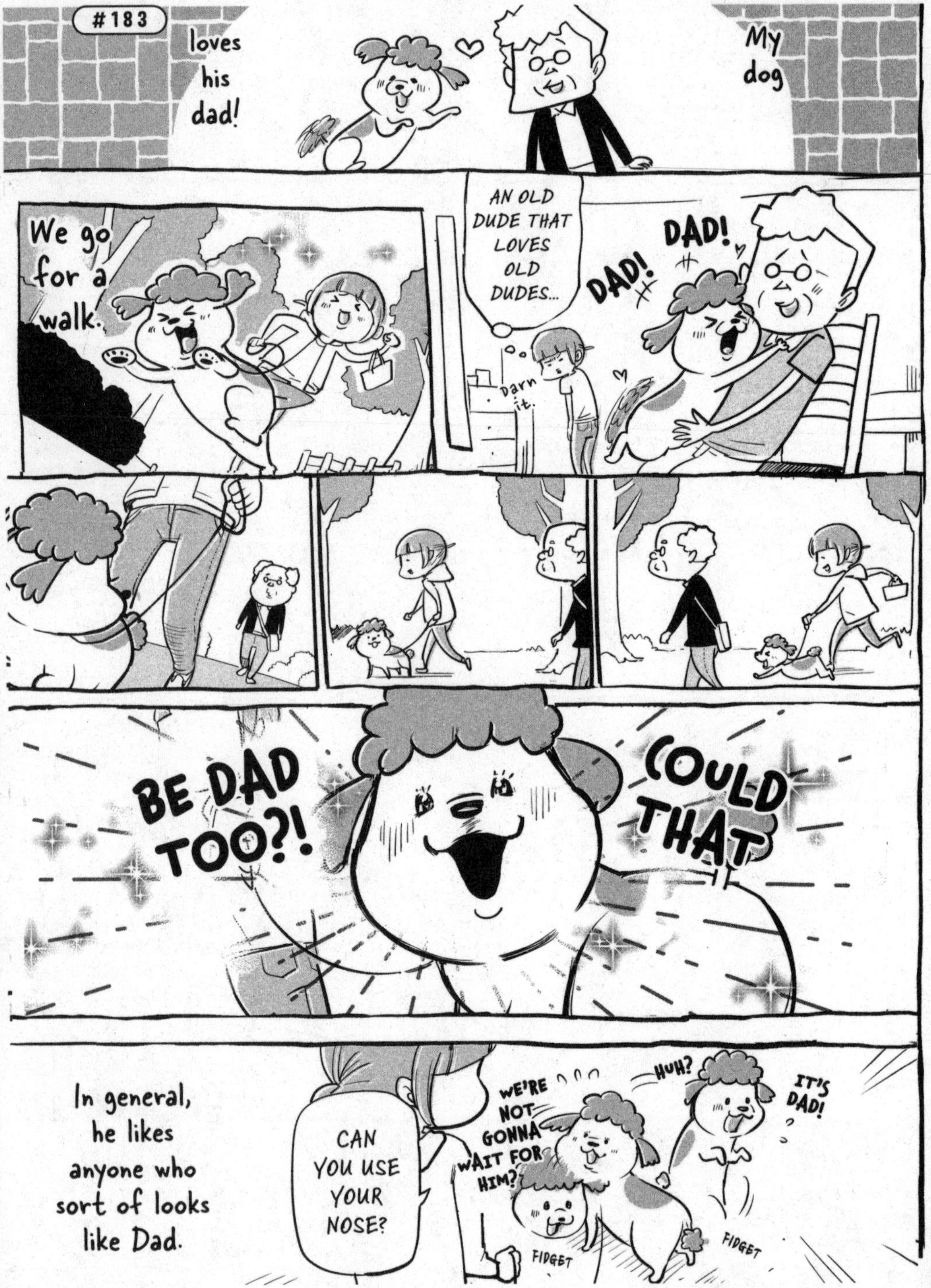
#183
My dog
loves his dad!
DAD!
DAD!
AN OLD DUDE THAT LOVES OLD DUDES...
Darn it.
We go for a walk.
COULD THAT
BE DAD TOO?!
IT'S DAD!
HUH?
WE'RE NOT GONNA WAIT FOR HIM?
FIDGET
FIDGET
CAN YOU USE YOUR NOSE?
In general, he likes anyone who sort of looks like Dad.

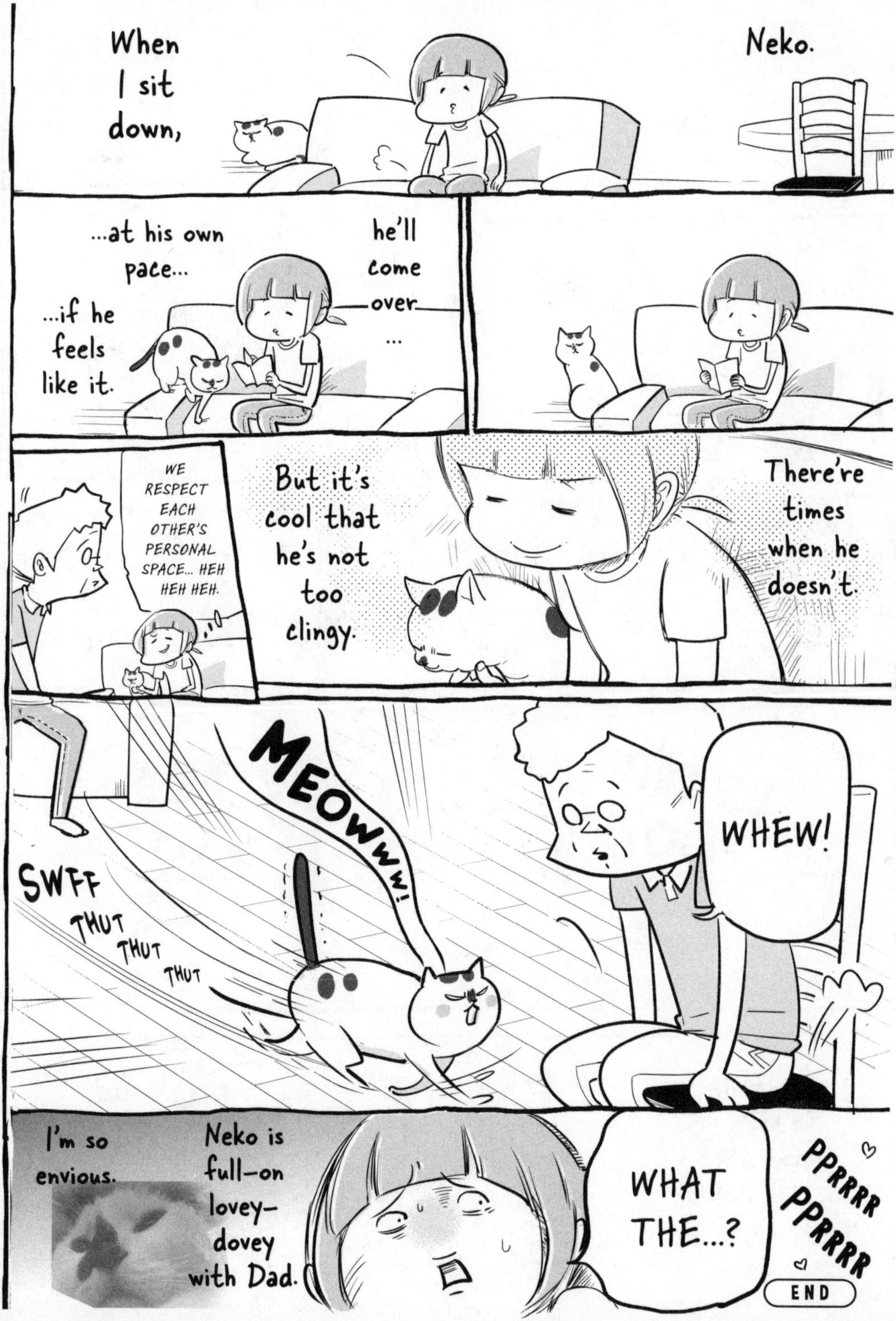
Neko.
When I sit down,
he'll come over...
...at his own pace...
...if he feels like it.
There're times when he doesn't.
But it's cool that he's not too clingy.
WE RESPECT EACH OTHER'S PERSONAL SPACE... HEH HEH HEH.
WHEW!
MEOWWWW!
SWFF
THUT
THUT
THUT
PPRRRR
PPRRRR
WHAT THE...?
Neko is full-on lovey-dovey with Dad.
I'm so envious.
END

Glistening.

Newly-Drawn 4-Panel Strip

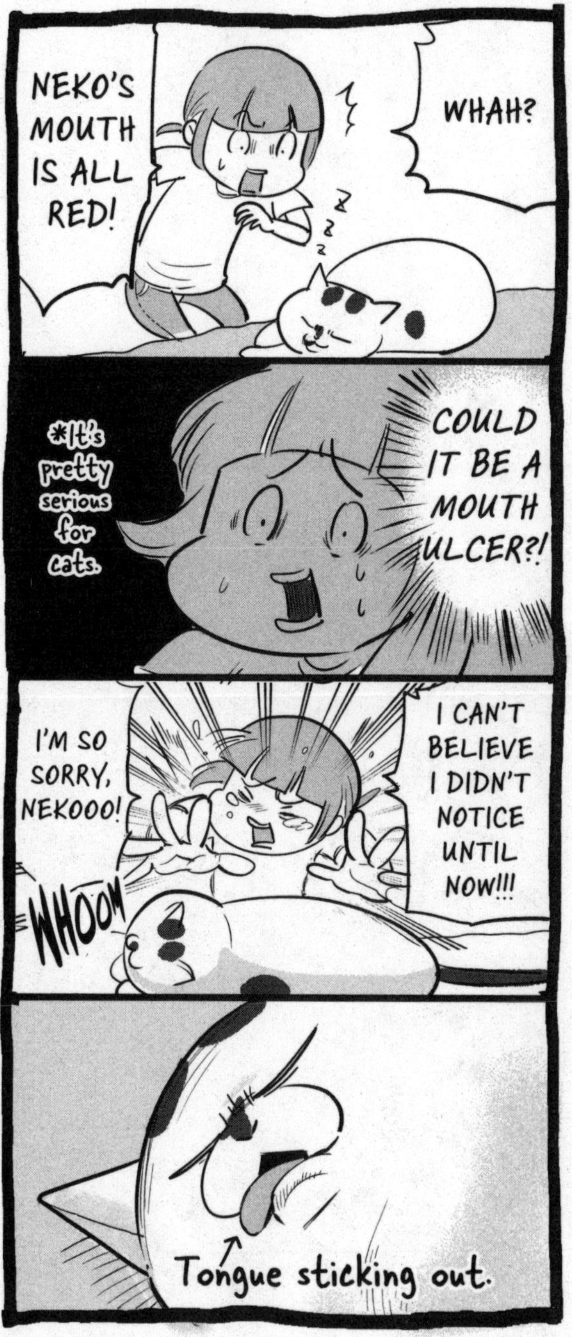
WHAH?
NEKO'S MOUTH IS ALL RED!
COULD IT BE A MOUTH ULCER?!
*It's pretty serious for cats.
I CAN'T BELIEVE I DIDN'T NOTICE UNTIL NOW!!!
I'M SO SORRY, NEKOOO!
WHOOM
Tongue sticking out.

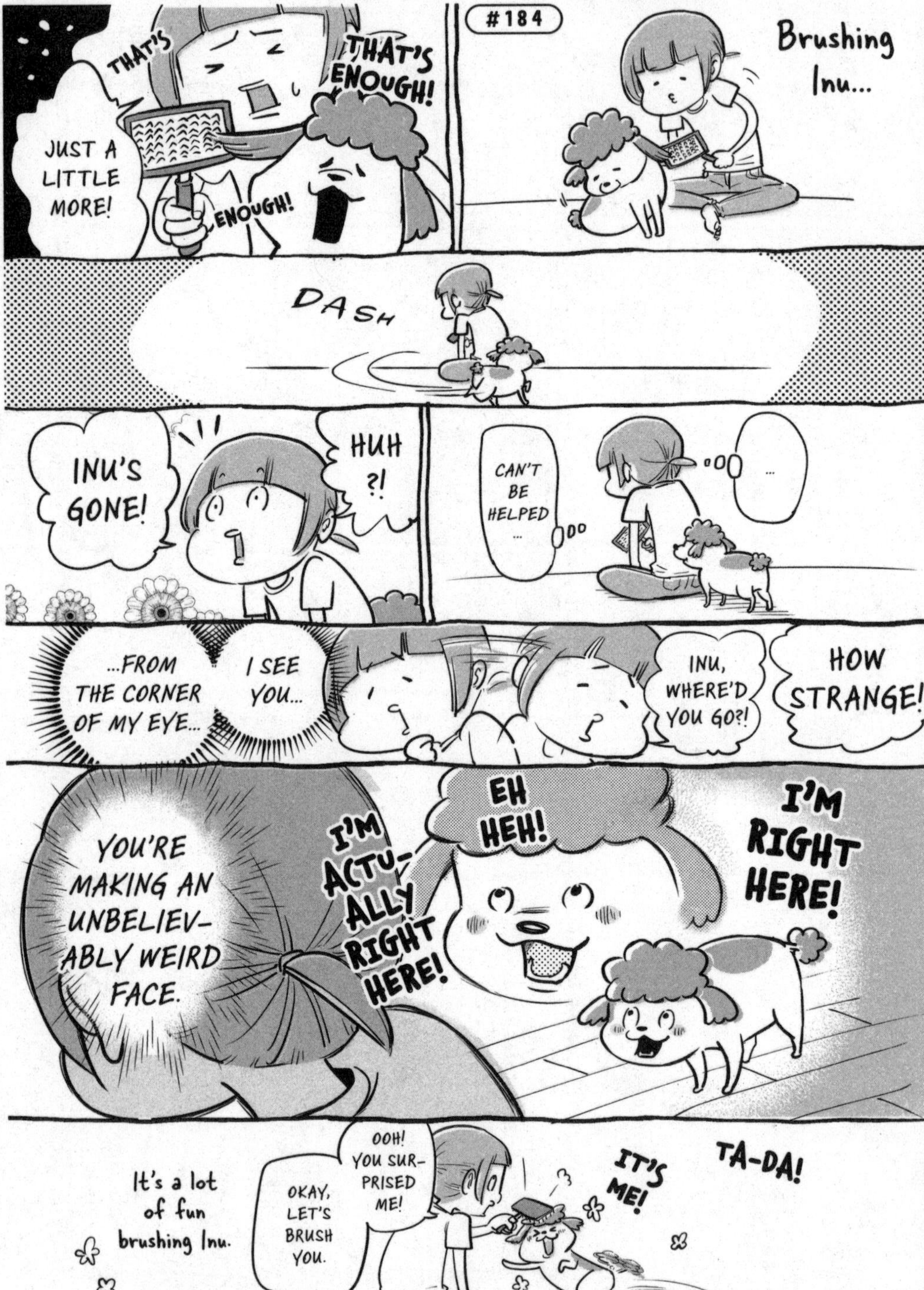
#184
Brushing Inu...
THAT'S ENOUGH!
THAT'S
JUST A LITTLE MORE!
ENOUGH!
DASH
...
CAN'T BE HELPED ...
HUH ?!
INU'S GONE!
HOW STRANGE!
INU, WHERE'D YOU GO?!
I SEE YOU...
...FROM THE CORNER OF MY EYE...
I'M RIGHT HERE!
EH HEH!
I'M ACTUALLY RIGHT HERE!
YOU'RE MAKING AN UNBELIEVABLY WEIRD FACE.
TA-DA!
IT'S ME!
OOH! YOU SURPRISED ME!
OKAY, LET'S BRUSH YOU.
It's a lot of fun brushing Inu.

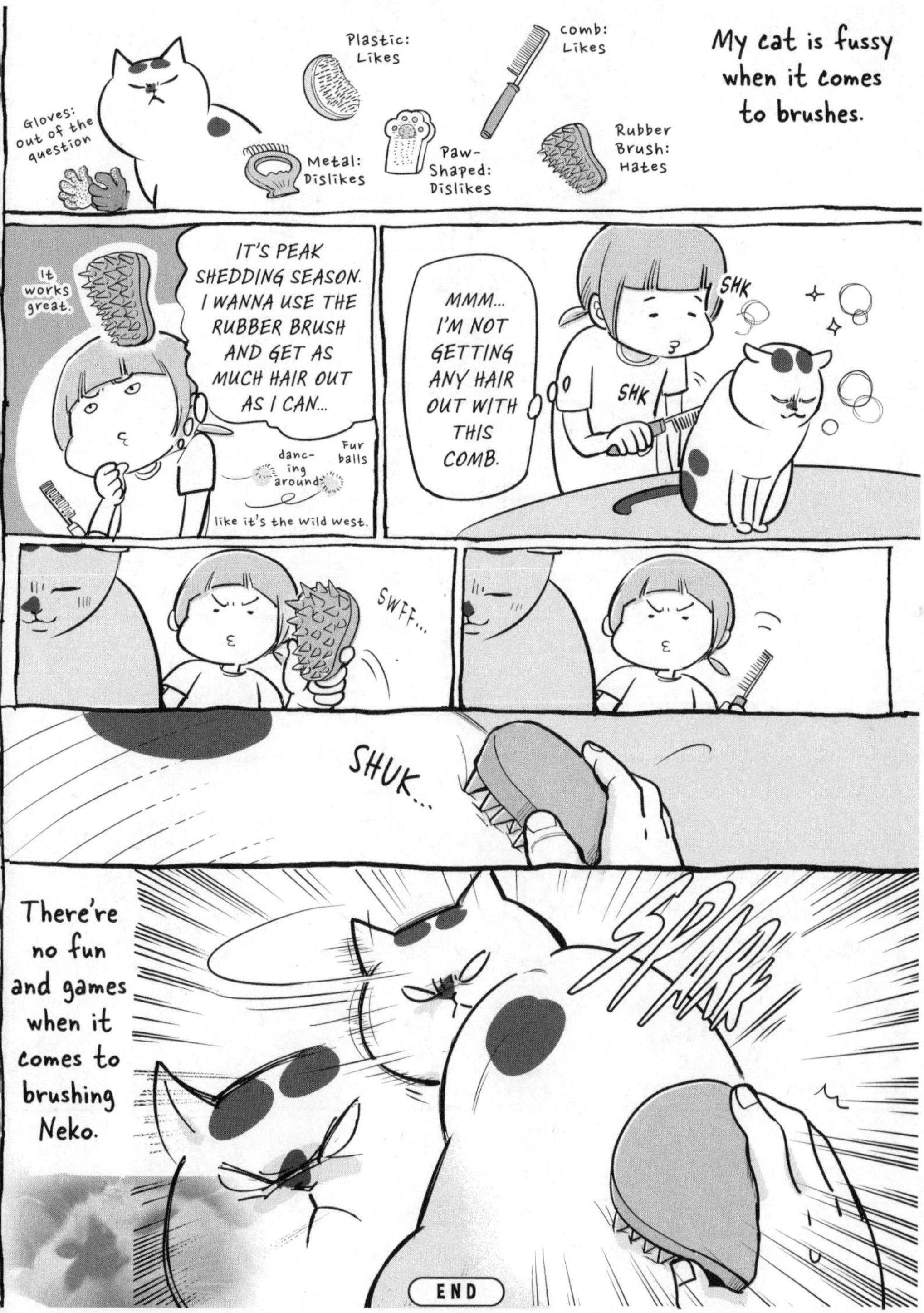
My cat is fussy when it comes to brushes.
Rubber Brush: Hates
comb: Likes
Paw-Shaped: Dislikes
Plastic: Likes
Metal: Dislikes
Gloves: out of the question
MMM... I'M NOT GETTING ANY HAIR OUT WITH THIS COMB.
SHK
SHK
IT'S PEAK SHEDDING SEASON. I WANNA USE THE RUBBER BRUSH AND GET AS MUCH HAIR OUT AS I CAN...
It works great.
Fur balls danc-ing around like it's the wild west.
SWFF...
SHUK...
There're no fun and games when it comes to brushing Neko.
END

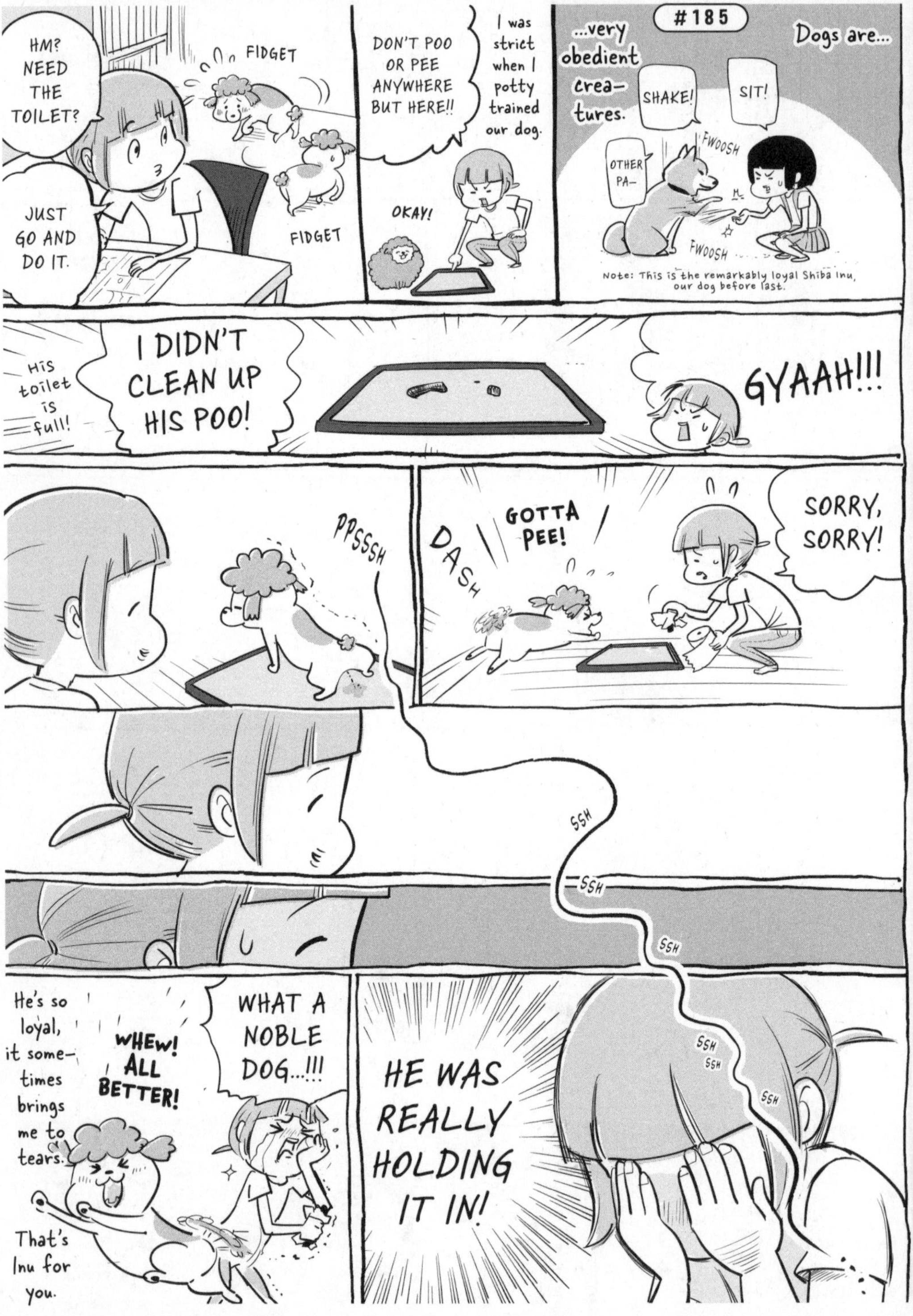
#185
Dogs are...
...very obedient creatures.
SIT!
SHAKE!
OTHER PA—
FWOOSH
FWOOSH
Note: This is the remarkably loyal Shiba Inu, our dog before last.
I was strict when I potty trained our dog.
DON'T POO OR PEE ANYWHERE BUT HERE!!
OKAY!
HM? NEED THE TOILET?
FIDGET
JUST GO AND DO IT.
FIDGET
GYAAH!!!
I DIDN'T CLEAN UP HIS POO!
His toilet is full!
SORRY, SORRY!
GOTTA PEE!
DASH
PPSSSH
SSH
SSH
SSH
HE WAS REALLY HOLDING IT IN!
SSH
SSH
SSH
WHAT A NOBLE DOG...!!!
WHEW! ALL BETTER!
He's so loyal, it sometimes brings me to tears.
That's Inu for you.

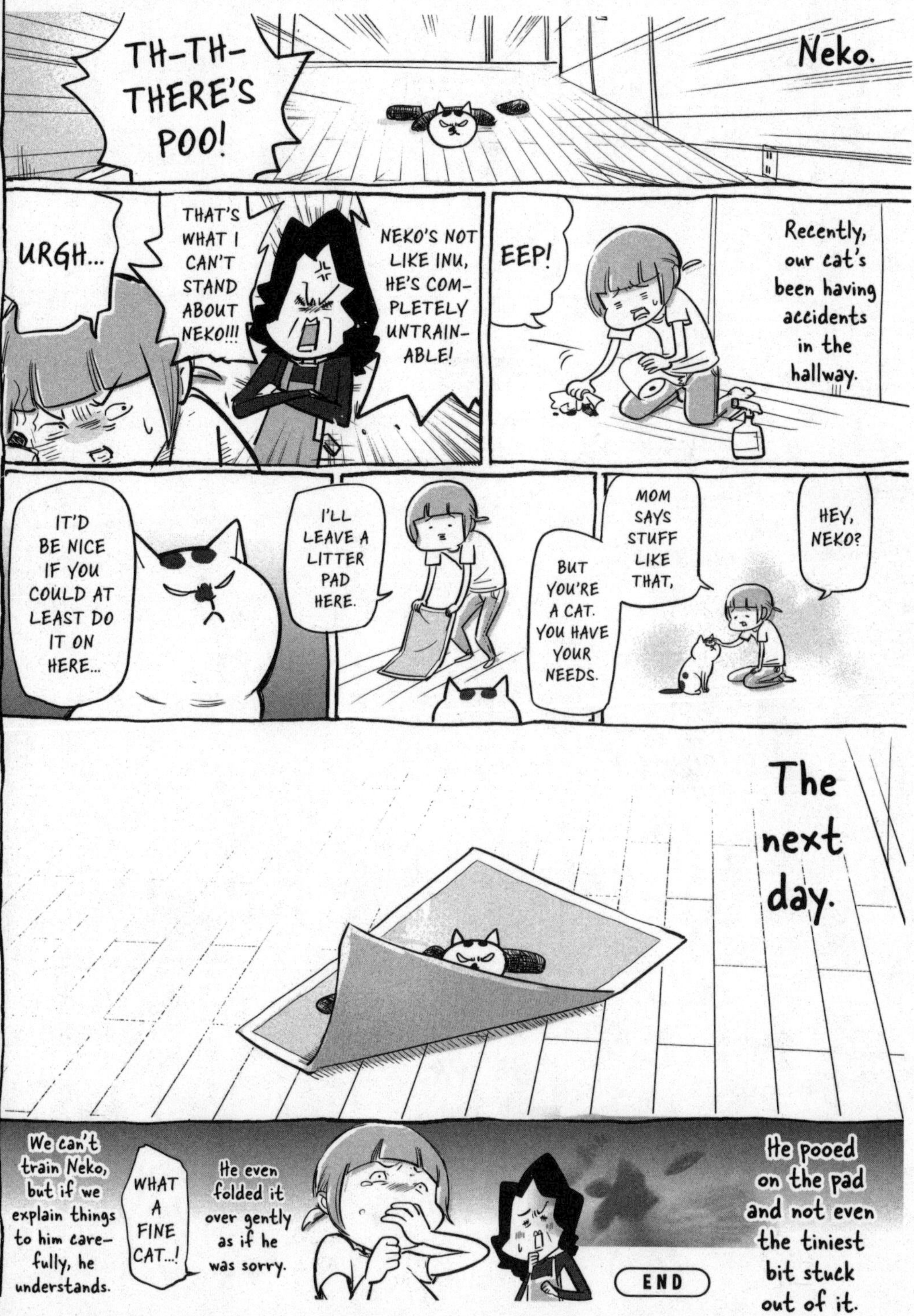
Neko.
TH-TH-THERE'S POO!
Recently, our cat's been having accidents in the hallway.
EEP!
NEKO'S NOT LIKE INU, HE'S COMPLETELY UNTRAINABLE!
THAT'S WHAT I CAN'T STAND ABOUT NEKO!!!
URGH...
HEY, NEKO?
MOM SAYS STUFF LIKE THAT,
BUT YOU'RE A CAT. YOU HAVE YOUR NEEDS.
I'LL LEAVE A LITTER PAD HERE.
IT'D BE NICE IF YOU COULD AT LEAST DO IT ON HERE...
The next day.
He pooed on the pad and not even the tiniest bit stuck out of it.
END
He even folded it over gently as if he was sorry.
WHAT A FINE CAT...!
We can't train Neko, but if we explain things to him carefully, he understands.

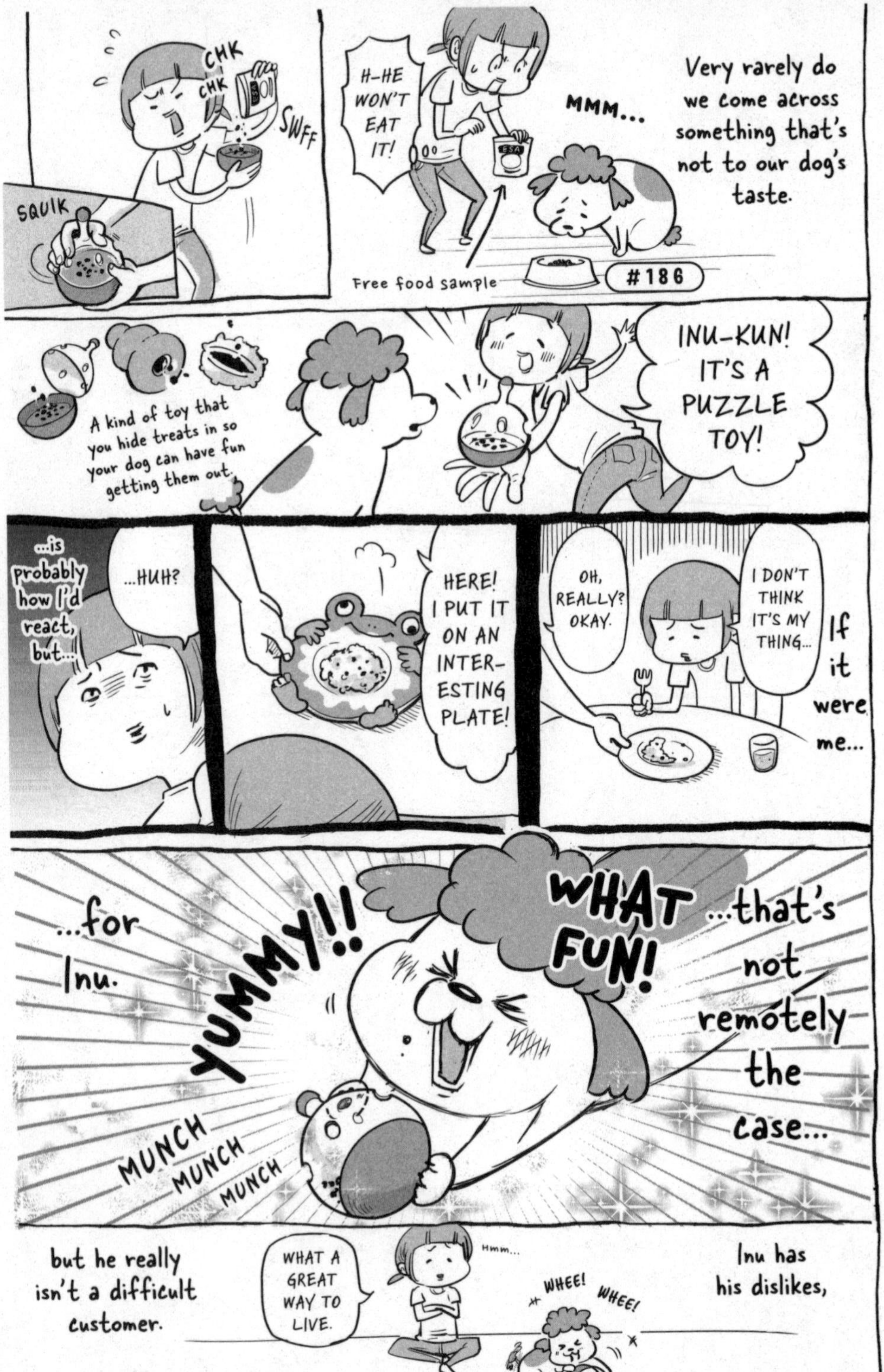

Very rarely do we come across something that's not to our dog's taste.
MMM...
H-HE WON'T EAT IT!
ESA
Free food sample
#186
CHK CHK
SWFF
SQUIK
INU-KUN! IT'S A PUZZLE TOY!
A kind of toy that you hide treats in so your dog can have fun getting them out.
If it were me...
I DON'T THINK IT'S MY THING...
OH, REALLY? OKAY.
HERE! I PUT IT ON AN INTERESTING PLATE!
...HUH?
...is probably how I'd react, but...
...that's not remotely the case...
WHAT FUN!
YUMMY!!
...for Inu.
MUNCH MUNCH MUNCH
Inu has his dislikes,
WHEE! WHEE!
Hmm...
WHAT A GREAT WAY TO LIVE.
but he really isn't a difficult customer.

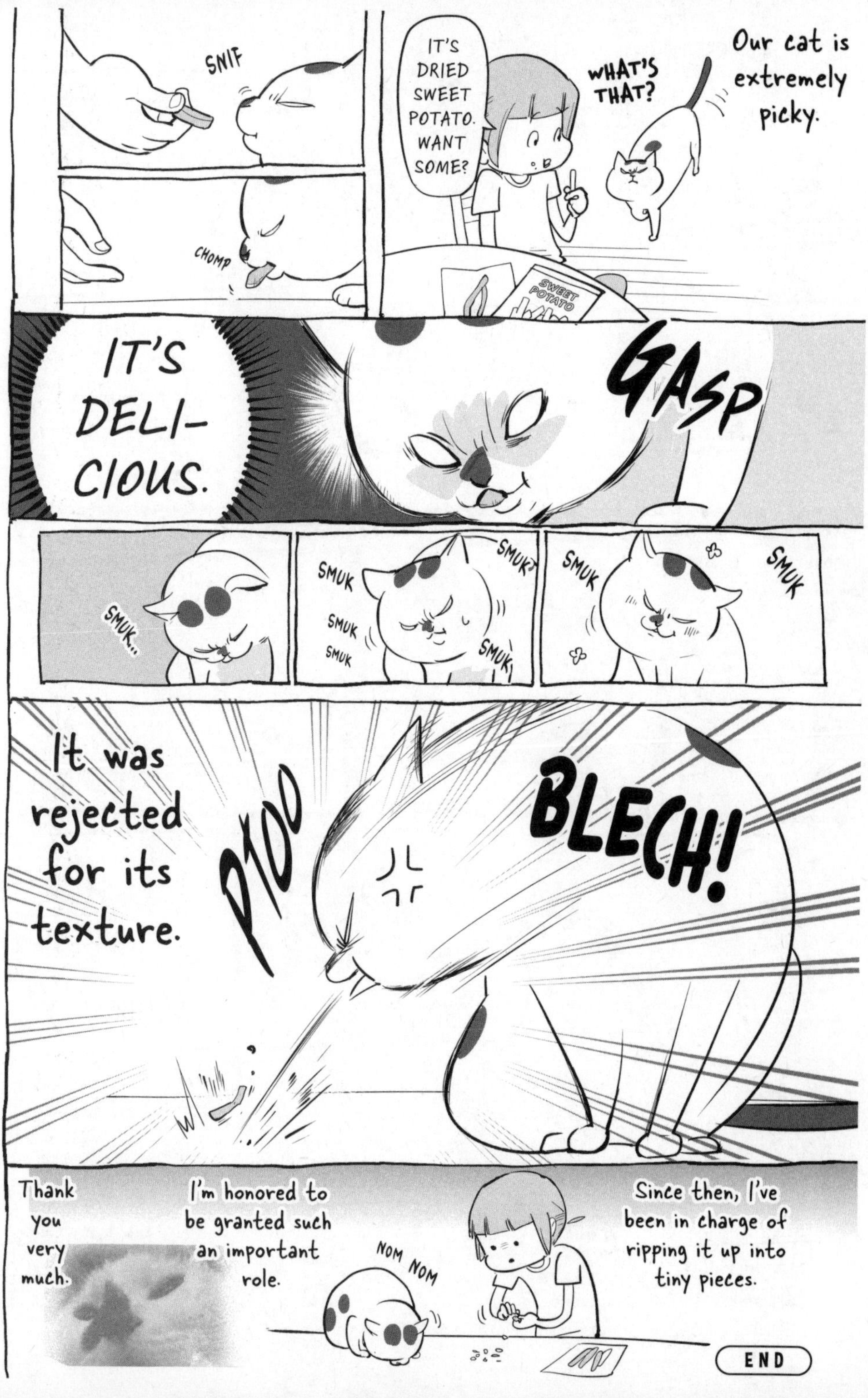
Our cat is extremely picky.
WHAT'S THAT?
IT'S DRIED SWEET POTATO. WANT SOME?
SWEET POTATO
SNIF
CHOMP
GASP
IT'S DELI-CIOUS.
SMUK
SMUK
SMUK?
SMUK
SMUK
SMUK
SMUK!
SMUK...
BLECH!
PTOO
It was rejected for its texture.
Since then, I've been in charge of ripping it up into tiny pieces.
NOM NOM
I'm honored to be granted such an important role.
Thank you very much.
END

Using an object for that funny face is unfair.

More About #186

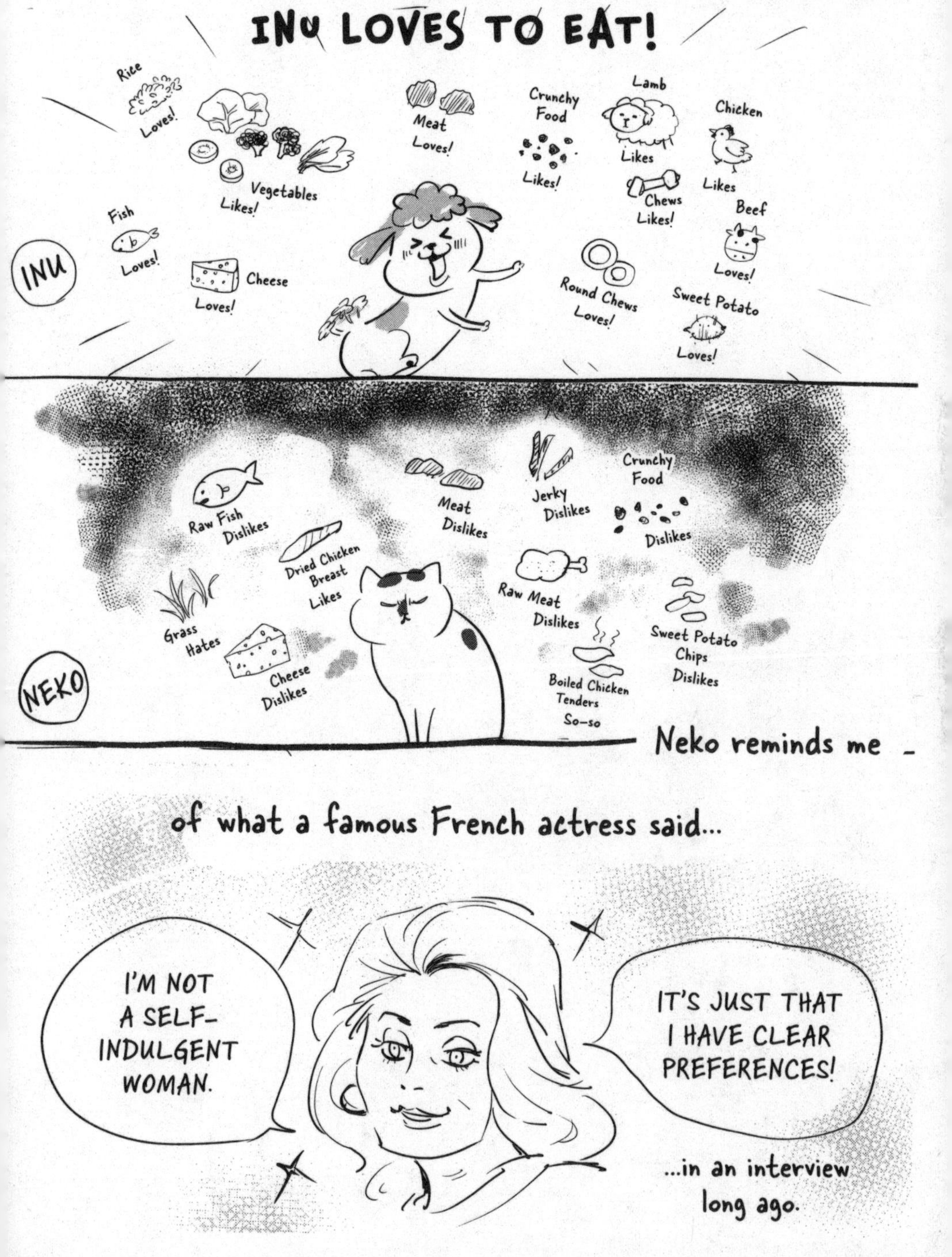
INU LOVES TO EAT!
INU
Rice Loves!
Vegetables Likes!
Meat Loves!
Crunchy Food Likes!
Lamb Likes
Chicken Likes
Chews Likes!
Fish Loves!
Cheese Loves!
Beef Loves!
Round Chews Loves!
Sweet Potato Loves!
NEKO
Raw Fish Dislikes
Dried Chicken Breast Likes
Meat Dislikes
Jerky Dislikes
Crunchy Food Dislikes
Grass Hates
Cheese Dislikes
Raw Meat Dislikes
Boiled Chicken Tenders So-so
Sweet Potato Chips Dislikes
Neko reminds me
of what a famous French actress said...
I'M NOT A SELF-INDULGENT WOMAN.
IT'S JUST THAT I HAVE CLEAR PREFERENCES!
...in an interview long ago.

Bonus

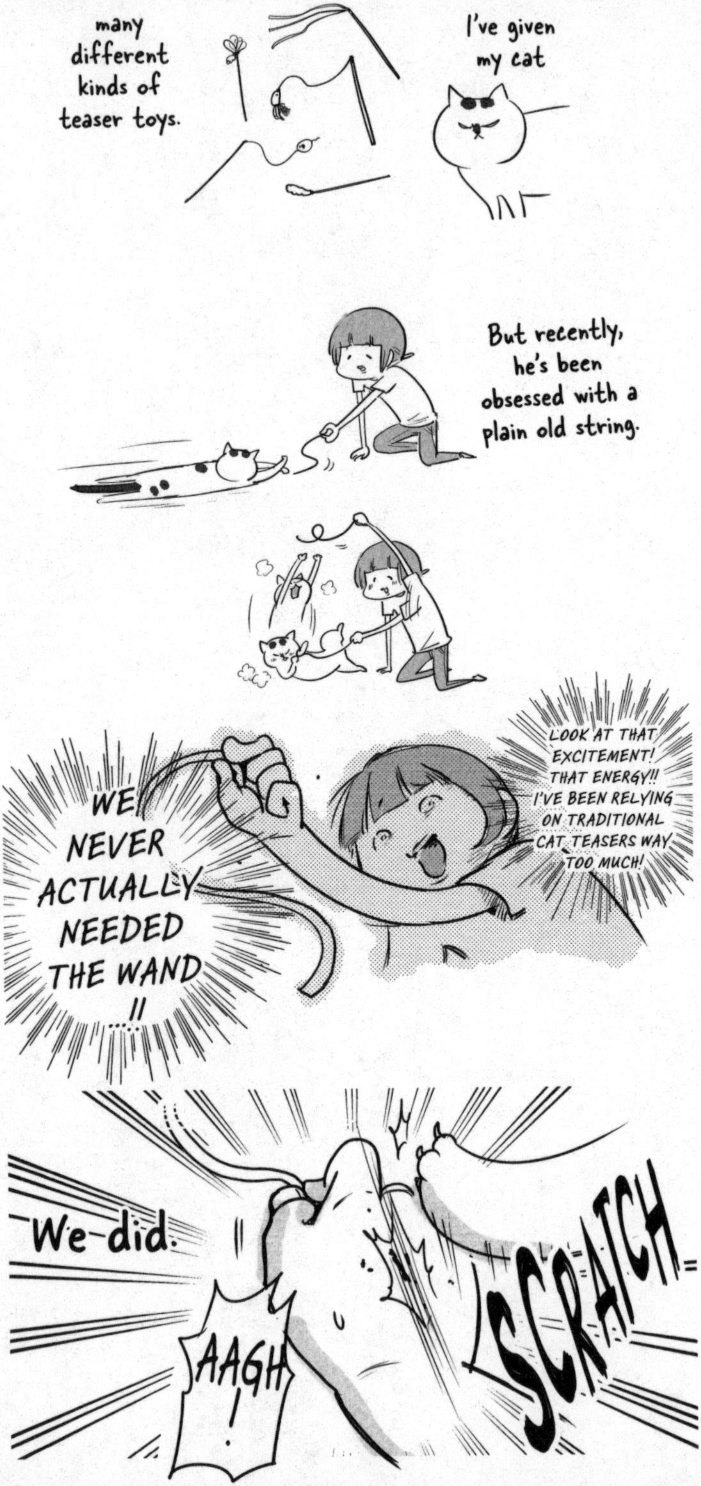
I've given my cat
many different kinds of teaser toys.
But recently, he's been obsessed with a plain old string.
LOOK AT THAT EXCITEMENT! THAT ENERGY!! I'VE BEEN RELYING ON TRADITIONAL CAT TEASERS WAY TOO MUCH!
WE NEVER ACTUALLY NEEDED THE WAND ...!!
SCRATCH
AAGH !
We did.

EEEK!
SOME-BODY, HELP!
YOU MON-STER!
CRASH
ARGH!
SPLASH
SPLASH
SPLASH
THAT'S A GOOD KID... GRAAH!
KRUNCH
JESUS!
DRAAG
SPARE ME!
RRRING
SPLATCH

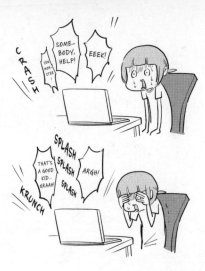

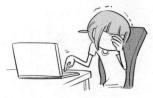

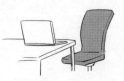

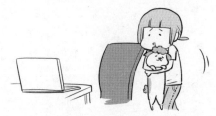

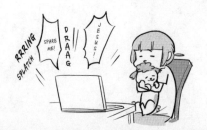

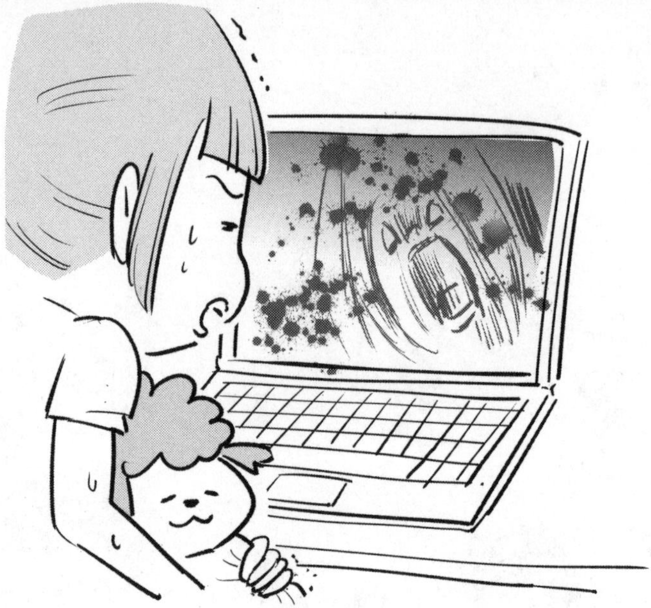

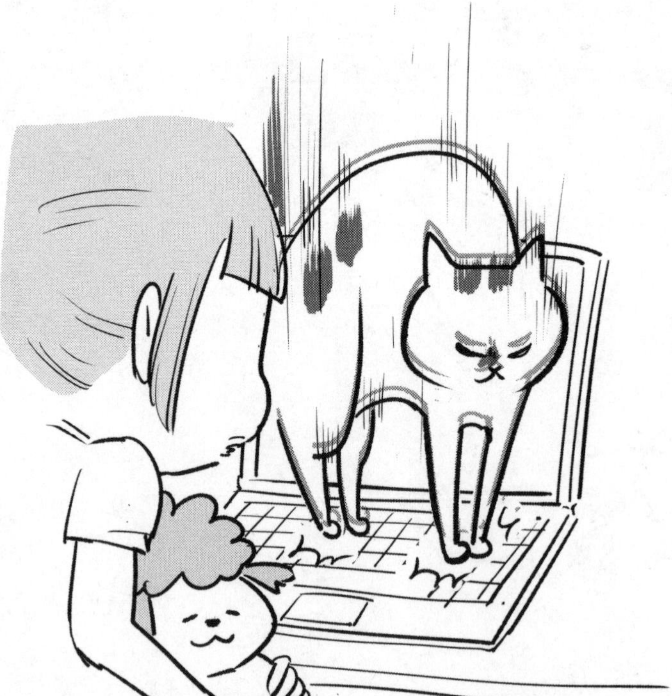

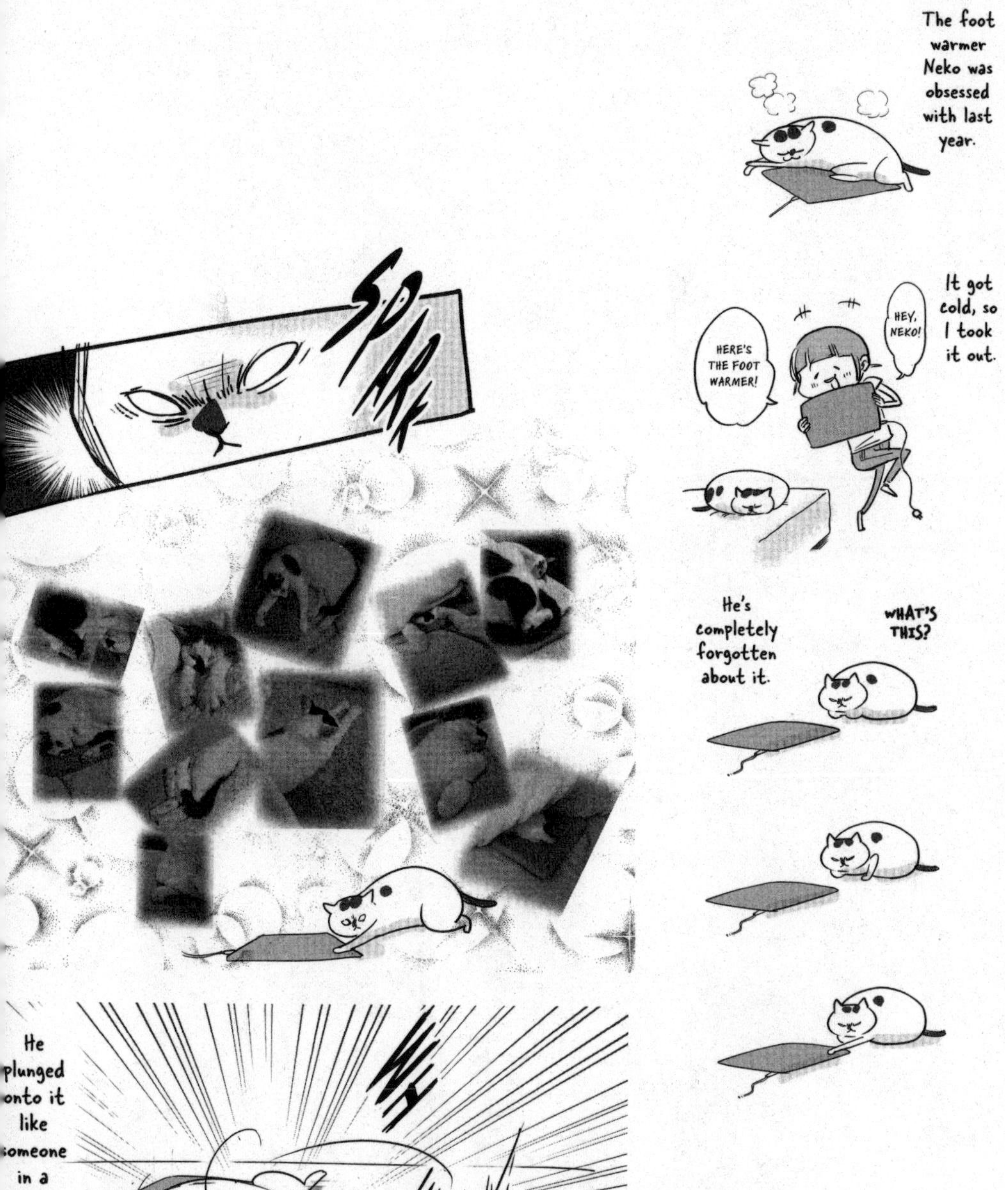
The foot warmer Neko was obsessed with last year.
It got cold, so I took it out.
HEY, NEKO!
HERE'S THE FOOT WARMER!
He's completely forgotten about it.
WHAT'S THIS?
SPARK
He plunged onto it like someone in a manga who uddenly ts their nemory back.
WHUMP

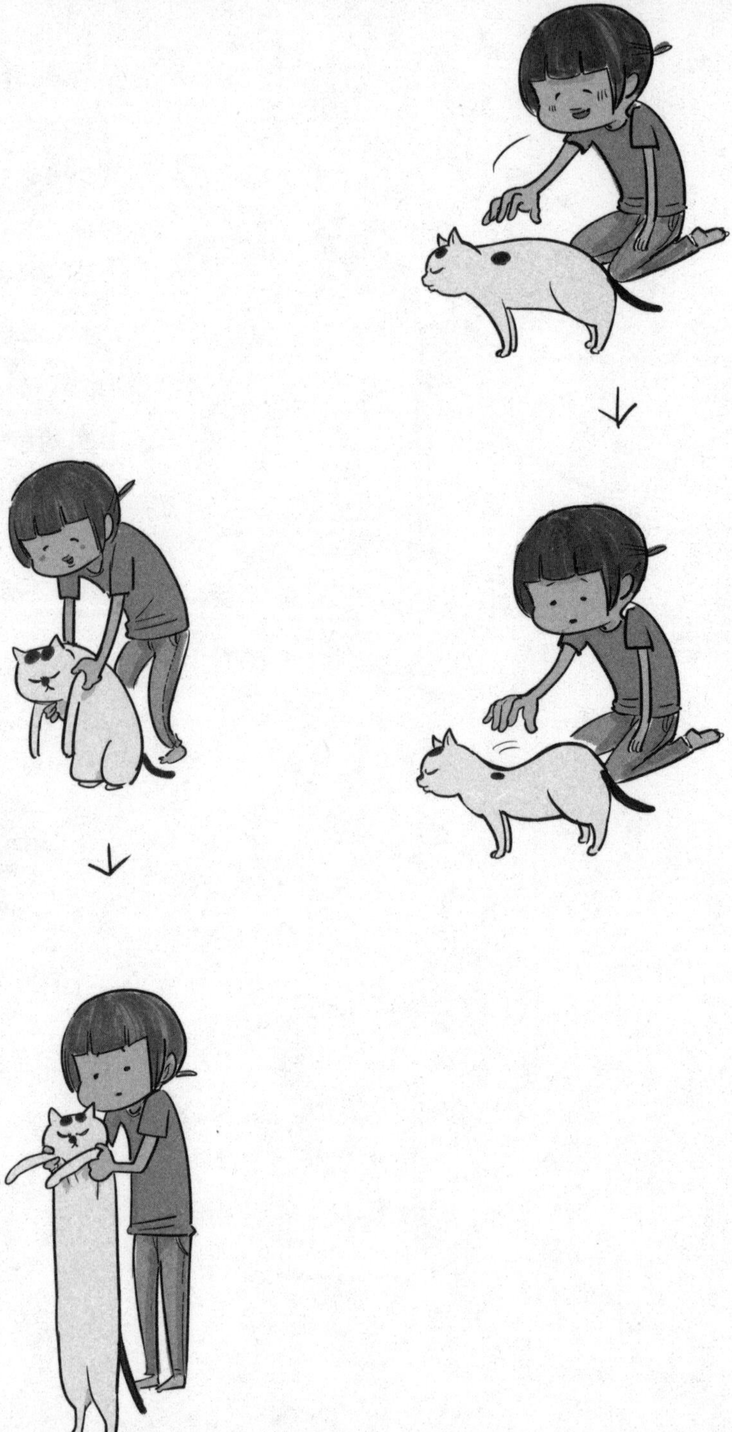

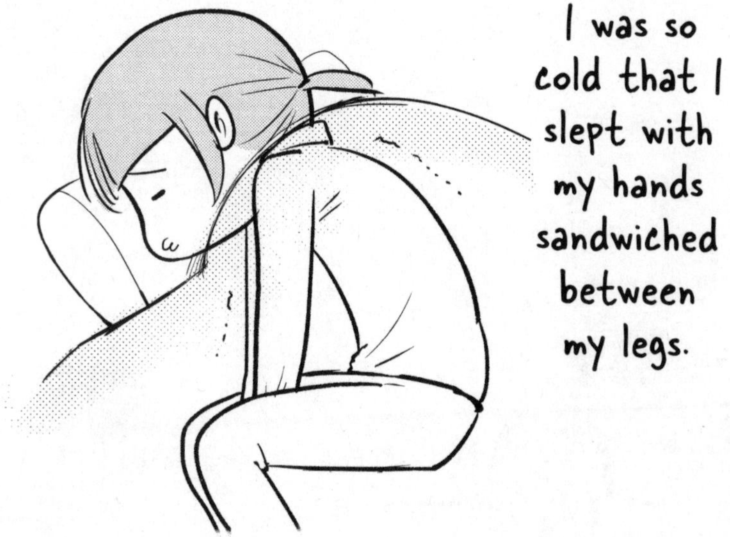
I was so cold that I slept with my hands sandwiched between my legs.

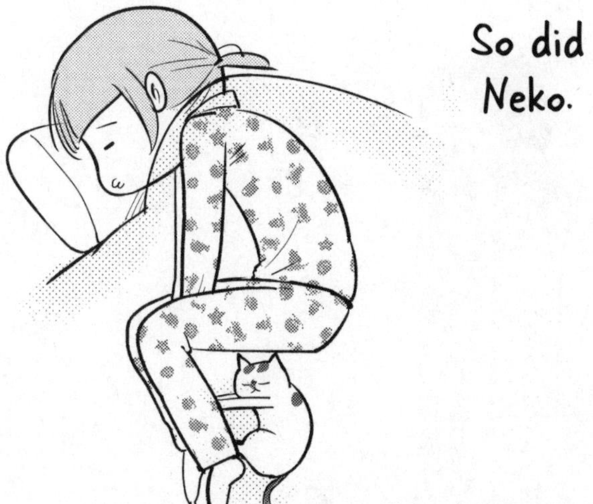
So did Neko.

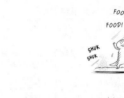

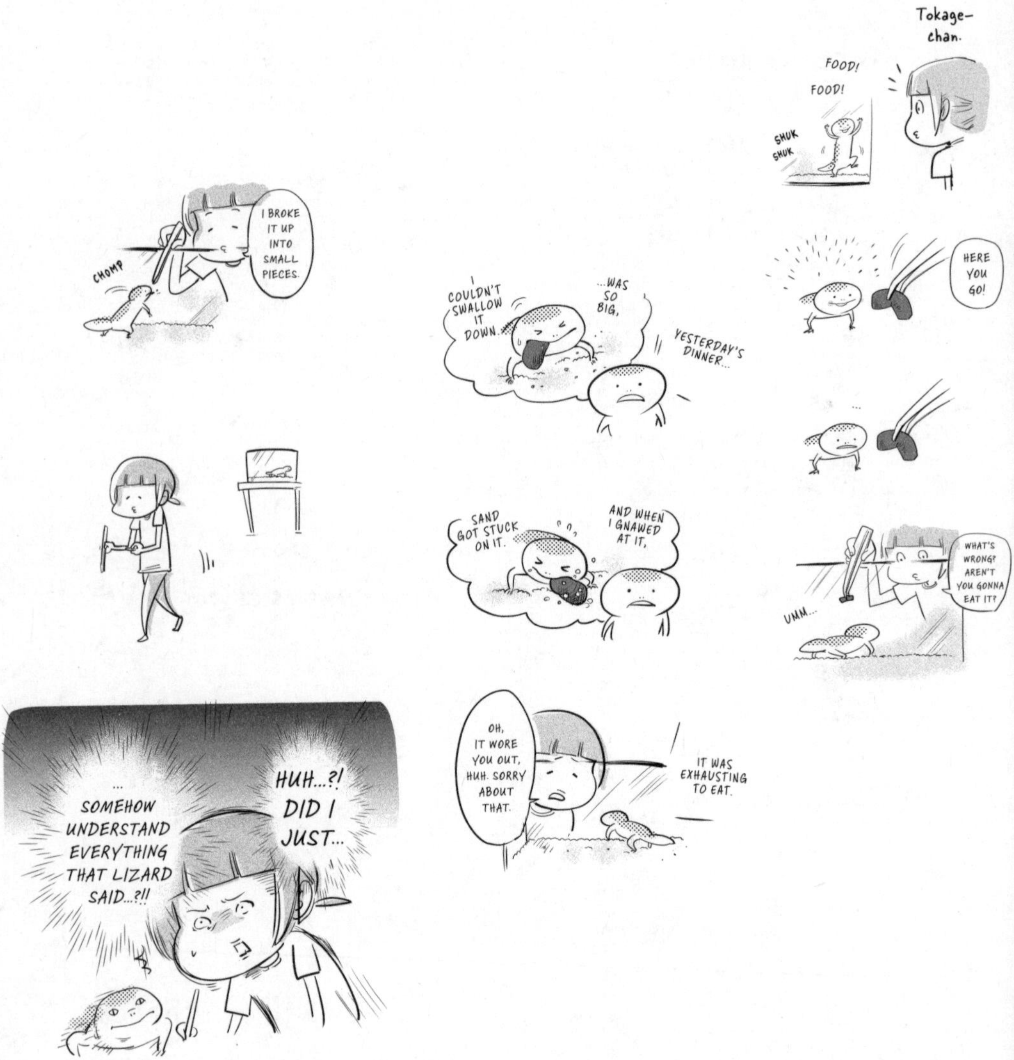
Tokage-chan.
FOOD!
FOOD!
SHUK SHUK
HERE YOU GO!
...
WHAT'S WRONG? AREN'T YOU GONNA EAT IT?
UMM...
YESTERDAY'S DINNER...
...WAS SO BIG,
I COULDN'T SWALLOW IT DOWN.
AND WHEN I GNAWED AT IT,
SAND GOT STUCK ON IT.
IT WAS EXHAUSTING TO EAT.
OH, IT WORE YOU OUT, HUH. SORRY ABOUT THAT.
I BROKE IT UP INTO SMALL PIECES.
CHOMP
HUH...?! DID I JUST...
... SOMEHOW UNDERSTAND EVERYTHING THAT LIZARD SAID...?!!

Daily Consumables

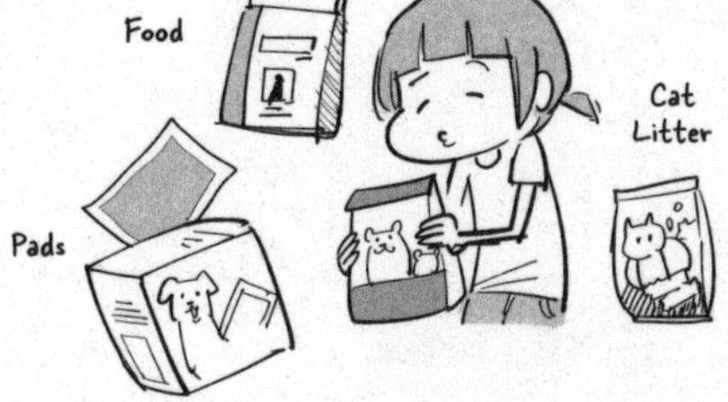
Food
Cat Litter
Pads

They seeemed expensive at first,
but I stopped thinking about it.

Usefulness ★★★★ / Excitement ★

Entertainment

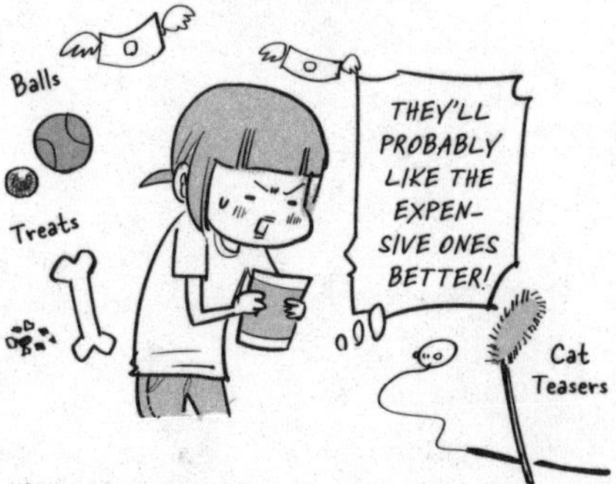
Balls
Treats
THEY'LL PROBABLY LIKE THE EXPEN-SIVE ONES BETTER!
Cat Teasers

I'm always drawn to things like goat cheese and organic or high-quality products, but animals don't care about the price. They'll probably enjoy things from a 100-yen store more.

Usefulness ★★ / Excitement ★★★

Things the Owner Uses to Force Her Fantasies on Her Pets

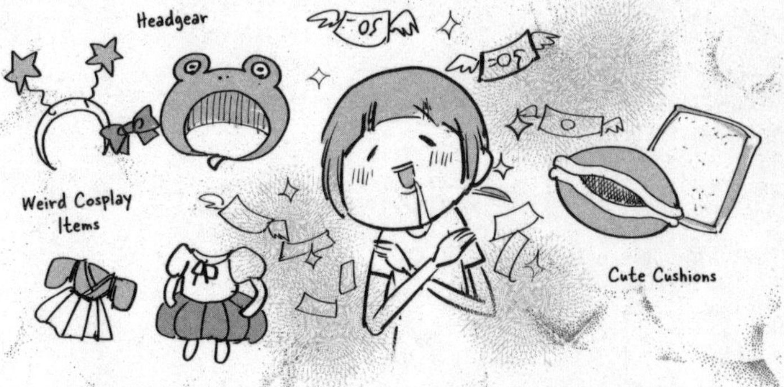
Headgear
Weird Cosplay Items
Cute Cushions

I turn into an ATM...

Usefulness 0 / Excitement ★★★★★

END

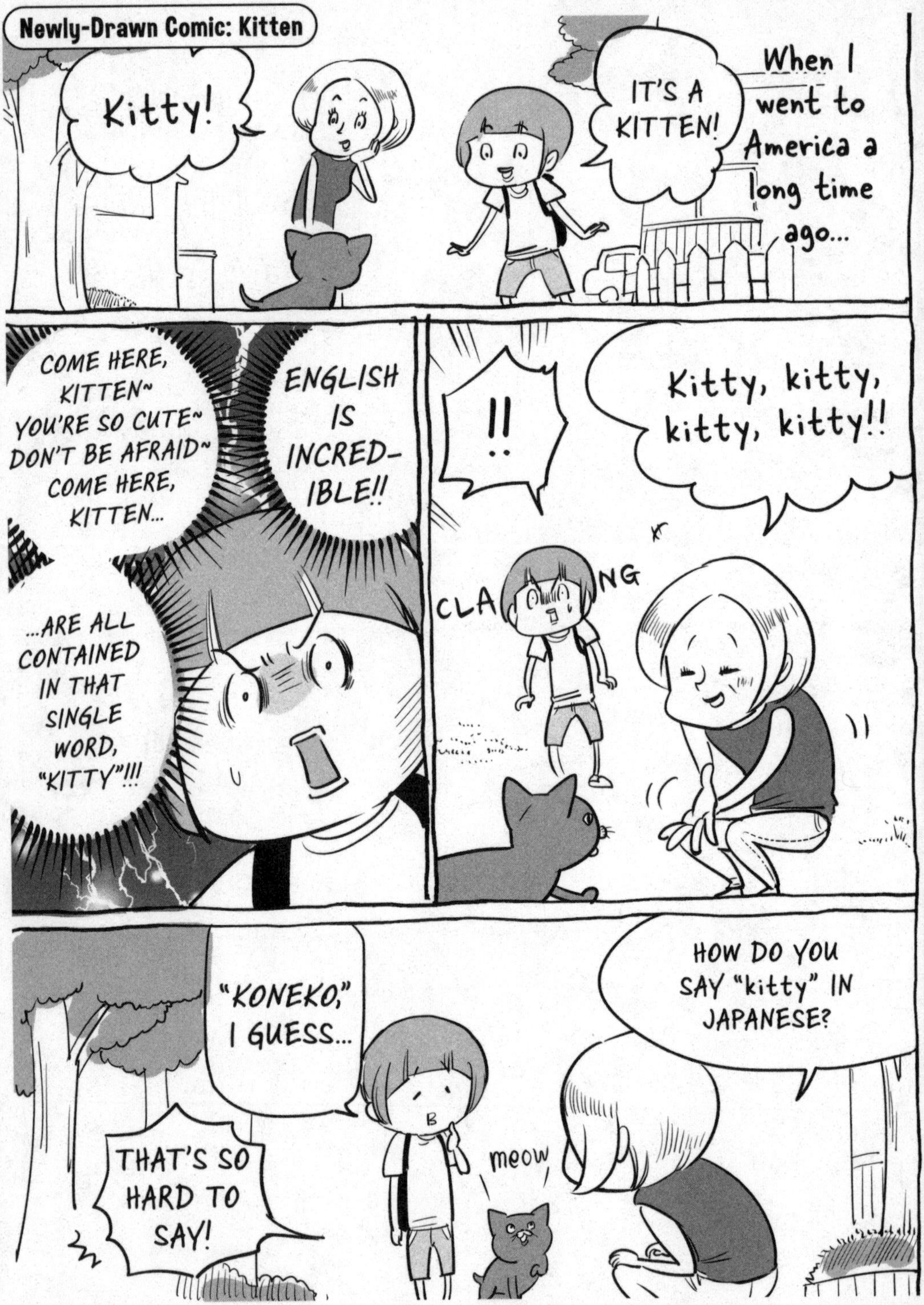
Newly-Drawn Comic: Kitten
When I went to America a long time ago...
IT'S A KITTEN!
Kitty!
Kitty, kitty, kitty, kitty!!
!!
CLANG
ENGLISH IS INCRED-IBLE!!
COME HERE, KITTEN~ YOU'RE SO CUTE~ DON'T BE AFRAID~ COME HERE, KITTEN...
...ARE ALL CONTAINED IN THAT SINGLE WORD, "KITTY"!!!
HOW DO YOU SAY "kitty" IN JAPANESE?
meow
"KONEKO," I GUESS...
THAT'S SO HARD TO SAY!

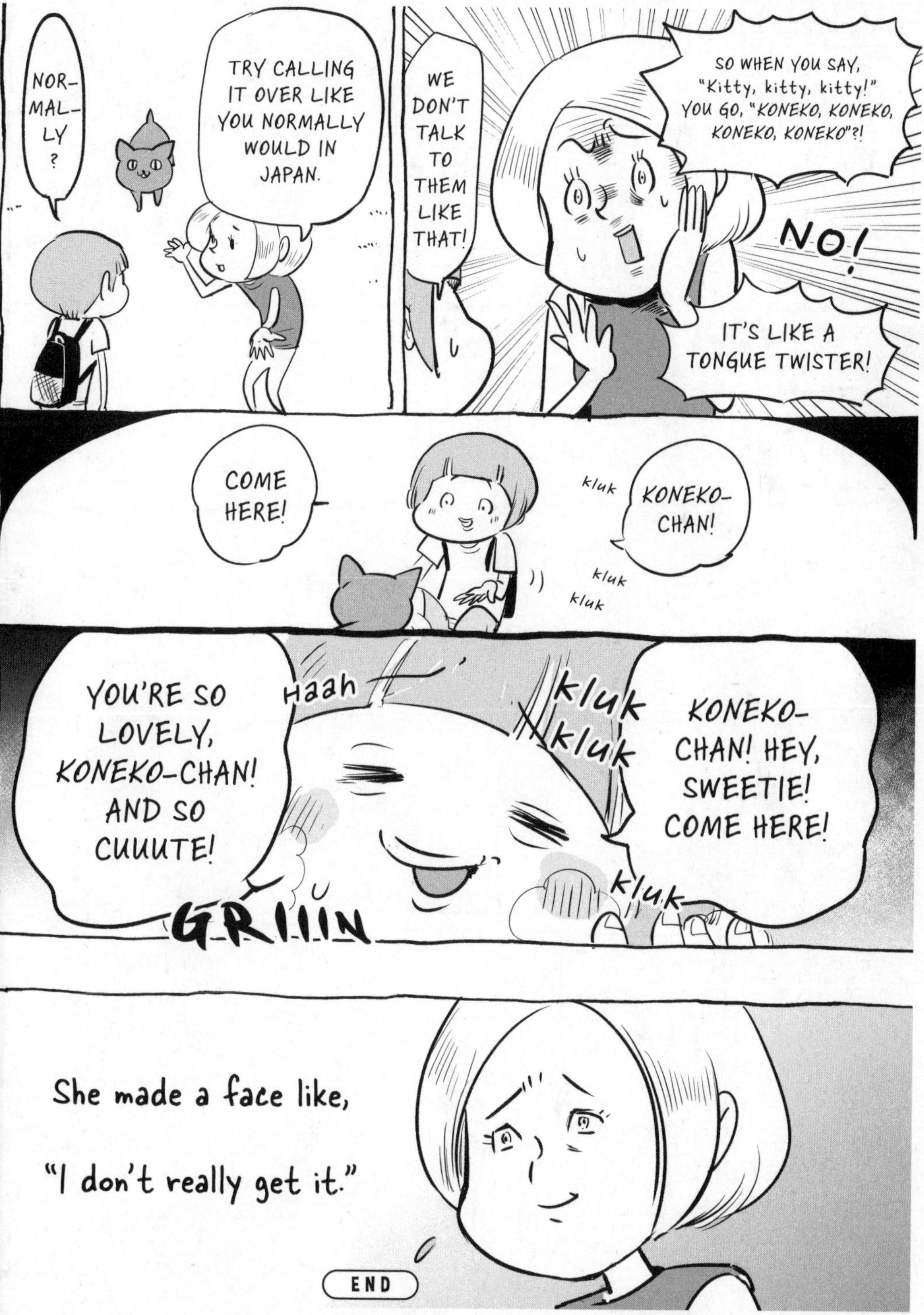
TRY CALLING IT OVER LIKE YOU NORMALLY WOULD IN JAPAN.
NOR-MAL-LY?
SO WHEN YOU SAY, "Kitty, kitty, kitty!" YOU GO, "KONEKO, KONEKO, KONEKO, KONEKO"?!
NO!
IT'S LIKE A TONGUE TWISTER!
WE DON'T TALK TO THEM LIKE THAT!
KONEKO-CHAN!
kluk
kluk
kluk
COME HERE!
KONEKO-CHAN! HEY, SWEETIE! COME HERE!
kluk
kluk
kluk
Haah
YOU'RE SO LOVELY, KONEKO-CHAN! AND SO CUUUTE!
GRIIIN
She made a face like,
"I don't really get it."
END

Afterword

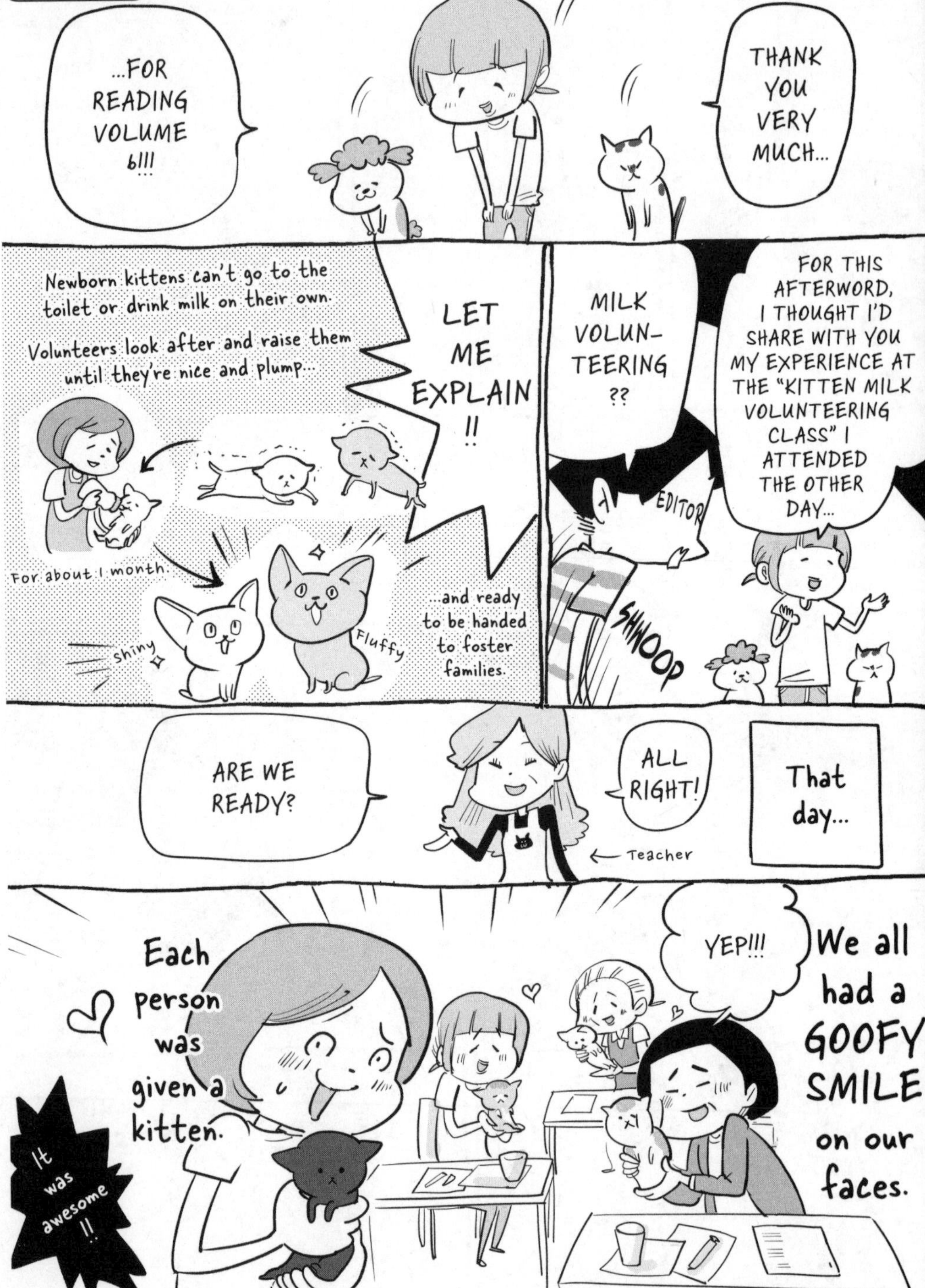
THANK YOU VERY MUCH...
...FOR READING VOLUME 6!!!
FOR THIS AFTERWORD, I THOUGHT I'D SHARE WITH YOU MY EXPERIENCE AT THE "KITTEN MILK VOLUNTEERING CLASS" I ATTENDED THE OTHER DAY...
MILK VOLUNTEERING ??
EDITOR
SHWOOP
LET ME EXPLAIN !!
Newborn kittens can't go to the toilet or drink milk on their own.
Volunteers look after and raise them until they're nice and plump...
For about 1 month.
Shiny
Fluffy
...and ready to be handed to foster families.
That day...
ALL RIGHT!
← Teacher
ARE WE READY?
We all had a GOOFY SMILE on our faces.
YEP!!!
Each person was given a kitten.
It was awesome !!

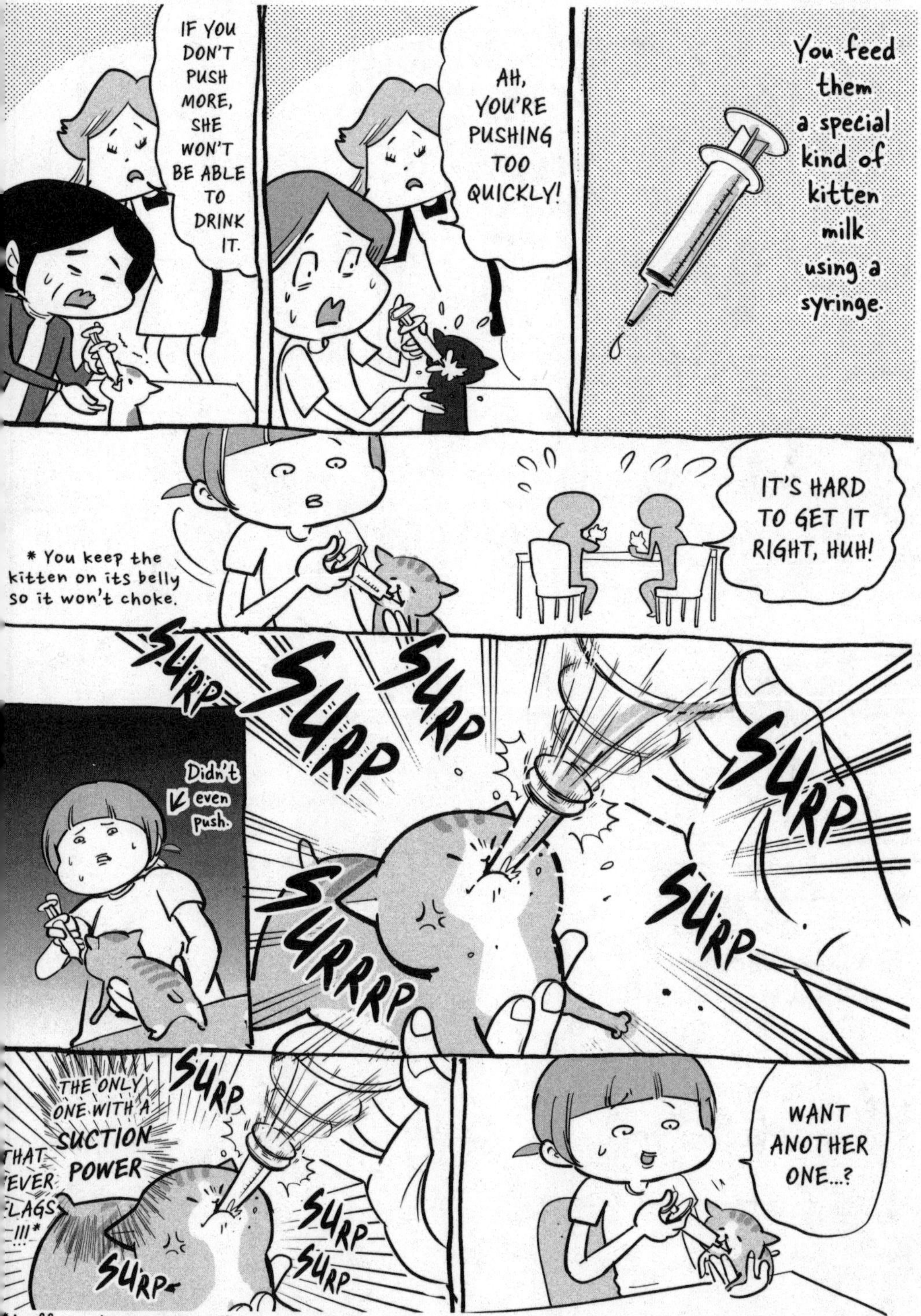
You feed them a special kind of kitten milk using a syringe.
AH, YOU'RE PUSHING TOO QUICKLY!
IF YOU DON'T PUSH MORE, SHE WON'T BE ABLE TO DRINK IT.
IT'S HARD TO GET IT RIGHT, HUH!
* You keep the kitten on its belly so it won't choke.
SURP
SURP
SURP
SURP
SURRRRP
SURP
SURP
Didn't even push.
WANT ANOTHER ONE...?
SURP
THE ONLY ONE WITH A SUCTION POWER
THAT EVER LAGS !!!*
SURP
SURP
SURP

*A riff on a Japanese vacuum cleaner commercial.

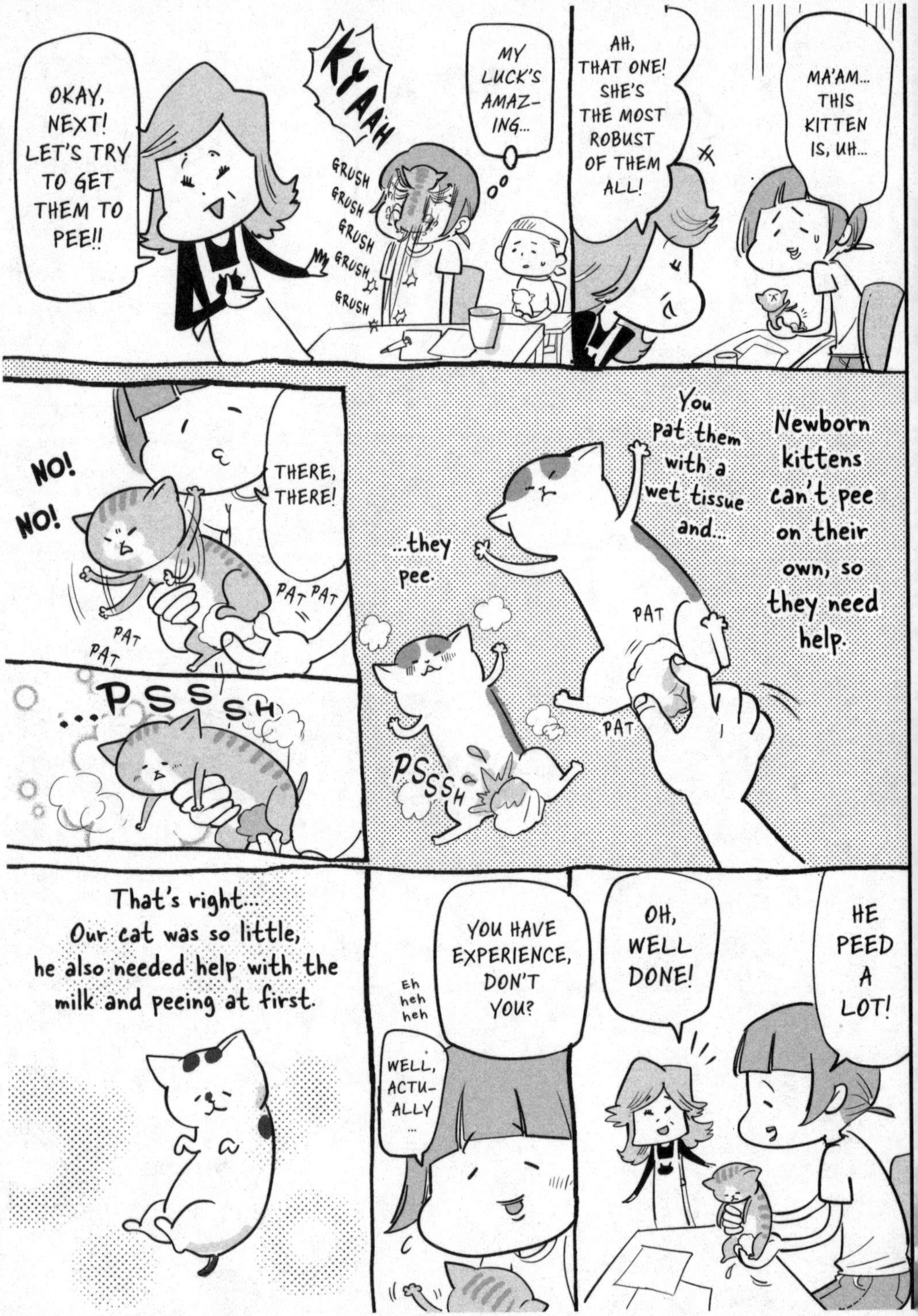
MA'AM... THIS KITTEN IS, UH...
AH, THAT ONE! SHE'S THE MOST ROBUST OF THEM ALL!
MY LUCK'S AMAZ-ING...
KYAAAH
GRUSH GRUSH GRUSH GRUSH GRUSH
OKAY, NEXT! LET'S TRY TO GET THEM TO PEE!!
Newborn kittens can't pee on their own, so they need help.
You pat them with a wet tissue and...
PAT
PAT
...they pee.
PSSSH
THERE, THERE!
NO!
NO!
PAT PAT
PAT PAT
...PSSSH
HE PEED A LOT!
OH, WELL DONE!
YOU HAVE EXPERIENCE, DON'T YOU?
Eh heh heh
WELL, ACTU-ALLY...
That's right... Our cat was so little, he also needed help with the milk and peeing at first.

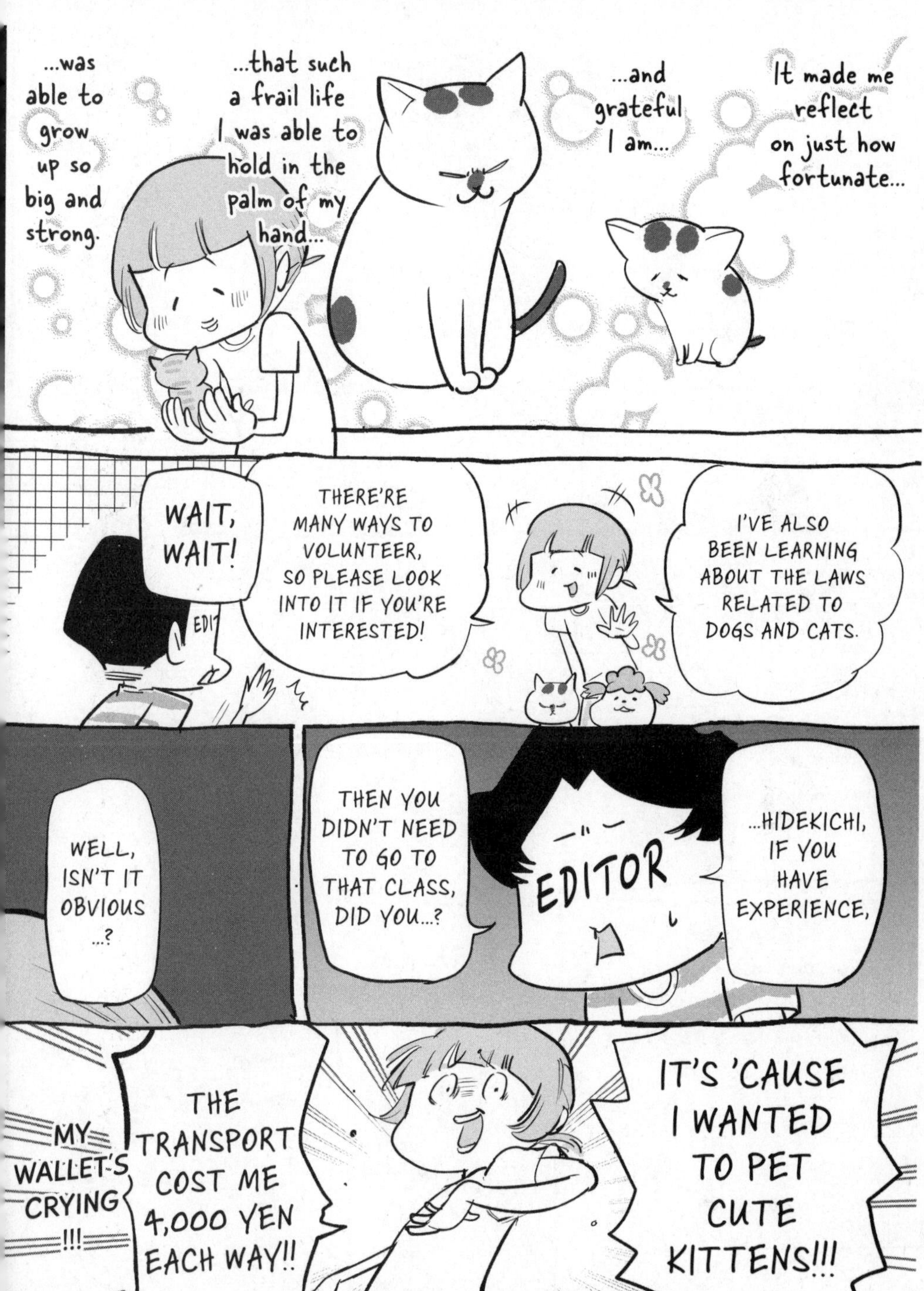
It made me reflect on just how fortunate...
...and grateful I am...
...that such a frail life I was able to hold in the palm of my hand...
...was able to grow up so big and strong.
I'VE ALSO BEEN LEARNING ABOUT THE LAWS RELATED TO DOGS AND CATS.
THERE'RE MANY WAYS TO VOLUNTEER, SO PLEASE LOOK INTO IT IF YOU'RE INTERESTED!
WAIT, WAIT!
...HIDEKICHI, IF YOU HAVE EXPERIENCE,
EDITOR
THEN YOU DIDN'T NEED TO GO TO THAT CLASS, DID YOU...?
WELL, ISN'T IT OBVIOUS ...?
IT'S 'CAUSE I WANTED TO PET CUTE KITTENS!!!
THE TRANSPORT COST ME 4,000 YEN EACH WAY!!
MY WALLET'S CRYING!!!
The End
To be continued in Volume 7

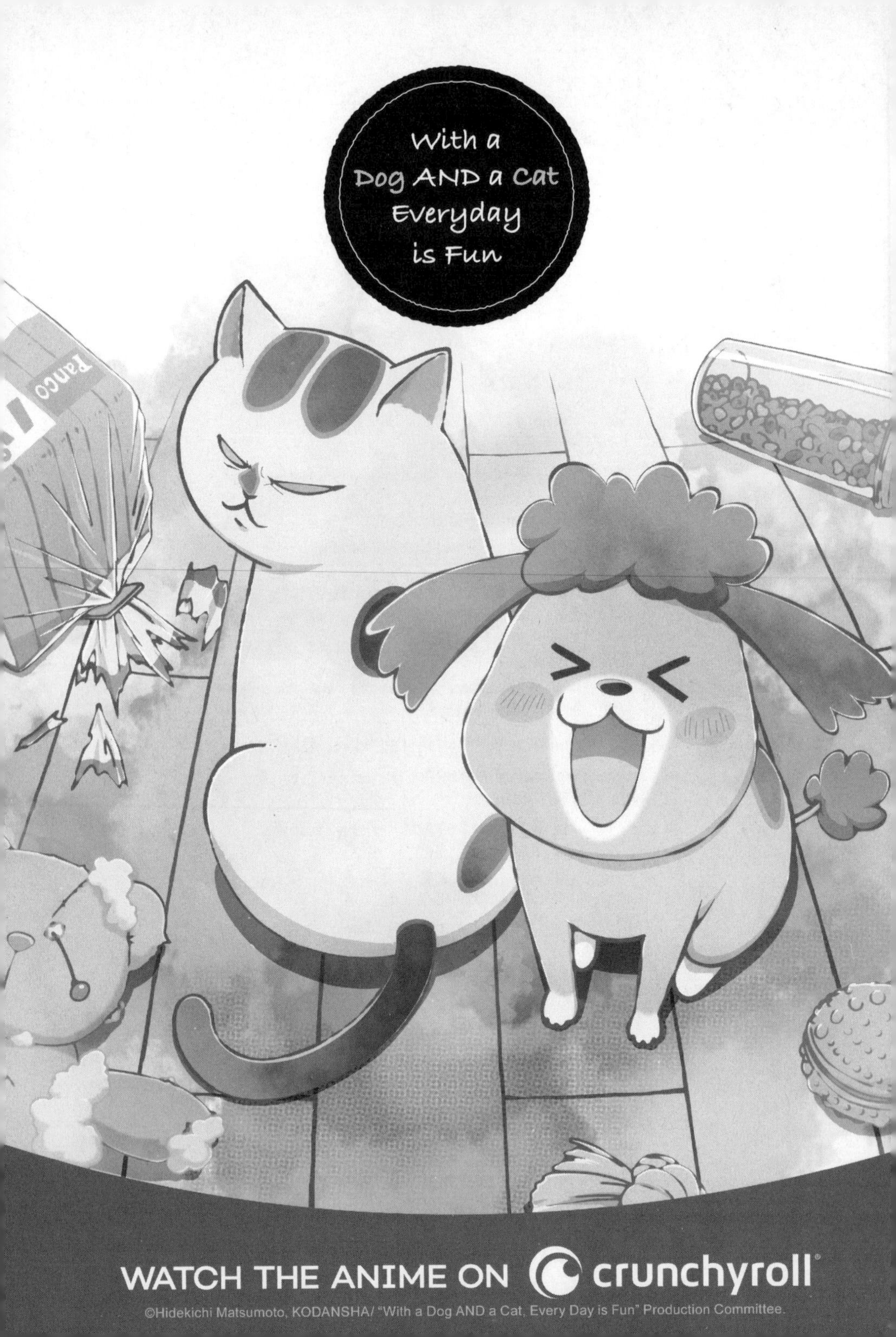

With a Dog AND a Cat Everyday is Fun
Ranco
WATCH THE ANIME ON crunchyroll
©Hidekichi Matsumoto, KODANSHA/ "With a Dog AND a Cat, Every Day is Fun" Production Committee.

IS BEING SERIALIZED ON TWITTER! Information

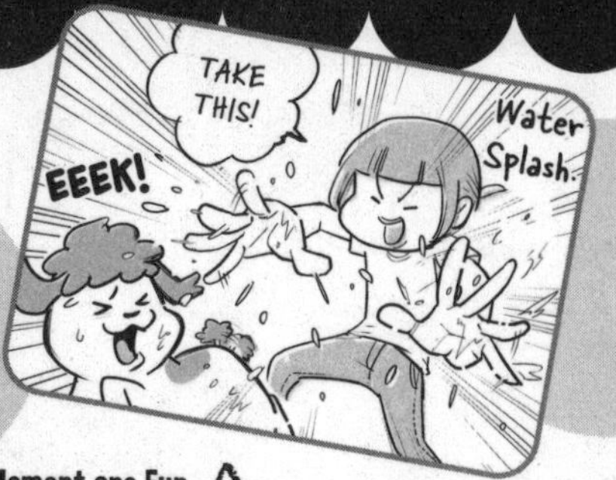
TAKE THIS!
Water Splash
EEEK!

VOLUME 6 EPISODE TITLES WHEN SERIALIZED ON TWITTER

#157 With a Dog AND a Cat, Getting Bitten is Totally Fun

#158 〃 Their Faces From Moment to Moment are Fun

#159 〃 The Hard Work That Goes Into Brushing Them Makes Every Day Fun

#160 〃 Family Members are Secretly Having Fun Every Day

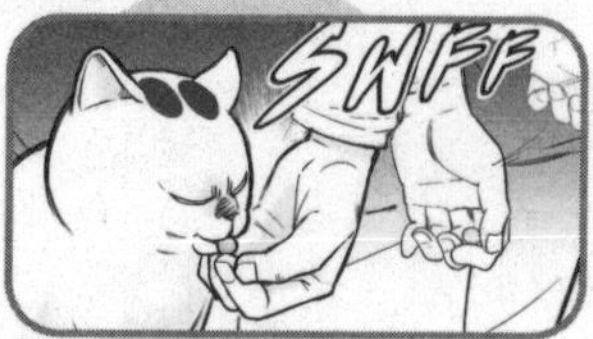
SNIFF

#161 〃 Even When They Stink, It's Totally Fun

#162 〃 Patting Their Bellies Makes Every Day Fun

#163 〃 The Times When They Try Extra Hard Make Every Day Fun

#164 〃 Their Positive and Negative Misunderstandings are Fun

#165 〃 They're Sometimes Cautious and Other Times Short-Sighted, So Every Day is Fun

#166 〃 Even When You Can't Help But Worry About Them, It's Totally Fun

#167 〃 The Laws of Physics Get Warped and Every Day is Fun

#168 〃 They Try to Act Cool At Surprising Times and Every Day is Fun

#169 〃 Their Indecisiveness, or Lack of It, Makes Every Day Fun

#170 〃 Giving Them Things is Always Fun

#171 〃 The Sudden Subtitles That Appear Make Every Day Fun

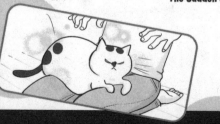

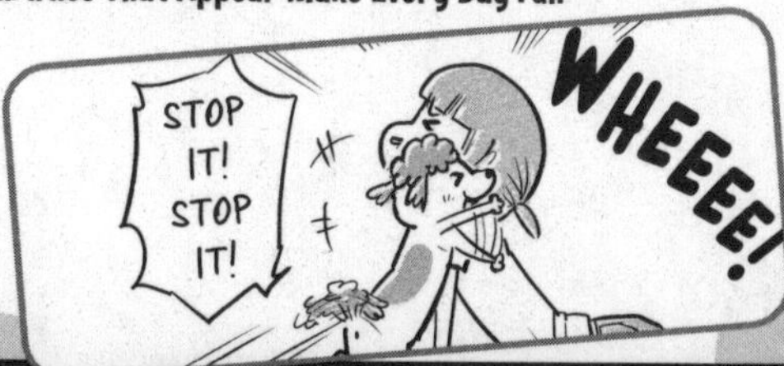
STOP IT! STOP IT!
WHEEEE!

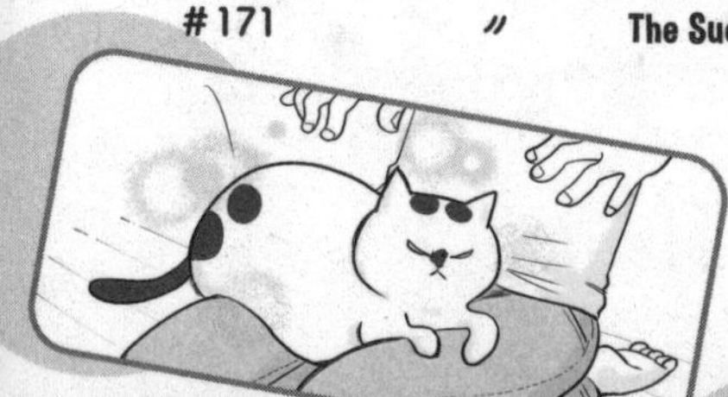

SUNDAY ☆

(AND TRYING NOT TO TAKE ANY WEEKS OFF!)

"WITH A DOG AND A CAT, EVERY DAY IS FUN"

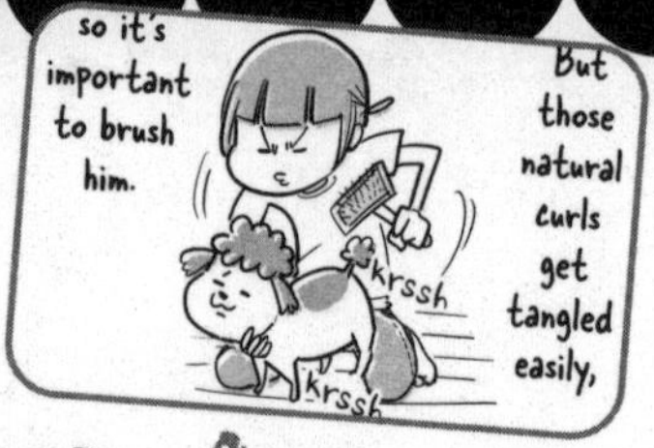
But those natural curls get tangled easily,
so it's important to brush him.
krssh
krssh

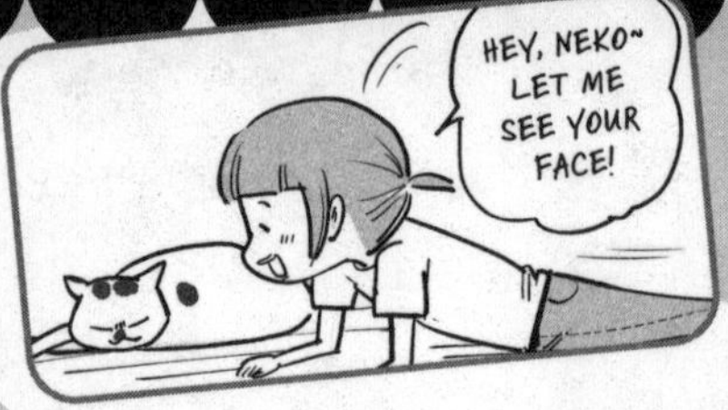
HEY, NEKO~ LET ME SEE YOUR FACE!

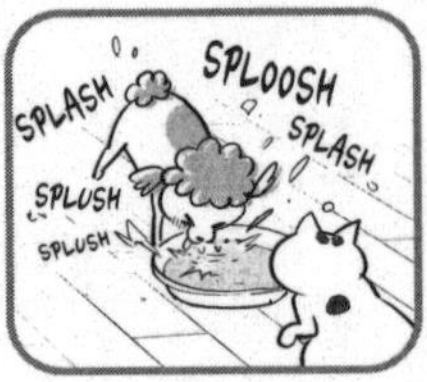
SPLOOSH
SPLASH
SPLASH
SPLUSH
SPLUSH

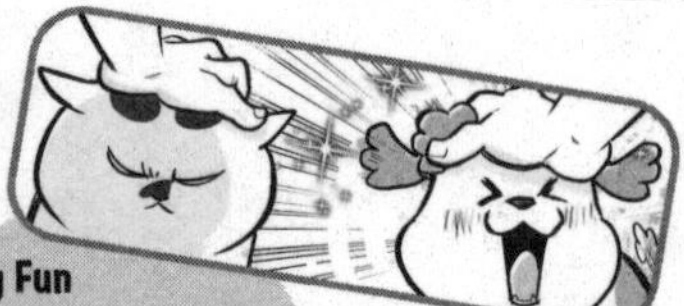

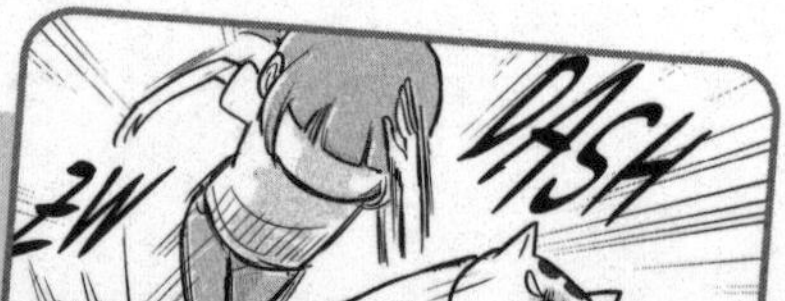
DASH
ZW
OOM

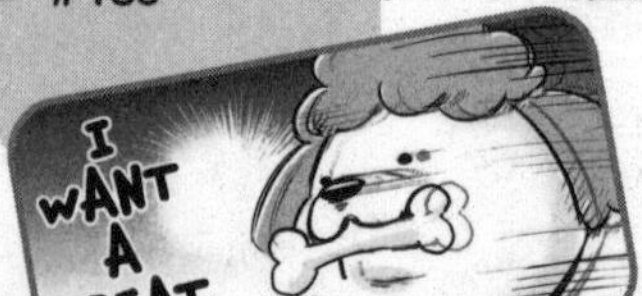
I WANT A TREAT, TOO!

Twitter @hidekiccan

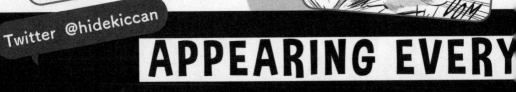

APPEARING EVERY

PORTING THE Dog AND Cat ANIME!

THE GREEDY OWNER, WHO ADORES BOTH DOGS AND CATS,
PRESENTS TO YOU THE LAVISH "WITH A DOG AND A CAT" ANIME!

WHICH DOG AND CAT...

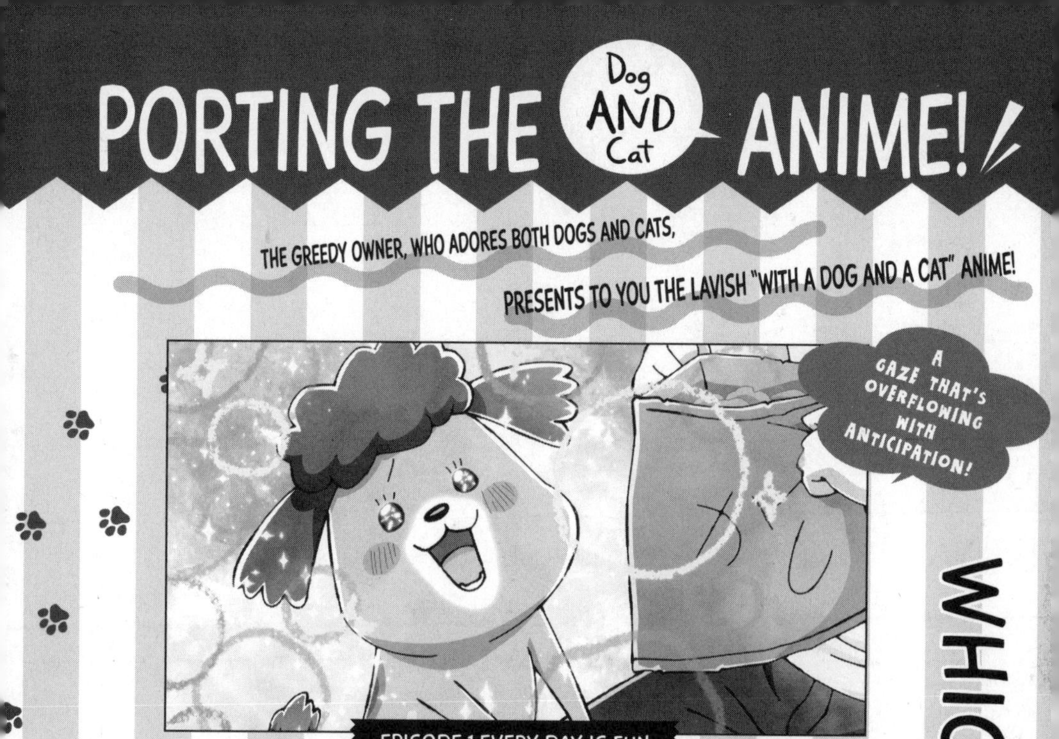
A GAZE THAT'S OVERFLOWING WITH ANTICIPATION!
EPISODE 1 EVERY DAY IS FUN

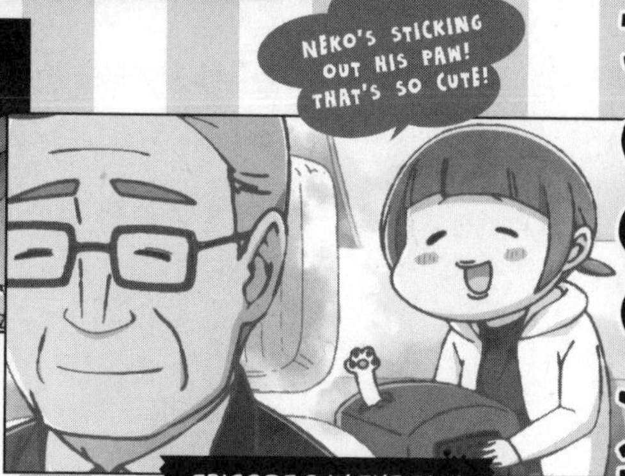
NEKO'S STICKING OUT HIS PAW! THAT'S SO CUTE!
EPISODE 3 IN THE TAXI

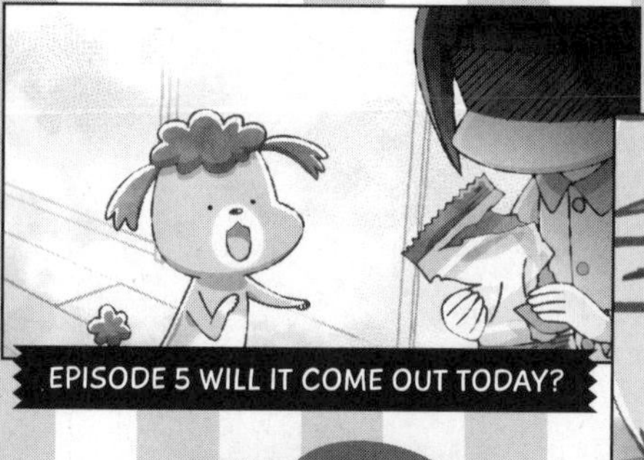
EPISODE 5 WILL IT COME OUT TODAY?

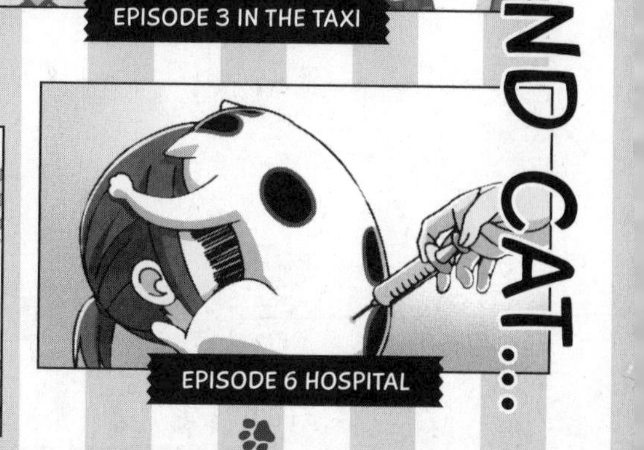
EPISODE 6 HOSPITAL

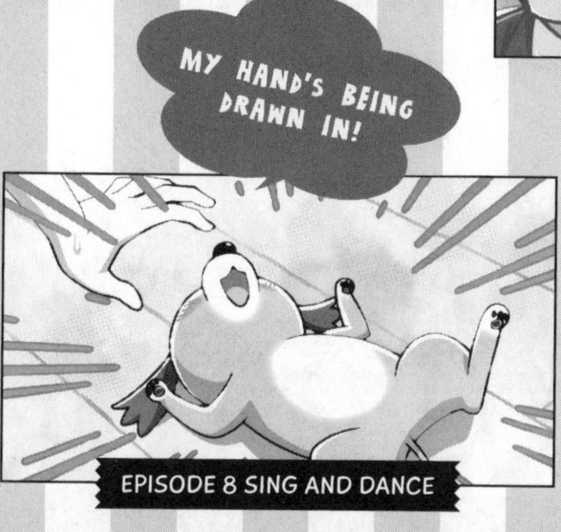
MY HAND'S BEING DRAWN IN!
EPISODE 8 SING AND DANCE

THANK YOU ALL FOR SUP

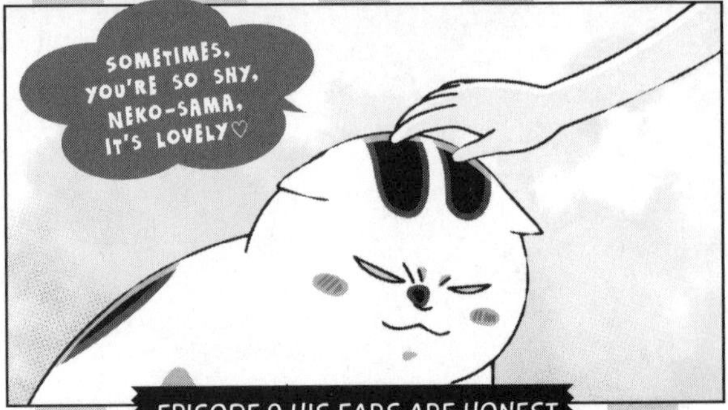
SOMETIMES, YOU'RE SO SHY, NEKO-SAMA, IT'S LOVELY♡

EPISODE 9 HIS EARS ARE HONEST

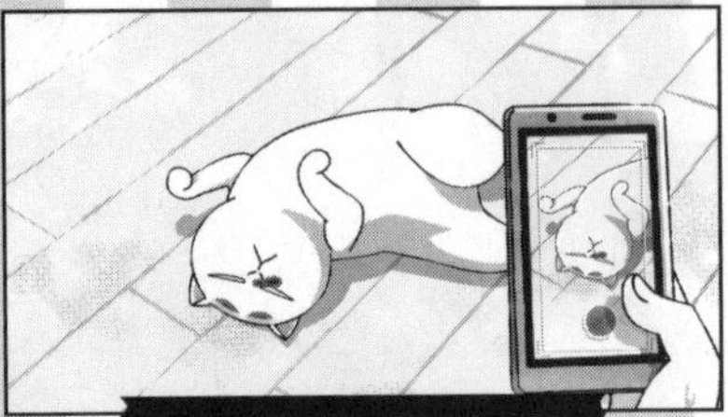

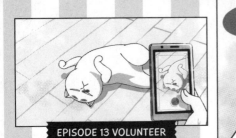

EPISODE 13 VOLUNTEER

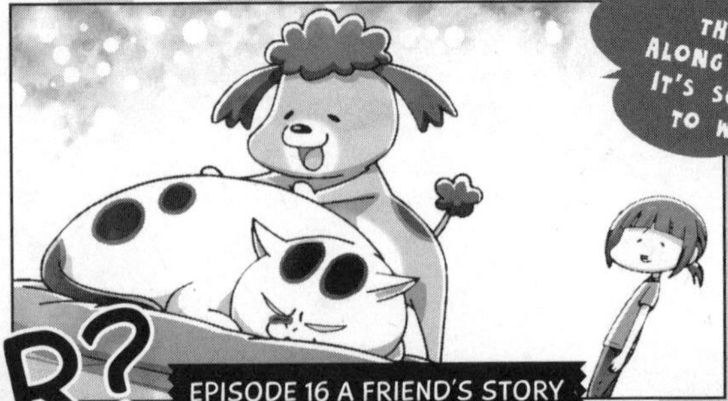
THEY GET ALONG SO WELL. IT'S SOOTHING TO WATCH.

EPISODE 16 A FRIEND'S STORY

...DO YOU PREFER?

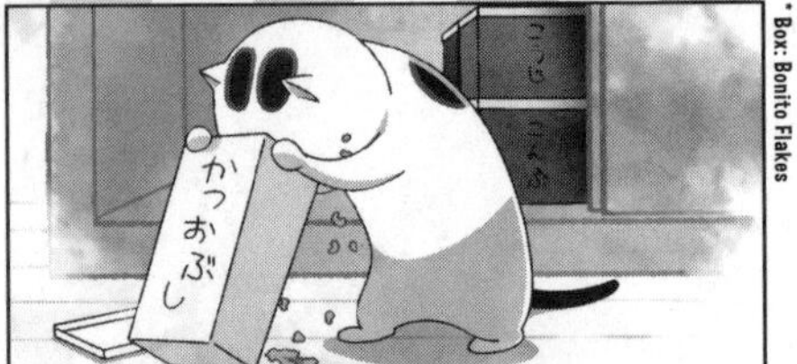
かつおぶし

EPISODE 17 THE VET

*Box: Bonito Flakes

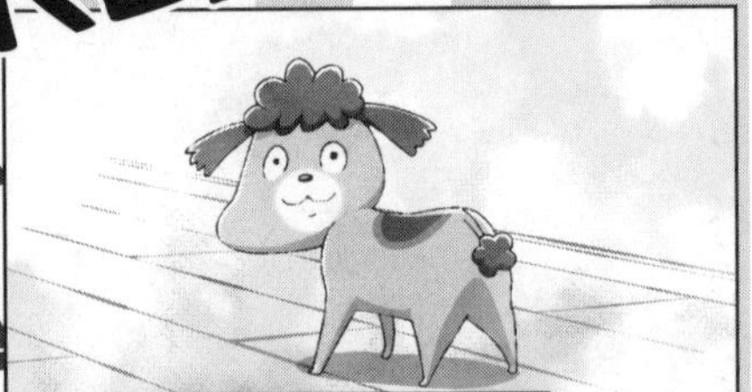

EPISODE 20 MOM

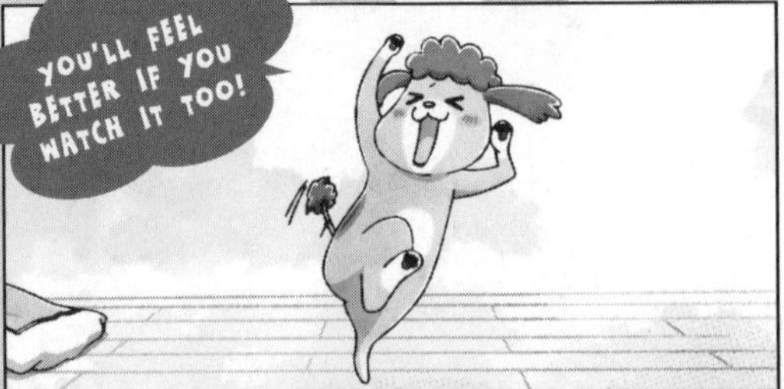
YOU'LL FEEL BETTER IF YOU WATCH IT TOO!

EPISODE 21 BRUSHING

CAST

INU-KUN — KANA HANAZAWA

NEKO-SAMA — TOMOKAZU SUGITA

HIDEKICHI MATSUMOTO — MAI KANAZAWA

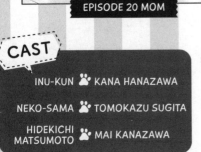

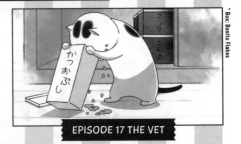

Chi returns to the US in a coloring book
featuring dozens of cute and furry illustrations from
award-winning cartoonist Konami Kanata.

Available Now!

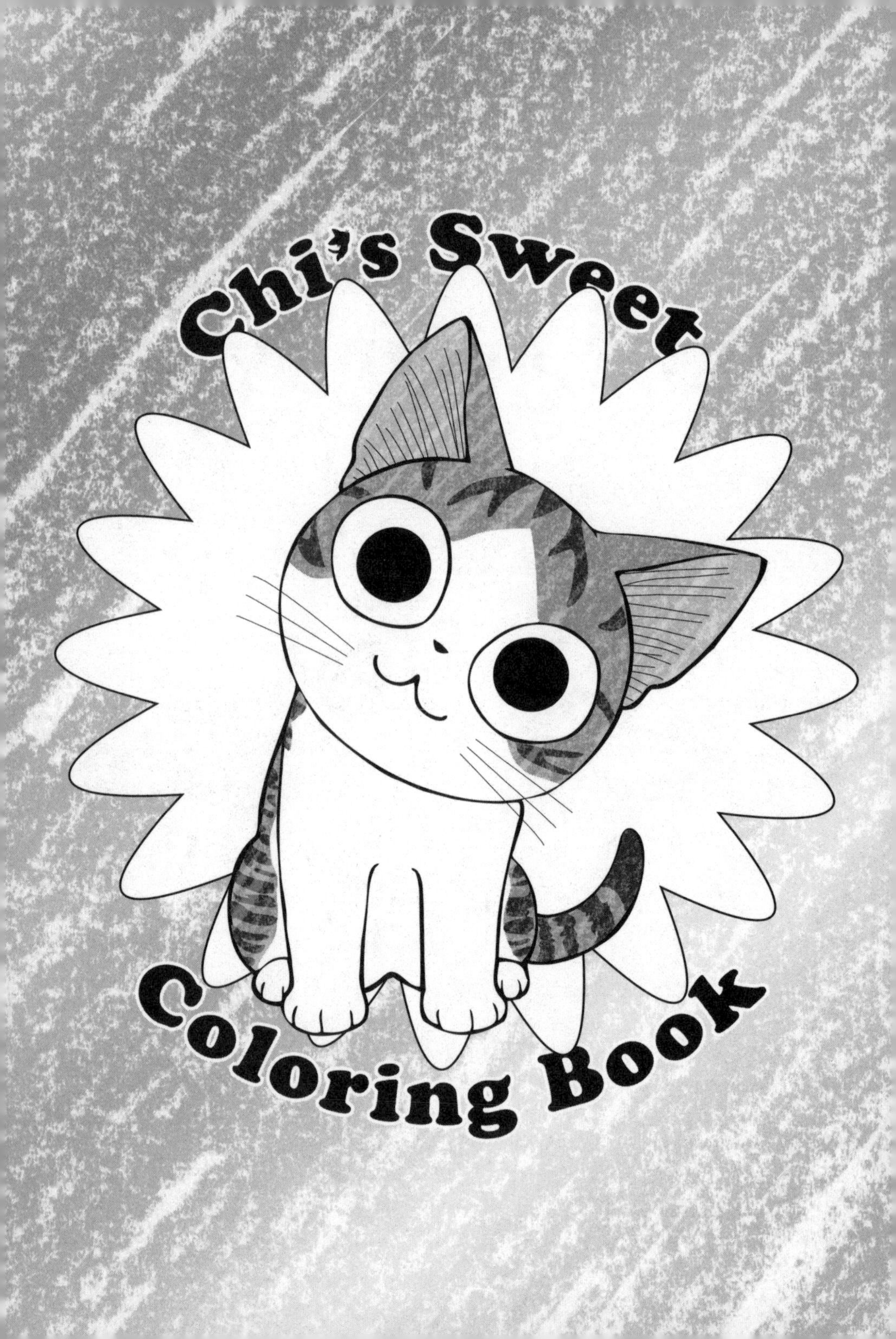
Chi's Sweet
Coloring Book

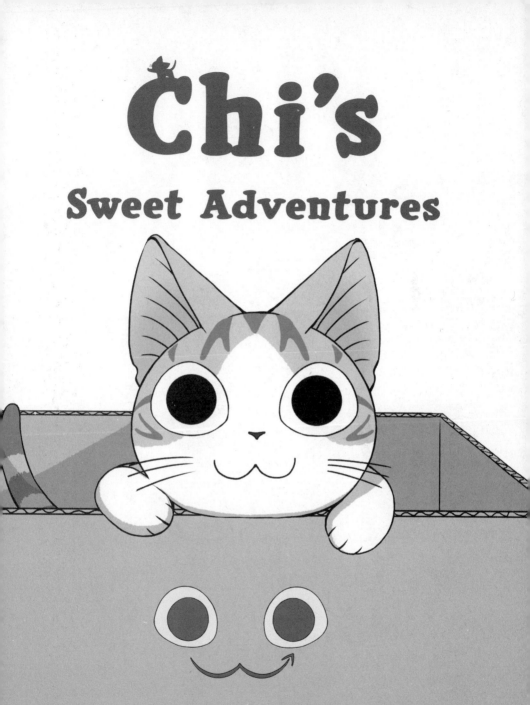

Chi's

Sweet Adventures

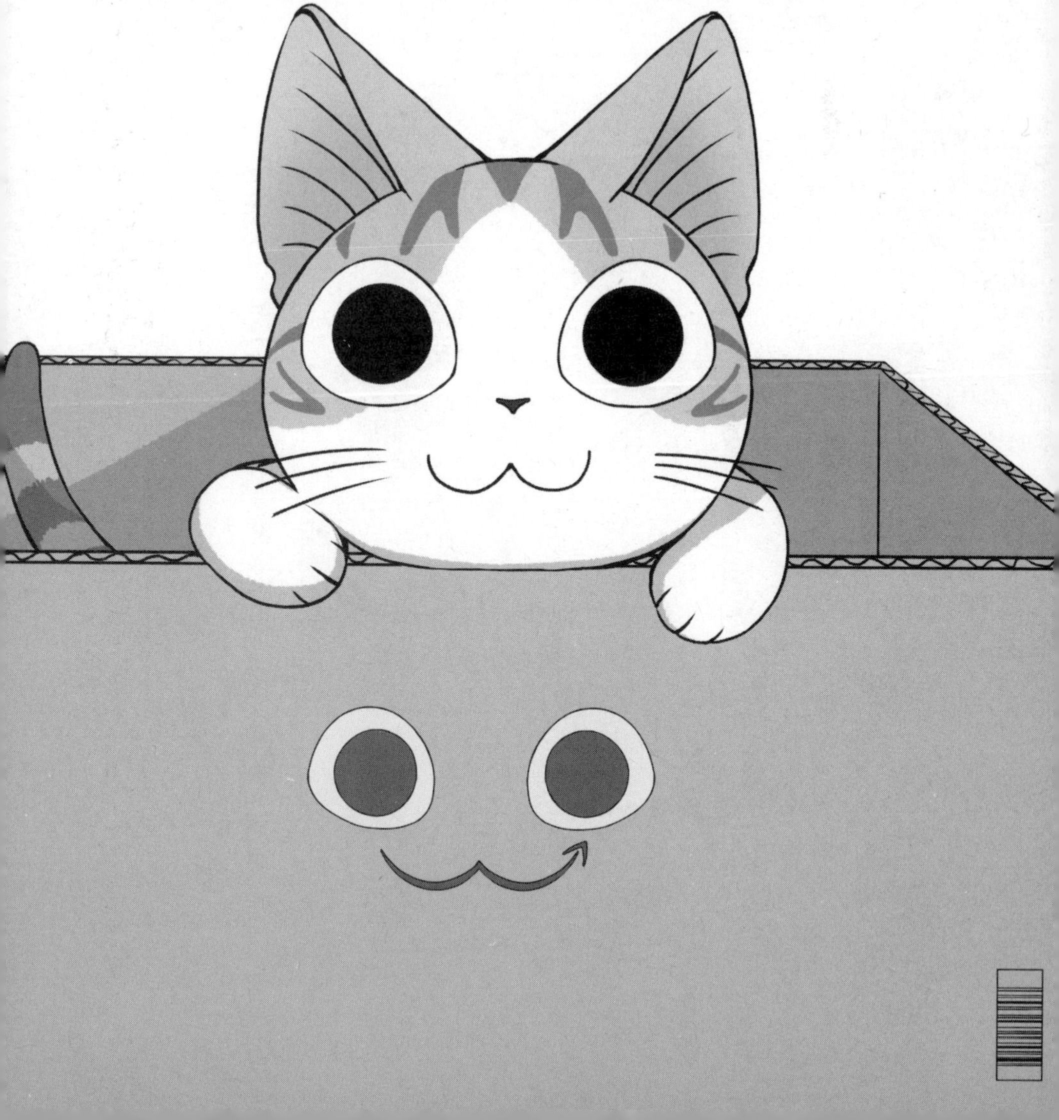

Created by Konami Kanata
Adapted by Kinoko Natsume

Chi is back! Manga's most famous cat
returns with a brand new series!
Chi's Sweet Adventures collects dozens
of new full-color kitty tales made
for readers of all ages!

Volumes 1-4
On Sale Now!

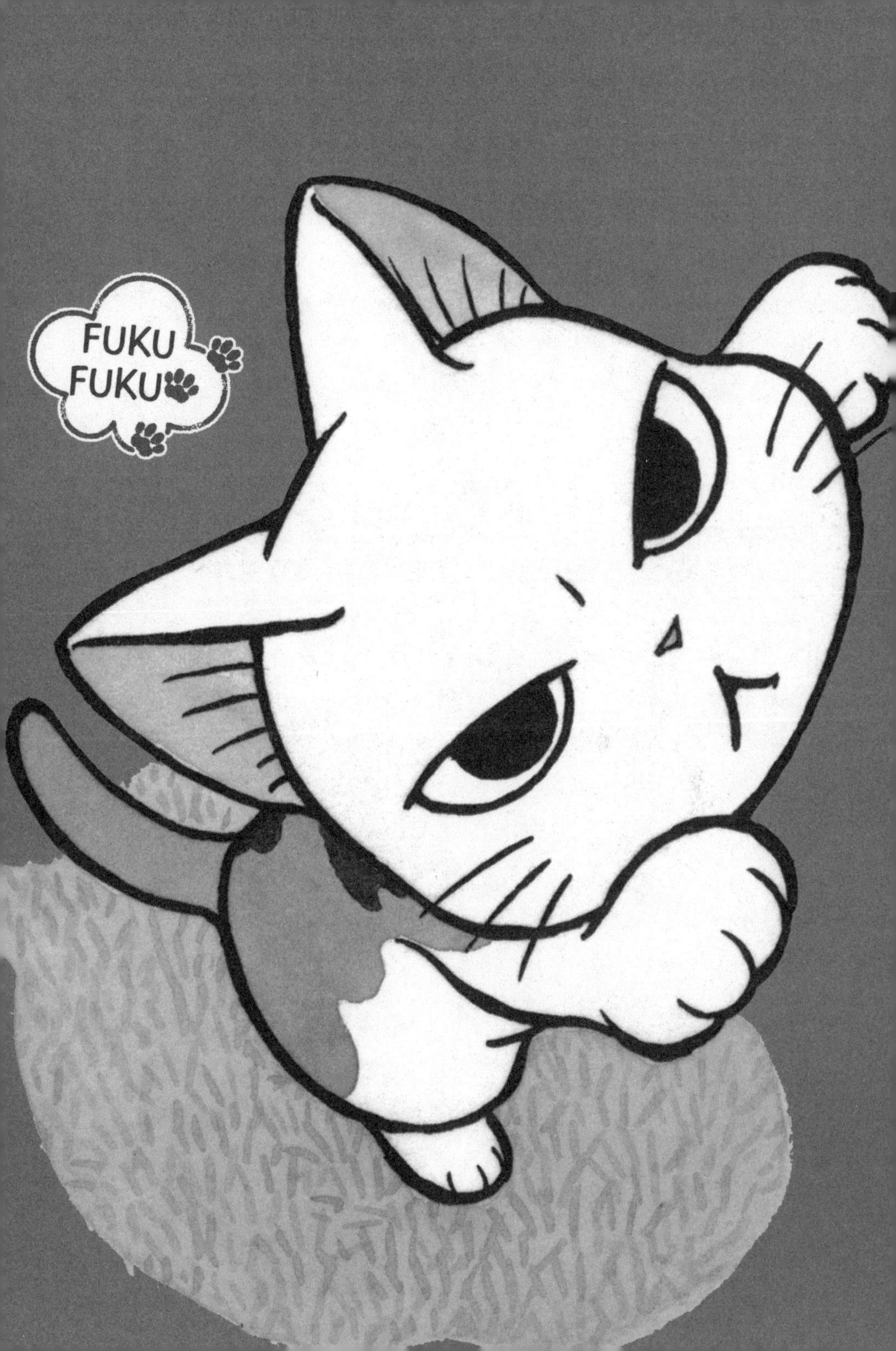
FUKU
FUKU

FUKU FUKU

Kitten Tales

Konami Kanata

Craving More Cute Cat Comics?

Want to see more furry feline antics? A new series by Konami Kanata, author of the beloved *Chi's Sweet Home* series, tells the story of a tiny kitten named FukuFuku who lives with a kindly old lady. Each day brings something new to learn, the change of the seasons leads to exciting discoveries and even new objects to shred with freshly-grown claws.

Join FukuFuku and her charming owner on this quietly heartwarming journey of kittenhood.

Oh, but you've already met FukuFuku, dear reader, as an adult! Can you recall which Chi story FukuFuku made a cameo in?

Parts 1 and 2 On Sale Now!

With a Dog AND a Cat, Every Day is Fun 6

A Vertical Comics Edition

Editor: Michelle Lin
Translation: Kumar Sivasubramanian
Production: Risa Cho
             Shirley Fang
             Eve Grandt
             Alexandra Swanson (SKY Japan Inc.)

© 2021 Hidekichi Matsumoto. All rights reserved.

First published in Japan in 2021 by Kodansha, Ltd., Tokyo
Publication rights for this English edition arranged through Kodansha, Ltd., Tokyo
English language version produced by Vertical Comics, an imprint of Kodansha USA Publishing, LLC

Translation provided by Vertical Comics, 2021
Published by Kodansha USA Publishing, LLC, New York

Originally published in Japanese as *Inu to Neko Docchimo Katteru to Mainichi Tanoshii 6* by Kodansha, Ltd., 2021

This is a work of fiction.

ISBN: 978-1-64729-075-7

Manufactured in the United States of America

First Edition

Kodansha USA Publishing, LLC
451 Park Avenue South
7th Floor
New York, NY 10016
www.kodansha.us

Vertical books are distributed through Penguin-Random House Publisher Services.

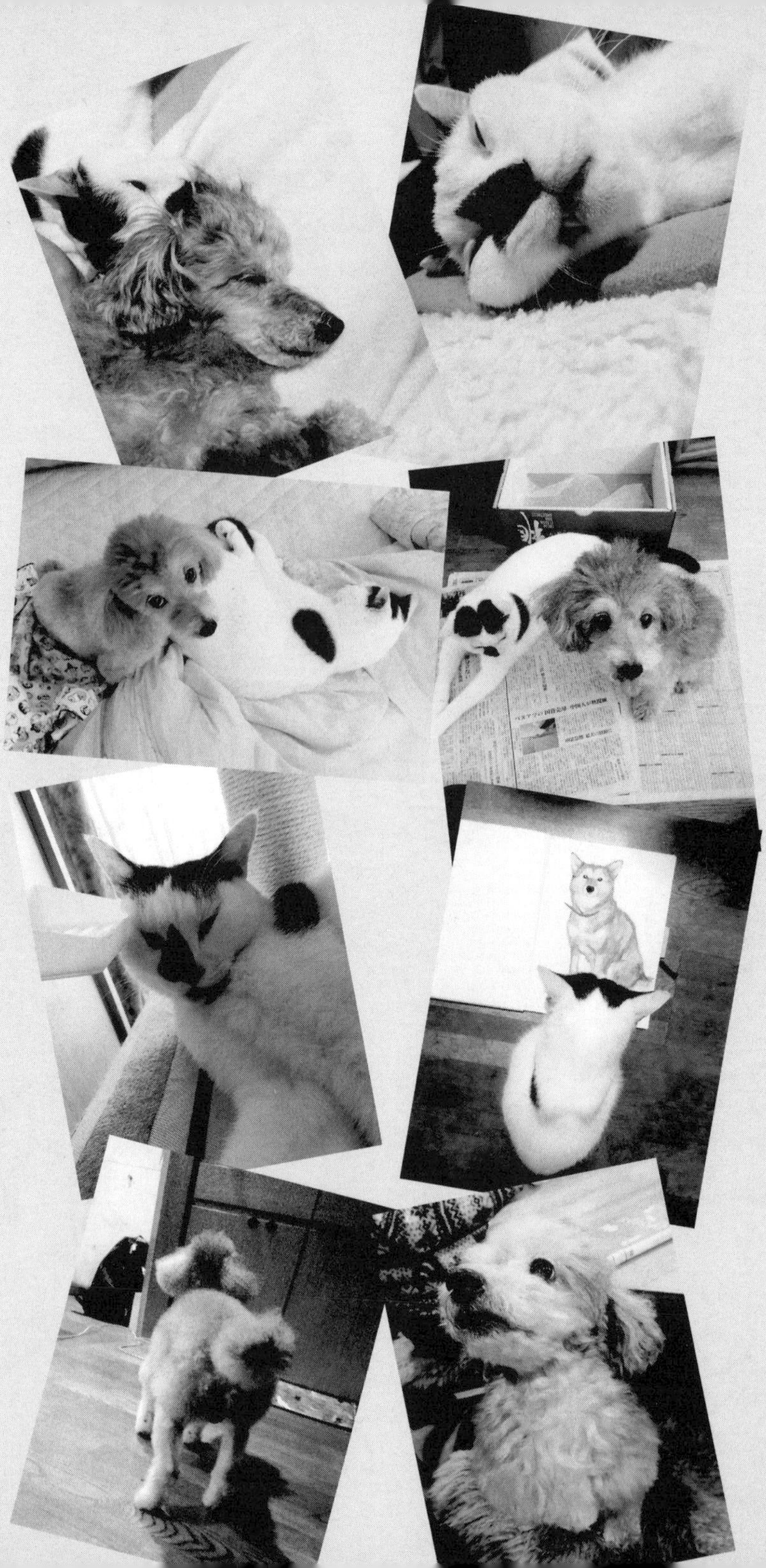

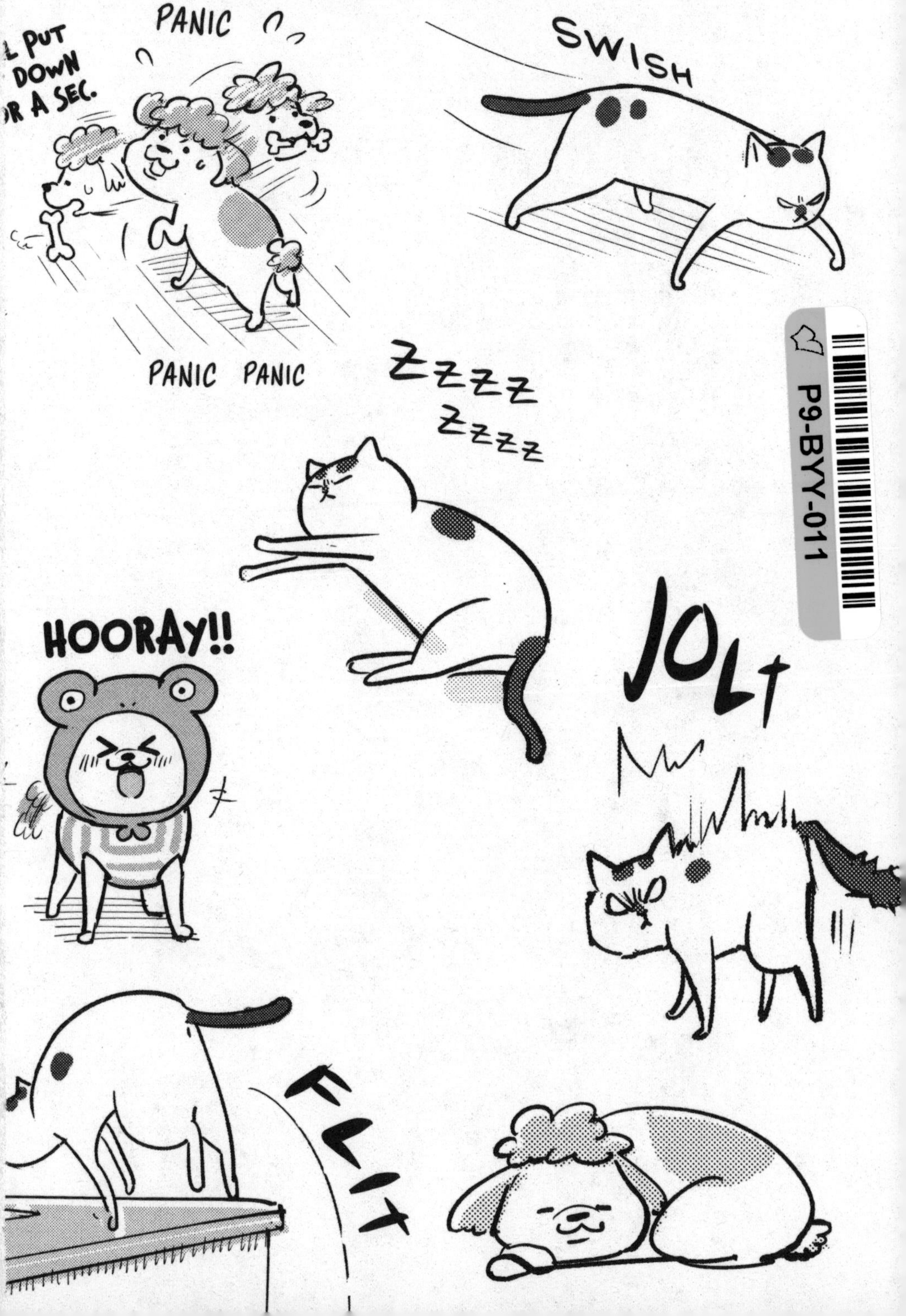
SWISH
L PUT
DOWN
OR A SEC.
PANIC
PANIC PANIC
ZZZZZ
ZZZZZ
JOLT
HOORAY!!
FLIT